SCIENTIFIC METHODS OF URBAN ANALYSIS

Published by
Leonard Hill Books
a division of
International Textbook Company Limited
24 Market Square, Aylesbury, Bucks., HP20 1TL

© 1972 by The Board of Trustees of the University of Illinois

First published in the USA 1972 by
The University of Illinois Press, Urbana.

ISBN 0 249 44127 6 √

Printed in Great Britain by Offset Lithography
by Billing & Sons Limited, Guildford and London

SCIENTIFIC METHODS
OF URBAN ANALYSIS

Anthony J. Catanese

Leonard Hill Books   An Intertext Publisher

In Memoriam

ÉVARIST GALOIS

FRENCH MATHEMATICIAN
BORN OCTOBER 25, 1811
DIED MAY 31, 1832

A delicate child, he twice failed exams to L'École Polytechnique, and entered L'École Normale in 1830, only to be expelled shortly thereafter for questioning his teachers and engaging in revolutionary activities. Imprisoned briefly for threatening the life of King Charles X, he was killed soon after in a duel sparked by insults to his politics and to a harlot he hardly knew. Galois was 20 years old when he was killed.

The night before he died, he wrote an incredible 31-page document in which he developed the *Galois Theory of Groups*. Largely esoteric to most people, it has emerged as one of the most advanced theories of mathematics. Group theory holds that pattern and structure exist in any real-world situation or phenomenon and that they can be discovered and described by borrowing tools from the various branches of mathematics. These tools are used to form groups of elements by which one can understand any problem and push ahead toward solution.

ACKNOWLEDGMENTS

Several publishers were most courteous and kind to allow me to use certain materials for the Appendices. Among these were Barnes and Noble for Appendices A, B, C; Van Nostrand for Appendix D; Holt, Rinehart, and Winston for Appendix F; RAND Corporation for Appendix G; and Technometrics for Appendix E. I would also like to thank the following for permission to use various materials in the text: the M.I.T. Press for Fig. 9:8; the American Institute of Planners for Figs. 10:1 and 10:2; and Environmetrics for Fig. 10:3.

Problems of urban systems are near, if not past, a critical mass. With more and more attention being paid to these problems, it is natural to expect a call for new approaches to problem-solving within an increasingly technological society. The result has been an infusion of new methods of analysis, as well as modification and improvement of classical methods, from the scientific disciplines. Such fields of pure and applied science as mathematics, general systems research, decision theory, operations research, and comprehensive planning have lent their existing methods and developed new methods for urban analysis.

As student, practitioner, and teacher concerned with urban systems, I have been aware of the lack of an integrated text or reference book which offered a concise presentation of the theory and application of scientific methods to the analysis of urban systems. This condition meant that reading lists for introductory courses on these matters, or courses which had significant sections devoted to these matters, had to be overly long, fragmented, and often irrelevant, since only theoretical bases were established and the student was asked to find applications on his own. Most of the literature on application of scientific methods to the various social sciences assumes that the reader is familiar with statistics, mathematics, and philosophy of science. This is rarely the case. This is not to say that the existing literature on introduction to and application of scientific methods is inadequate for the general educational mission; rather, the student of urban systems is overlooked. This book is an attempt to remedy the oversight, but by no means do I wish to detract from the need for the serious student to pursue such courses as statistics, operations research, calculus, algebra, etc.

This book is intended for use as a textbook for advanced undergraduate and graduate courses concerned with an introduction to scientific methods for the urban branches of planning, political science, sociology, economics, geography, public administration, architecture, engineering, applied mathematics, applied statistics, business administration, operations research, and systems analysis. A further use of the book could be for continuing education and special educational programs as well as for personal understanding and learning by students, researchers, teachers, and practitioners from any of the above or related fields.

A broad range of subjects is examined in this book. It is meant to serve as an introductory guide to the subject areas. One should by no means expect to be an expert in scientific methods of urban analysis by virtue

Preface

of mastering the material presented here. One would have to refer to many of the original works cited and perhaps undertake additional work in given areas where one is weakest. The book should provide, however, a wide-ranging introduction that would bring familiarity with most of the scientific methods of urban analysis. This book should be acceptable in most courses in urban analysis as a basic text, to be used in conjunction with the original materials cited herein as examples of basic texts, as well as supplementary materials suggested by the instructor. The same approach might be useful for continuing education courses and, indeed, for self-education.

There are two perspectives within which this book has been framed: (1) urban and (2) applied. The book is oriented to urban problems, issues, and possibilities and is not a general presentation of scientific methods for nonurban disciplines. The second perspective means that the applied nature of scientific methods weighs more heavily than the theoretical nature. Together, the two perspectives mean that this is a book which attempts to introduce the student or practitioner of urban analysis to as much of the theory of scientific methods as he needs to know, and also to demonstrate what these applications are and can be with further development.

The content of the book is divided into five parts for convenience and simplicity. The first part is a basic examination of the scientific method and its relevance and utility for urban systems. The remaining four parts are concerned with specific scientific methods from various fields as well as with new and synthetic methods. The presentation of this latter material takes the form of sections on theory, applications, recommended exercises, and further reading. The second part of the book covers predictive and estimating models: matrix methods, linear models, nonlinear and probability models. The third part covers optimizing models: basic optimization, calculus, and mathematical programming. The fourth part is a general overview of simulation and gaming. The final part is a general overview of urban information systems: automated systems within the context that they serve as integrative mechanisms for scientific methods of urban analysis.

Atlanta, Georgia

January, 1972

Contents

Tables

Figures

When a student is first introduced to those sciences which have come under the dominion of mathematics, a new and wonderful aspect of Nature bursts upon his view. He has been accustomed to regard things as essentially more or less vague.

William Kingdon Clifford, *The Exactness of Mathematical Laws* (1872)

PART I

SCIENTIFIC METHOD

There are many ways to consider the meaning of *urban* which are more or less valid according to the purpose for such a consideration. If we are concerned with some quantitative measure, it is sufficient to accept the U.S. Bureau of the Census definition of *urban* as constituting incorporated municipalities which have reached a population of 2,500 with certain densities and socioeconomic characteristics. If we are concerned with a general definition, it is sufficient to consider urban *systems* — entities with interrelated parts or components — as having four components: (1) the physical features and characteristics of the area as delimited; (2) the political structure and distribution of legal and political powers within the area; (3) the economic basis and supporting structure for the area; and (4) the complex interrelationships between individuals and groups of individuals within the social order of the area.

Analysis involves the process of separating systems into parts or components so that we can understand the nature, function, interrelationship, and proportion of the parts within the whole. In *mathematics,* the queen of sciences, analysis involves the solution of problems through equations or the examination of characteristics of equations. In urban problems it is often necessary to extend the concept of analysis to include an examination of the quality, by some reasonable measure, of the urban system. *Urban analysis* is the breakdown of urban systems into their physical, political, economic, and social parts in order to understand them, determine their problems, and seek solutions to these problems, which are usually interdependent.

Science is a word which is Latin in origin (*scientia*), being derived from the verb *scire* (to know). The original meaning of the word was "the state or fact of knowing." The contemporary use of the word *science* is to indicate a body of systematic knowledge and a method of analysis. Science is a systematic body of knowledge which is recorded and preserved, arising through observation, experimentation, and study. Science is a method of analysis, since this recorded and preserved knowledge is used to discover new knowledge, usually by the form of (1) inquiry, (2) problem-solving, and (3) development of methods for analysis.

CHAPTER 1

Scientific Method and Urban Analysis

All knowledge and methods of analysis are obviously not scientific. Non-scientific knowledge and methods are referred to as *common sense,* a simple if misleading term. Common sense is a collection of insights, prejudices, and feelings that an individual accumulates over the years through his experiences. *Intuition* is sometimes considered to be artistic or unrestrained creativity and thought. We can assume, however, that no activity of an individual is completely unrestrained. Even the most "happening"-type artist is using an inwardly ordered structure of analysis that may not be explicit even to himself. There is little evidence to show that completely unrestrained activity exists anywhere in the physical universe.

A major distinction between scientific and nonscientific knowledge and methods is the ability to make explicit and to reiterate. Intuitive analysis may be sound in that an analyst can "feel" that one approach to an urban problem is better than all others. In the early days of city planning, for example, architects developed plans more by intuition than by scientific or even quasi-scientific reasoning. People accepted their plans because the "expert knew what was best." Urban problems have become sufficiently complex and interrelated that more than intuition is generally needed for solution. Intuitive analysis is difficult to use as a basis for solutions to urban problems which must gain public approval. The public, in general, is leery about spending money on solutions that are not fully convincing, and the public, like many subgroups within it, is somewhat awed by scientific analysis. The ability to reiterate findings from analysis is particularly relevant to this argument. Scientific knowledge comes from findings that could be undertaken by any analyst using the same environment and conditions. Scientific experiments will always produce more or less similar results within similar conditions, something which is rarely insured through intuitive analysis.

There is a distinction between intuitive and scientific knowledge, yet there is virtually no way that the two can be separated in practice. Intuitive knowledge is an absolute necessity in the undertaking of any scientific analysis. Intuition is essential in scientific analysis of urban problems because many characteristics and features of urban problems cannot be quantified or related in mathematical terms. The "softness" of urban data and functions necessitates that certain compromises, assumptions, and hybrid analyses be made.

The basic quality which enables scientific knowledge to be more ordered and consistent than intuitive knowledge is the amount of control possible over conditions and environments. Scientific experiments always involve some sort of control over the environment and conditions — the more the better. Since control over urban environment and conditions is difficult to attain, it is necessary to state rigorously what the environment and conditions were during the conduct of an analysis. Consequently, loss of control will diminish the reiterative capabilities of discovered knowledge in different environments and conditions. The presence of these complicating impediments to control in urban systems requires that intuitive analysis be used in conjunction with scientific analysis for problems in these areas.

SCIENTIFIC METHOD

There is a *method* of analysis which has been derived from the scientific knowledge of the ages. Method is used in the context of an orderly, rational, and consistent approach to the analysis of problems — in other words, it is a *process*. There are several methods or techniques which are used in varying degrees within the scientific method or process, but we are concerned presently with the procedures.

The term *scientific method* is a common one and is used interchangeably with many other terms to express similar concepts. In a purist sense, however, there are two branches of scientific method: (1) basic research and (2) research and development. Another way of expressing this same distinction is to consider the difference between pure science and applied science.

BASIC RESEARCH

Basic research is the discovery of scientific knowledge for its own sake. Basic research is undertaken with the principal objective of adding to the recorded and preserved body of knowledge that has arisen from science. The basic research branch of the scientific method relevant to urban systems is a modification of a classical three-stage process:

1. *Observation.* Under various conditions and environments, urban systems can be studied using various methods to try to understand more about them.

2. *Generalization.* Observation of urban systems under varying environments and conditions allows for an ordering and generalization into hypotheses or theories.

3. *Experimentation.* While it is rarely possible or advisable to vary urban

system conditions and environments for experimental purposes only, it is possible to represent systems by various methods and to perform experiments on these representations to determine what the effects and side effects of changes would be, as well as to test various intuitive notions. We can call these methods either *models* (*representations* of reality) or *simulations* (*imitations* of reality), the latter being essentially a way of using the former.

Basic research into urban systems is an important branch of the scientific method. It often results in meaningful additions to our incomplete and scant knowledge of urban systems. The inherent limitation in this branch of the scientific method is that it does not allow for application without further analysis. On the other hand, it is often the case that basic research into urban systems must precede any attempts to apply scientific knowledge.

RESEARCH AND DEVELOPMENT

Research and development, or the application of scientific knowledge and methods to the solution of urban problems, involves another branch of the scientific method. Research and development has the principal objective of using the body of knowledge, which is usually scientific knowledge, and any new knowledge that can be discovered to reach certain goals and objectives that have been predetermined. Research and development is basically a problem-solving process, but there is sufficient latitude in the process to have major applications to the interrelated, multiproblem nature of urban systems. The research and development branch of the scientific method is a classical five-stage process which can be modified for urban analysis as follows:

1. *Problem Definition.* Solutions or resolutions can be found by formulating the problem or set of interrelated problems. This is especially important; many urban problems are insolvable not because of their inherent characteristics but because of the inadequate manner in which they have been defined. This first stage is a quantitative/qualitative definition of the problems in terms of conditions, environments, measures, interrelationships, and human values in such a frame of reference that solutions or resolutions may be discovered.

2. *Representation.* Through several methods, usually modeling or simulation, the urban system is represented and defined problems are incorporated into this representation of the real world. This allows for observation

and experimentation under conditions of control which are either impossible or prohibitively expensive if done in reality.

3. *Testing.* Since there are many ways to represent real-world urban systems, various attempts should be tested against past and present observations to insure that the most accurate representation is utilized. While it is generally impossible to devise a perfect representation, and since greater accuracy always entails higher costs and efforts, some reasonable level of compromise must be reached depending upon the nature of the problem.

4. *Deriving Solutions.* The major value of the representation lies in its ability to test alternative courses of action that can be employed to solve or resolve the defined problems. These alternative courses of action are formed by intuitive analysis and then tested, or they are formed through some mechanism within the representation itself. The representation is used to evaluate the courses of action under various conditions, environments, and measures of problem-solving in order to reach a classification of alternative courses of action by varying levels of performance and effectiveness.

5. *Development.* The classification of alternative courses of action that can be used to solve the defined problems, if determinable, can be developed into applications or implementations in various ways. The development stage varies greatly with the nature of the analysts and their professional orientations to urban problems. More or less typical examples of development for urban systems are recommendations to decision-makers; administrative rules, regulations, and guidelines; legislative acts; dissemination of findings; continuing research; and educational programs.

The research and development branch of the scientific method is relevant to urban affairs because it offers a process which is interesting to persons charged with the development of administrative, legislative, and planning programs, as well as to analysts who aid these persons. It is often difficult to decide when incomplete or inaccurate knowledge exists about a problem. Basic research may be needed before research and development can be employed for certain problems in urban systems.

MATHEMATICAL FOUNDATIONS

Modern mathematics is considered to have originated in the sixteenth century with the work of René Descartes (1596-1650), if we can agree that the concepts of *variable* and *function* are characteristic of modern mathematics.[1] This is not to say that there were no important predecessors of Descartes but, rather, that these mathematical scholars were more concerned with Aristotelian logic and geometrical analysis. Descartes initiated the use of variables and functional relationships in mathematics, further developed by such mathematical logicians as Gottfried Wilhelm von Leibniz, J. H. Lambert, George Boole, Augustus de Morgan, and others.

Mathematics is the study of relationships between entities which do not have to remain fixed. The methods of mathematics have served as the natural language and logical basis for science. The commonly held beliefs of the exactitude, rigor, and conciseness of mathematics are usually offered as the reasons for science's use of the discipline, but it is also the basic flexibility of mathematics to deal with simple or complex variables and simple or complex relationships in the most direct and generic manner.

VARIABLES

The concept of variables is a foundation of mathematics as used in scientific methods. A variable is a quantity which does not have to be fixed. Variables can take on any one of a set of values which falls within a *range* of values delimited by the set boundaries.

Let us assume that we are analyzing the population living within cities of various sizes within the United States. Let χ represent the number of people living in a city — it is a variable. Let us confine our analysis to cities having a population of at least 2,500 and no more than 1,000,000. Since χ can be anywhere from 2,500 to 1,000,000, we consider this to be the range of the variable χ.

There are obviously many cities in the country which fall within this range. We find that the designation of our variable as χ is too restrictive. We can overcome this apparent restriction by using a mathematical shorthand called *subscripted variables*. We will let the subscript stand for a category of similar entities, e.g., cities within a range of population in our case. In essence, we are merely giving a code name to each city and its population.

[1] For an excellent review of modern mathematics, see Phillip E. B. Jourdain, "The Nature of Mathematics," in James R. Newman, ed., *The World of Mathematics,* 1 (New York: Simon and Schuster, 1956), 4-74.

TABLE 1:1. Subscripted variables.

City	Subscripted Variable
1	χ_1
2	χ_2
3	χ_3
.	.
.	.
.	.
30	χ_{30}
etc.	etc.

If we want to refer to any one of the cities in general, we can use the subscripted variable χ_i and let $i = 1, 2, 3, \ldots, 30$, etc.

The usual way of adding up the population of all the cities to find the total population would be:

$$\chi_1 + \chi_2 + \chi_3 + \ldots + \chi_{30}, \text{ etc.} = \text{total population.}$$

A more convenient method is to use the mathematical shorthand Σ, which means "the summation of":

$$\text{total population} = \sum_{i=1}^{30+} \chi_i.$$

This equation is read "the total population is equal to the summation of the ith number of χ variables within the range of i between 1 and more than 30." As a matter of standard convention, a subscript such as i is always a positive *integer* (whole number), but it is not necessary to start the range of consideration for summation at 1.

Let us assume that we want to analyze the population of all cities within certain classes by state. Assuming that we have established ten classes of population size, we can form a table of values, or a *matrix,* in a rectangle.

TABLE 1:2. Matrix of states by population class.

$(j\rightarrow)$

	1	2	3	. . .	10
1	χ_{11}	χ_{12}	χ_{13}	. . .	χ_{110}
2	χ_{21}	χ_{22}	χ_{23}	. . .	χ_{210}
3	χ_{31}	χ_{32}	χ_{33}	. . .	χ_{310}
.	.	.	.		.
.	.	.	.		.
.	.	.	.		.
50	χ_{501}	χ_{502}	χ_{503}	. . .	χ_{5010}

State $(\leftarrow i)$

The shorthand for any population in our matrix would be χ_{ij}, where i is the row number and j is the column number. Since there are 50 rows and 10 columns in the matrix, we have a "50 by 10 matrix." If we wanted to find the total population living in cities by class, we would solve $\Sigma \chi_j$ for each class; similarly, the population of each state would be $\Sigma \chi_i$ for each state. If we wanted to determine the total population of all classes of cities in all states, we would use a double summation form:

$$\text{total population} = \sum_{i=1}^{i=50} \sum_{j=1}^{j=10} \chi_{ij}.$$

The same effect could be obtained in longhand by adding each of the elements in the matrix, i.e., $\chi_{11} + \chi_{12} + \ldots + \chi_{5010}$. An important point to remember when using double-subscripted variables such as χ_{ij} is that the first subscript stands for the row position and the second subscript stands for the column position.

These mathematical foundations provide sufficient basis for expressing quantities subject to change as variables. The selection of variables, and the measurement criteria to be used, are difficult problems which vary greatly from subject to subject. While the mathematical foundations are convenient for expression of variables, intuitive analysis is often required to select and measure variables.

FUNCTIONS

The concept of functions is a basic tenet of modern mathematics which has much relevance for urban analysis. A function is a rule to show the association of one set of variables with another. Since we have chosen to consider variables within sets, we can call the ranges of the variables of all sets the *domain* of the function. Urban analysis almost always deals with domains of *real numbers* (not *imaginary* numbers). For example, if we were to consider $y = f(x)$, which is read "y is equal to a function of x," and further consider $y = 2x$, which is read "y is equal to twice the value of any value of x," we could conclude that $y = f(x) = 2x$ and that the function denoted by f can be stated "take any value of x and multiply by 2."

Another way of studying functions is the *predicative* approach. For example, we can say

St. Louis is a city

is the same as

$$f(x),$$

where

x is a set of urban settlements, in this case only one,
f is a function, in this case "is a city."

In another example we can have multiple functions:

Atlanta is a city $[f_1(x)]$,
Atlanta is young $[f_2(x)]$,

so that

Atlanta is a young city $[f_1(x) + f_2(x)]$.

Functions can be used to *classify* variables in this way.

Functions can also be used to *compare* sets of variables. For example,

New York is larger than Atlanta $[f(x_1,x_2)]$,

where

f is a function, "is larger than,"
x_1 = New York,
x_2 = Atlanta.

This type of comparison is sometimes called *nonsymmetric* because one set of variables is different from the others. A *symmetric* comparison function is of the kind

Philadelphia is near New York $[f(x_1,x_2)]$,

where

f is a function, "is near,"
x_1 = Philadelphia, a city,
x_2 = New York, a city.

Symmetric functions imply that $f(x_1,x_2)$ is the same as $f(x_2,x_1)$; for example, New York is near Philadelphia. Nonsymmetric functions do not make this implication; for example, Atlanta is not larger than New York.

The most common use of the concept of functions for urban analysis is to express *relations*. For example, we often see such relations as

$$dp_i = p_i/a_i,$$

where

dp_i = density of population for any city in the set i,
p_i = population of city i,
a_i = geographical area of city i,

and, in this case, the function is division of the population variable by the area variable.

Functions are used commonly in urban analysis to show three basic types of relations, usually though not always expressed in mathematical terms:

1. *Deterministic.* The cause-and-effect relation which holds that χ will always occur or be absent when y occurs.

2. *Probabilistic.* The chance relation that χ may or may not occur or be absent when y occurs, but we can say that there is a probability p_x that χ may or may not occur when y occurs.

3. *Pseudo.* We know that χ and y are often present or absent in the same way time after time, but we doubt that one causes the other. For example, umbrellas are usually opened on city streets when it is raining, yet we know that opened umbrellas do not cause it to rain and we know that rain does not cause umbrellas to open — and we also know that umbrellas are opened sometimes on city streets when it is gloriously sunny. To deal with such problems, we can devise pseudo relationships which may not have cause-and-effect characteristics.

We have stated that the domain of functions (of any of the types) is usually all real numbers in urban analysis. In order to work with functions efficiently, we try to limit the range of consideration by looking at only a certain part of the domain — this is called an *interval*. Since the range of a function is usually $-\infty \rightarrow +\infty$, or minus infinity to plus infinity, we must place restrictions on values to be considered, as seen in Fig. 1:1. We will only consider values for our function which lie between a and b in our example because all other values of the function are not interesting to us. There are three types of intervals:

1. *Closed.* We will consider $[a,b]$, which means all values between a and b including a and b.

2. *Open.* All values in the interval (a,b), which means any real number in the interval except a and b.

3. *Mixed.* It is sometimes found that one end of an interval may be open and the other closed, such as $(a,b]$ or $[a,b)$.

As a practical matter in urban analysis, we try to deal only with closed intervals. Open intervals are often impossible to analyze because of the impossibility of determining how close you can get to a value such as a or b without ever reaching it (there are an infinite number of steps which get smaller and smaller). As a matter of practicality, we often use inequality signs to express the interval we are considering:

$$a \leq y \leq b \text{ denotes a closed interval,}$$
$$a < y < b \text{ denotes an open interval.}$$

Mixed intervals can be expressed as

$$a \leq y < b,$$
$$a < y \leq b.$$

This is an important foundation of mathematics which is useful in simplifying the application and, in some cases, the costs of scientific methods to urban analysis. It also requires that the urban analyst has a good understanding of what is relevant in a problem and what is irrelevant.

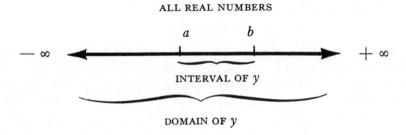

Fig. 1 : 1. Domain and interval.

Models

The basic tenets and foundations of modern mathematics are most significant in both the basic research and research and development branches of scientific methods in the manner that they are used for representation of real-world entities. Using the foundations of science and mathematics, representations of the real world are developed and tested — the activity often called modeling — and the representations are usually called models.

There are some cases where models may not be mathematical. We can assume that there are three basic types of models:

1. *Analog.* This type of model uses one physical entity to represent another. For example, there have been cases where traffic on city streets has been represented by the flow of electrons through wires and circuits.

2. *Iconic.* These are common models whereby a scale representation of the real world is made. For example, groups of buildings are often built at a small scale so that a designer can analyze them; maps are drawn to scale to show the location of physical and nonphysical characteristics of cities.

3. *Symbolic.* The most significant type of model is the symbolic model, usually in mathematical terms, which uses symbolism to express the real world. We will be concerned primarily with symbolic models, but we are aware of the significance of analog and iconic models in urban analysis.

BASIC SYMBOLIC MODEL

Russell L. Ackoff has stated that all symbolic models for scientific methods have the same basic form:[2]

$$v = f(x_i, y_j),$$

where v is some measure of performance of the real-world phenomenon that is being represented; x_i is a set of variables which represents decisions or other aspects of the situation that can be controlled by either the analyst or decision-makers in the real world; and y_j is a set of variables which represents decisions, environment, conditions, or other aspects of the situation that cannot be controlled or arise from outside the urban system and are called exogenous.

This basic form of the symbolic model is interesting in that it clearly shows that the analyst must have many insights and must exercise sound judgment if he is to develop a model effectively. The analyst must determine what measure of performance is to be analyzed or what group of measures is to be interrelated and analyzed. Control variables must be selected that both allow experimentation with various alternatives for the urban system and serve as a means of possible resolution of the problem in the real world. The noncontrol or exogenous variables must be carefully considered — they indicate what conditions cannot be changed and what possible side effects may arise. The determination of the functions which relate these variables is often the most difficult job for the analyst, and it is often the reason for inadequate models, since the function is usually based on incomplete knowledge of the urban system.

OPTIMAL SOLUTIONS

Models have much significance in scientific methods because they enable analysts to determine solutions to questions addressed to models. These

[2] Russell L. Ackoff, *Scientific Method: Optimizing Applied Research Decisions* (New York: Wiley, 1962), pp. 108-140.

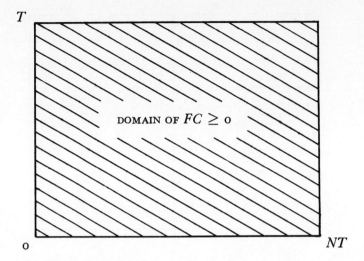

FIG. 1:2. Domain of *FC* function.

questions usually pertain to the control variables, and the answers to the model show what the effects of certain alternative decisions may be. Since urban problems always involve noncontrol variables and are usually limited to a certain interval of solutions, they are said to be under conditions of *constraint*. Whenever a symbolic model is constrained, and we seek the best solution to the model (or the problem that the model represents), we seek the *optimal solution*. The optimal solution is the best answer to our question within the constraints that have been set.

A simple example may help to clarify the concept of optimal solutions. Assume that the fiscal capability for a city in a given year is the total of its tax and nontax revenues. We can model this situation by

$$FC = T + NT,$$

where

FC = fiscal capability in dollars,
T = tax collections in dollars,
NT = nontax revenues in dollars.

Assuming that the city is not losing money, the domain of *FC* is any real-number value which is positive, as shown in Fig. 1:2. In a given year let us assume that political leaders have imposed a tax ceiling of a (on T), and the economy, population, and characteristics of the city will probably limit NT to b or less. This means that *FC* is constrained by $0 \leq T \leq a$ and

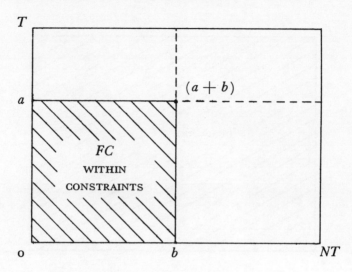

Fig. 1:3. Constrained domain of *FC* function.

$0 \leq NT \leq b$. The interval is shown in Fig. 1:3. We can now test several possibilities. We can see that the minimum fiscal capability of the city (denoted as Min *FC*) is 0 at $T = 0$, $NT = 0$. The maximum fiscal capability of the city (denoted as Max *FC*) is $a + b$ at $T = a$, $NT = b$. This sets up several decision situations. If we seek the maximum fiscal capability of the city within the constraints, we would say that Max *FC* = $a + b$ is the optimal solution. On the other hand, if we wanted to maximize *FC* without imposing taxes, we see that Max *FC* would be b at $T = 0$. Similarly, Max *FC* would be a if $NT = 0$. The selection of an optimal solution, then, depends upon some criteria established by the analyst.

Symbolic models can have maximum, minimum, and optimum solutions. A general table (1:3) of solution types can help illustrate this. This table

TABLE 1:3. Types of solutions.

| Solution | Time | Criteria | |
		Resources	Effectiveness
Maximum	Longest	Highest	Greatest
Minimum	Shortest	Lowest	Least
Optimum	Middle	Medium	Medium

somewhat oversimplifies the case, but it is useful for explanatory purposes. It shows simply that the optimum solution for models which also have maximum and minimum solutions tends to be a compromise between the extremes. The compromise is determined both by the constraints placed upon the solution and the model and by the criteria for selection of optimality selected by the analyst. The optimum solution does not necessarily mean the best answer to the problem that the model imitates. In most cases the optimal solution means the best answer with "all things considered" or within the constraints set for deriving any answer.

There is another set of alternatives, or perhaps a single alternative, which exists for dealing with urban problems. The *utopian solution* is considered to be the best solution to urban problems without constraints. If the constraints for solution can be removed or minimized, whether they consist of resources, time, effectiveness, or human values, we can develop an ideal solution to an urban problem. The utopian solution can be arrived at through solution of symbolic models with all constraints removed or through intuitive analysis. The utopian solution has been a factor in urban planning for many years and continues to offer both insight and perspective. An operational role for utopian solutions can be made by including it in the array of alternatives that the analyst will examine.[3] It may emerge that a utopian solution is a valid course of action and that the main concern of decision-makers should be to eliminate constraints which impede the attainment of such a solution. It is also possible that utopian solutions can assist the analyst in determining the effect of constraint relaxation on other solutions.

VALUES AND SCIENTIFIC METHODS

A *value* is an inherent worth of any entity or belief. Values are held by humans as individuals and humans in groups with common interests, such as communities. Issues and very real differences often arise between what individuals and communities in urban systems value and what scientific methods show to be the optimal solution to problems. The optimal solution to a problem rests on the consideration of all things and the constraints as they have been defined for the model. Individuals and communities often will disagree about the need for consideration of all things or all con-

---

[3] For further examination of this concept, see Anthony J. Catanese and Alan W. Steiss, *Systemic Planning: Theory and Application* (Boston: D. C. Heath, 1970).

straints. As has been noted, in its purest sense the scientific method tends to produce relatively conservative solutions to problems. Human and community values may demand other than conservative solutions.

A common example in urban systems is found with freeway locations. Most freeways are located by scientific methods which evaluate the costs and the benefits of several variables (usually in terms of reduced time and costs of travel). It is not uncommon to find freeways planned to traverse fine residential areas, parks, historic areas, and natural areas. In terms of which variables were considered, the solution may be valid, yet in terms of human and community values about such nonquantifiable variables as mentioned, the optimal solution may be completely unacceptable. What then becomes the "best" solution? Who determines what is the "best" solution? Such issues lie at the heart of many urban problems.

C. West Churchman has written about the general nature of *scientific methods and human and community values.*[4] Churchman argues that ethics — the science of what society wants a decision to be or behavior to be — has not been developed enough to serve as a sufficient basis for resolving conflicts between optimal solutions and human and social values. There should be an input of freedom into the scientific methods that will help determine when optimal solutions must be tempered with other alternatives that arise from values, politics, morality, etc. On the assumption that our greatest failure has been the inability to determine and measure human and community values, Churchman concludes, "What seems to be the distinctive contribution of the twentieth century to the theory of human progress is the recognition that there can be no progress without conflict. The challenge is to develop a science of values or ethics which can understand what this means."[5] Thus he argues that science can be of only limited assistance to human progress, especially in urban areas, without the development of a science which understands human and community values.

The conflict between human and community values and optimal solutions to urban problems formulated through scientific methods is a major problem of urban analysis. This perspective should be deeply held by all those who labor to improve urban systems. Progress is being made gradually toward the kind of challenge that Churchman has raised, but there is much to be done. Scientific methods of urban analysis are only valid

[4] C. West Churchman, *Prediction and Optimal Decision: Philosophical Issues of a Science of Values* (Englewood Cliffs, N.J.: Prentice-Hall, 1964).
[5] Ibid., p. 380.

when they are tempered with an intuitive understanding of human and community values.

RECOMMENDED EXERCISES

1. To the question "Should black children be transported to predominantly white suburban schools in order to achieve a racial balance?" the following responses were found in one area:

i \ j	1 (Yes)	2 (No)	3 (Undecided)
1 (Students)	313	157	125
2 (Teachers)	56	65	10
3 (Parents)	117	200	60

Assuming that any cell can be represented as n_{ij}, calculate and interpret:

(A) $\sum_{i=1}^{3} n_{i1}$

(B) $\sum_{j=1}^{2} n_{2j}$

(C) $\sum_{j=2}^{3} \sum_{i=1}^{2} n_{ij}$

(D) $\dfrac{\sum_{i=1}^{3} n_{i1}}{\sum_{j=1}^{3} \sum_{i=1}^{3} n_{ij}}$

(E) $\dfrac{\sum_{i=1}^{3} n_{i2}}{\sum_{j=1}^{3} \sum_{i=1}^{3} n_{ij}}$

2. Write a brief essay on the differences between the scientific method and the general planning process that exists in most urban areas.

3. Population (P) is a function of such key variables as births, deaths, in-migration, and out-migration. For any given city in any given year develop a population model. What variables are related to population that cannot be measured? How accurate is the model?

4. Formulate and execute a survey to determine what human and community values exist concerning a given problem in a given city. Analyze the conflicts, if any, that arise between these values and an optimal solution developed by analysts.

FURTHER READING

Ackoff, Russell L. *Scientific Method: Optimizing Applied Research Decisions.* New York: Wiley, 1962.

One of the foremost students of science and scientific method develops an exhaustive analysis of both in this book. General in its orientation, it is useful for a basic understanding of scientific methods and problems of optimal decisions.

Churchman, C. West. *Prediction and Optimal Decision: Philosophical Issues of a Science of Values.* Englewood Cliffs, N.J.: Prentice-Hall, 1964.

The author is a pioneer in the application of scientific methods to management problems and explores in this book the issues and conflicts that arise between values and optimal solutions. The book is concerned with the major problems of determination, analysis, and measurement of values, and it concludes with a profound challenge to science to take values into consideration.

I shall claim the privilege of a Freethinker; and take the liberty to inquire into the object, principles, and method of demonstration admitted by mathematicians of the present age, with the same freedom that you presume to treat the principles and mysteries of Religion; to the end that all men may see what right you have to lead, or what encouragement others have to follow you.

Bishop Berkeley, *The Analyst: A Discourse Addressed to an Infidel Mathematician* (1734)

PART **II**

PREDICTIVE AND ESTIMATING MODELS

Most examples of scientific methods of urban analysis that already exist in the real world, in a fully operational and practical perspective, are relatively simple deterministic (rarely probabilistic) models. These models involve variables that are set in some observed or theoretical functional relationship and can be solved to find solutions to problems. It is this succinct simplicity of deterministic models that accounts for their popularity and validity. When processed by digital computers, the additional dimension of speed is added.

The expression of models in matrix terms is especially advantageous for digital computer processing. The digital computer solves problems in an electrological sense that is not unlike matrix methods. Most library programs for computers require, in fact, that input be set in matrix terms in order to provide valid and efficient output.

THE MATRIX APPROACH

The matrix approach, or the more traditional matrix algebra, further simplifies and facilitates deterministic (and probabilistic) models. Matrix methods are ordinarily used when subscripted variables or numerous data observations exist in deterministic functional relationships for urban problems. Matrix methods provide a foundation for more advanced models in addition to the simple manipulation facilitation in deterministic models. Matrix methods are useful for the solution of many models, such as input/output, linear programming, and simultaneous equations. The use of matrix methods for probabilistic models has been of growing importance in recent years, especially in demographic analyses, such as age-cohort-survival projections, which we will explore later.

RUDIMENTS OF MATRIX METHODS

A matrix is any rectangular array of values. A matrix consists of rows and columns. Symbolically, this is usually shown through the use of capital

CHAPTER 2

Matrix Methods

letters for the matrix and subscripted lower-case letters for the elements of the matrix:

$$A = \begin{pmatrix} a_{11} & a_{12} \\ a_{21} & a_{22} \end{pmatrix}.$$

We say that a matrix is $m \times n$ in size, where m represents the number of rows and n represents the number of columns. For example,

$$B = \begin{pmatrix} 1 & 2 & 3 \\ 4 & 5 & 6 \end{pmatrix}$$

is a 2×3 matrix. When a matrix has only one row and several columns, or one column and several rows, it is called a *vector*. For example,

$$a = \begin{pmatrix} 1 \\ 2 \\ 3 \\ 4 \end{pmatrix},$$

$$b = (5, 6, 7).$$

Vectors

Vectors have many interesting properties in the social sciences. It is important to remember, however, that we are talking about vectors as *points in space*. For example, Fig. 2:1 is the *mapping* of the vector

$$c = \begin{pmatrix} a_1 \\ b_1 \end{pmatrix}.$$

We can have n-dimensional vectors as well as our simple two-dimensional example in Fig. 2:1. In Fig. 2:2 a three-dimensional vector is shown for

$$d = \begin{pmatrix} a_1 \\ b_1 \\ c_1 \end{pmatrix}.$$

Regardless of the dimensions, a vector for urban and social science analysis will always start at origin in a mapping.[1] (It is possible to conceive of cases in economics, planning, and other problem areas where vectors start away from origin, but solution is improved by reconstructing the axes to form a new origin.)

---

[1] It is important to distinguish vectors as used in physics to represent *magnitude* and *direction* from our intended use of the concept.

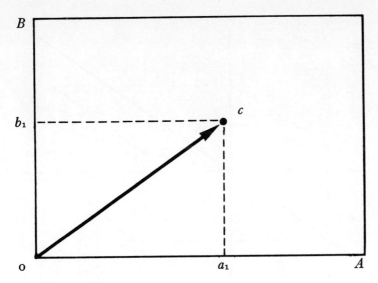

FIG. 2:1. Points in space.

We usually call a vector of the form

$$p = \begin{pmatrix} x_1 \\ x_2 \\ \cdot \\ \cdot \\ \cdot \\ x_n \end{pmatrix}$$

a *column vector*. If we wanted to treat it as a *row vector*, we can *transpose* the vector:

$$p' = (x_1, x_2, \ldots, x_n).$$

It may be recalled from plane geometry that vectors can be added, subtracted, and multiplied. This is, of course, true algebraically. We can add and subtract vectors:

$$p_1 = \begin{pmatrix} x_{11} \\ x_{21} \\ \cdot \\ \cdot \\ \cdot \\ x_{n1} \end{pmatrix}, \ p_2 = \begin{pmatrix} x_{12} \\ x_{22} \\ \cdot \\ \cdot \\ \cdot \\ x_{n2} \end{pmatrix},$$

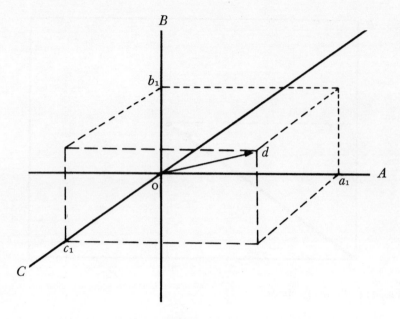

FIG. 2:2. Three-dimensional points in space.

and

$$p_1 \pm p_2 = \begin{pmatrix} x_{11} \pm x_{12} \\ x_{21} \pm x_{22} \\ \cdot \quad\quad \cdot \\ \cdot \quad\quad \cdot \\ \cdot \quad\quad \cdot \\ x_{n1} \pm x_{n2} \end{pmatrix}.$$

When a vector is multiplied by a single value, often called a *scalar*, the following rule holds:

$$kp_1 = \begin{pmatrix} kx_{11} \\ kx_{21} \\ \cdot \\ \cdot \\ \cdot \\ kx_{n1} \end{pmatrix}.$$

Column vectors can be multiplied by other vectors with the same number of elements by a process called the *inner product*. Take two column vectors,

$$p_1 = \begin{pmatrix} a_1 \\ a_2 \\ \cdot \\ \cdot \\ \cdot \\ a_n \end{pmatrix}, \; p_2 = \begin{pmatrix} b_1 \\ b_2 \\ \cdot \\ \cdot \\ \cdot \\ b_n \end{pmatrix},$$

as a matter of convention, transpose the first vector, or multiplicand, and calculate according to the general form:

$$p'_1 p_2 = \sum_{i=1}^{n} a_i b_i.$$

Note that the result of an inner product is always a scalar; for example,

$$p_1 = \begin{pmatrix} 1 \\ 2 \\ 3 \end{pmatrix}, \; p_2 = \begin{pmatrix} 4 \\ 5 \\ 6 \end{pmatrix};$$

hence

$$p'_1 p_2 = (1 \times 4) + (2 \times 5) + (3 \times 6) = 32.$$

Column vectors can be multiplied by row vectors with the same number of elements by taking the inner product without the necessity of transposing.

Matrix Addition and Subtraction

If we consider a matrix to be a set of vectors, many of its mathematical properties can be easily understood. It is possible to add and subtract matrices if and only if they have the same *shape,* that is, the same number of rows and columns. If two matrices have different shapes, they cannot be added or subtracted. Consider, for example,

$$A = \begin{pmatrix} a_{11} & a_{12} & \cdots & a_{1n} \\ a_{21} & a_{22} & \cdots & a_{2n} \\ \cdot & \cdot & & \cdot \\ \cdot & \cdot & & \cdot \\ \cdot & \cdot & & \cdot \\ a_{m1} & a_{m2} & \cdots & a_{mn} \end{pmatrix}, \; B = \begin{pmatrix} b_{11} & b_{12} & \cdots & b_{1n} \\ b_{21} & b_{22} & \cdots & b_{2n} \\ \cdot & \cdot & & \cdot \\ \cdot & \cdot & & \cdot \\ \cdot & \cdot & & \cdot \\ b_{m1} & b_{m2} & \cdots & b_{mn} \end{pmatrix},$$

and adding or subtracting:

$$A \pm B = \begin{pmatrix} a_{11} \pm b_{11} & a_{12} \pm b_{12} & . & . & . & a_{1n} \pm b_{1n} \\ a_{21} \pm b_{21} & a_{22} \pm b_{22} & . & . & . & a_{2n} \pm b_{2n} \\ . & . & & & & . \\ . & . & & & & . \\ . & . & & & & . \\ a_{m1} \pm b_{m1} & a_{m2} \pm b_{m2} & . & . & . & a_{mn} \pm b_{mn} \end{pmatrix}.$$

The general rule is that a matrix A which is the same shape as matrix B can be added or subtracted to form a new matrix C with the same shape: $A + B = C$, in which $c_{ij} = a_{ij} \pm b_{ij}$.

Matrix Transposition

A matrix can be transposed by exchanging rows and columns, so that row 1 becomes column 1, row 2 becomes column 2, etc. For example,

$$A = \begin{pmatrix} a_{11} & a_{12} & . & . & . & a_{1n} \\ a_{21} & a_{22} & . & . & . & a_{2n} \\ . & . & & & & . \\ . & . & & & & . \\ . & . & & & & . \\ a_{m1} & a_{m2} & . & . & . & a_{mn} \end{pmatrix}$$

can be transposed so that

$$A' = \begin{pmatrix} a_{11} & a_{21} & . & . & . & a_{m1} \\ a_{12} & a_{22} & . & . & . & a_{m2} \\ . & . & & & & . \\ . & . & & & & . \\ . & . & & & & . \\ a_{1n} & a_{2n} & . & . & . & a_{mn} \end{pmatrix}.$$

As can be seen, if A is $m \times n$, then A' is $n \times m$. Transposed matrices have many useful properties which will be explored later.

Matrix Multiplication

Any matrix A can be multiplied by a scalar k; for example,

$$k \begin{pmatrix} a_{11} & a_{12} & . & . & . & a_{1n} \\ a_{21} & a_{22} & . & . & . & a_{2n} \\ . & . & & & & . \\ . & . & & & & . \\ . & . & & & & . \\ a_{m1} & a_{m2} & . & . & . & a_{mn} \end{pmatrix} = \begin{pmatrix} ka_{11} & ka_{12} & . & . & . & ka_{1n} \\ ka_{21} & ka_{22} & . & . & . & ka_{2n} \\ . & . & & & & . \\ . & . & & & & . \\ . & . & & & & . \\ ka_{m1} & ka_{m2} & . & . & . & ka_{mn} \end{pmatrix}.$$

It can be readily seen that A and kA or Ak have the same shape.

A matrix A can be multiplied by a column vector x if the number of elements in x is equal to the number of rows in A. For example, matrix A multiplied by vector x is equal to vector y, or $Ax = y$:

$$\begin{pmatrix} a_{11} & a_{12} & \cdots & a_{1p} \\ a_{21} & a_{22} & \cdots & a_{2p} \\ \cdot & \cdot & & \cdot \\ \cdot & \cdot & & \cdot \\ \cdot & \cdot & & \cdot \\ a_{m1} & a_{m2} & \cdots & a_{mp} \end{pmatrix} \begin{pmatrix} x_1 \\ x_2 \\ \cdot \\ \cdot \\ \cdot \\ x_p \end{pmatrix} = \begin{pmatrix} a_{11}x_1 + \cdots + a_{1p}x_p \\ a_{21}x_1 + \cdots + a_{2p}x_p \\ \cdot \\ \cdot \\ \cdot \\ a_{m1}x_1 + \cdots + a_{mp}x_p \end{pmatrix}.$$

To put this another way, we are taking the inner product of p columns and m rows with vector x to form a new vector y. Another example is to take matrix B and multiply by row vector a:

$$(a_1, a_2, \ldots, a_p) \begin{pmatrix} b_{11} & b_{12} & \cdots & b_{1n} \\ b_{21} & b_{22} & \cdots & b_{2n} \\ \cdot & \cdot & & \cdot \\ \cdot & \cdot & & \cdot \\ \cdot & \cdot & & \cdot \\ b_{p1} & b_{p2} & \cdots & b_{pn} \end{pmatrix}$$

$$= \left(\sum_{i=1}^{p} a_i b_{i1}, \sum_{i=1}^{p} a_i b_{i2}, \ldots, \sum_{i=1}^{p} a_i b_{in} \right).$$

If matrix A has the same number of columns as matrix B has rows, then this process can be extended in order to multiply matrix A by matrix B to form matrix AB. Unlike real-number multiplication, however, products are not always *commutative*: $AB \neq BA$. In order to multiply A by B, the number of rows in A must be equal to the number of columns in B. If we say $AB = C$, then

$$c_{ij} = a_{i1}b_{1j} + a_{i2}b_{2j} + \ldots + a_{ip}b_{pj},$$

where

$$\begin{pmatrix} a_{11} & \cdots & a_{1p} \\ \cdot & \cdot & \cdot \\ a_{i1} & \cdots & a_{ip} \\ \cdot & \cdot & \cdot \\ a_{m1} & \cdots & a_{mp} \end{pmatrix} \begin{pmatrix} b_{11} & \cdots & b_{ij} & \cdots & b_{1n} \\ \cdot & \cdot & \cdot & \cdot & \cdot \\ \cdot & \cdot & \cdot & \cdot & \cdot \\ \cdot & \cdot & \cdot & \cdot & \cdot \\ b_{p1} & \cdots & b_{pj} & \cdots & b_{pn} \end{pmatrix} = \begin{pmatrix} c_{11} & \cdots & c_{1n} \\ \cdot & \cdot & \cdot \\ \cdot & c_{ij} & \cdot \\ \cdot & \cdot & \cdot \\ c_{m1} & \cdots & c_{mn} \end{pmatrix}.$$

An example may illustrate matrix multiplication:

$$A = \begin{pmatrix} 1 & 2 \\ 3 & 4 \end{pmatrix}, B = \begin{pmatrix} 5 & 6 \\ 7 & 8 \end{pmatrix};$$

therefore

$$AB = \begin{pmatrix} 1\times5+2\times7 & 1\times6+2\times8 \\ 3\times5+4\times7 & 3\times6+4\times8 \end{pmatrix} = \begin{pmatrix} 19 & 22 \\ 43 & 50 \end{pmatrix};$$

however,

$$BA = \begin{pmatrix} 5\times1+6\times3 & 5\times2+6\times4 \\ 7\times1+8\times3 & 7\times2+8\times4 \end{pmatrix} = \begin{pmatrix} 23 & 34 \\ 31 & 46 \end{pmatrix},$$

and

$$AB \neq BA.$$

There is a major exception to this rule.[2] When we have an $n \times n$ or *square matrix* with ones along the diagonal and zeros elsewhere, it is called an *identity matrix* and is denoted by I. For example,

$$I = \begin{pmatrix} 1 & 0 & 0 & 0 \\ 0 & 1 & 0 & 0 \\ 0 & 0 & 1 & 0 \\ 0 & 0 & 0 & 1 \end{pmatrix}$$

is a 4×4 identity matrix. The identity matrix multiplied by any matrix A which fits multiplication rules always results in product matrix A; that is,

$$AI = IA = A.$$

Inverses

One may recall from algebra that for every real number $n \neq 0$, there is an inverse, n^{-1} or $1/n$, such that

$$n \cdot n^{-1} = n^{-1} \cdot n = 1.$$

Some, but not all, matrices have inverses. A matrix may have an inverse only if it is (1) square and (2) *nonsingular*.[3] If matrix A is square and nonsingular, then it has an inverse A^{-1} such that

$$A^{-1} \cdot A = A \cdot A^{-1} = I.$$

There are several ways to compute an inverse matrix — the simplest

[2] There are also some minor cases where $AB = BA$ due largely to coincidence; for example,

$$\begin{bmatrix} 2 & 1 \\ 3 & 4 \end{bmatrix} \times \begin{bmatrix} 1 & 2 \\ 6 & 5 \end{bmatrix} = \begin{bmatrix} 1 & 2 \\ 6 & 5 \end{bmatrix} \times \begin{bmatrix} 2 & 1 \\ 3 & 4 \end{bmatrix} = \begin{bmatrix} 8 & 9 \\ 27 & 20 \end{bmatrix}.$$

[3] A matrix A is nonsingular if its *determinant* $d(A) \neq 0$. A determinant is computed by adding all right diagonals and subtracting all left diagonals, the result being $\neq 0$. Most matrices in urban problems are nonsingular and have determinants, which is another way of saying that the rows and columns of the matrices are not the same. For further development, see readings listed at end of chapter.

way is through *row operations*. In row operations we use the mathematical nature of *augmented* matrices to manipulate the matrix on the left side so as to form its identity matrix — the resultant on the right side being its inverse. For example,

$$A = \begin{pmatrix} 1 & 2 \\ 3 & 4 \end{pmatrix};$$

we want A^{-1}, so we use the augmented form:

Step 1

$$\begin{pmatrix} 1 & 2 & | & 1 & 0 \\ 3 & 4 & | & 0 & 1 \end{pmatrix}.$$

We want the left-hand side to be I. Row operations require that we use any real combination of rows or any multiple of rows to make the first row become (1,0) and the second row become (0,1).

Step 2: row 2 − 3 (row 1)

$$\begin{pmatrix} 1 & 2 & | & 1 & 0 \\ 0 & -2 & | & -3 & 1 \end{pmatrix}.$$

Step 3: row 2 multiplied by $(-\frac{1}{2})$

$$\begin{pmatrix} 1 & 2 & | & 1 & 0 \\ 0 & 1 & | & \frac{3}{2} & -\frac{1}{2} \end{pmatrix}.$$

Step 4: row 1 − 2 (row 2)

$$\begin{pmatrix} 1 & 0 & | & -2 & 1 \\ 0 & 1 & | & \frac{3}{2} & -\frac{1}{2} \end{pmatrix}.$$

Thus

$$A^{-1} = \begin{pmatrix} -2 & 1 \\ \frac{3}{2} & -\frac{1}{2} \end{pmatrix},$$

and as proof:

$$AA^{-1} = \begin{pmatrix} 1 & 2 \\ 3 & 4 \end{pmatrix} \begin{pmatrix} -2 & 1 \\ \frac{3}{2} & -\frac{1}{2} \end{pmatrix} = \begin{pmatrix} 1 & 0 \\ 0 & 1 \end{pmatrix}.$$

Buried in the process of row operations is the mathematical concept which proves that we can multiply, add, or subtract rows in an augmented matrix without changing the inherent mathematical meaning of the matrix. This provides urban analysts with a most useful tool.

Solution of Equations

A practical application of matrix operations is the solution of *simul-*

taneous equations. Let us develop a problem concerned with incomplete data. We are considering felonies (x_1) and misdemeanors (x_2) for a week in a given city in two police precincts or reporting units, but the reporting practices do not make the distinction we seek. In precinct A there were six arrests which officers say were in the same proportion of felonies to misdemeanors. Precinct B reported nine arrests with twice as many felonies as precinct A. This can be shown as

$$\text{A:} \quad x_1 + x_2 = 6,$$
$$\text{B:} \quad 2x_1 + x_2 = 9.$$

In matrix notation this can be shown as

$$Kx = n$$

or

$$\begin{pmatrix} 1 & 1 \\ 2 & 1 \end{pmatrix} \begin{pmatrix} x_1 \\ x_2 \end{pmatrix} = \begin{pmatrix} 6 \\ 9 \end{pmatrix}.$$

While this example could be solved by simultaneous equations, it can also be solved by matrix operations, since

$$K^{-1}Kx = K^{-1}n \text{ and}$$
$$Ix = K^{-1}n, \text{ or}$$
$$x = K^{-1}n.$$

This yields a vector which is the solution for the unknown x elements. It is solved by the use of row operations on the augmented matrix.

Step 1

$$\left(\begin{array}{cc|c} 1 & 1 & 6 \\ 2 & 1 & 9 \end{array} \right).$$

Step 2: row 2 − 2 (row 1)

$$\left(\begin{array}{cc|c} 1 & 1 & 6 \\ 0 & -1 & -3 \end{array} \right).$$

Step 3: row 2 multiplied by (−1)

$$\left(\begin{array}{cc|c} 1 & 1 & 6 \\ 0 & 1 & 3 \end{array} \right).$$

Step 4: row 1 − row 2

$$\left(\begin{array}{cc|c} 1 & 0 & 3 \\ 0 & 1 & 3 \end{array} \right).$$

Thus the solution vector shows that $x_1 = 3$ and $x_2 = 3$. This allows us to complete our missing data in the example.

MATRIX APPLICATIONS

It is not possible or practical to explore all of the applications of matrix operations to urban analysis. There has been increased emphasis on these applications in recent years in deterministic models. Many everyday analytical problems of urban systems can be better handled through matrix methods.

AGE-COHORT-SURVIVAL MODEL

A particularly interesting application of matrix methods has been for demographic estimates and projections. Demographic models tend to be inadequate in many urban analyses and fail to utilize efficient mathematics. The matrix approach, coupled with the probabilistic *age-cohort-survival model,* is a most sensible approach to correcting this situation.

The age-cohort-survival model evaluates the population by age groups according to the pattern of fertility and mortality that has been observed or predicted and introduces an explicit effect of net migration (regardless of whether it is an increase or a decline). The age cohorts are analyzed over time, often in five-year cohorts, as they change according to appropriate fertility, mortality, and net migration. Further refinements may be made for race, sex, income, etc., depending on data availability and necessity. The conceptual age-cohort-survival model can be shown symbolically as

$$P_{t+n} = P_t + (BP_t + G) - (DP_t + L),$$

where

P_t = base population in year t,
n = number of years beyond t for estimate,
B = birth rates,
D = death rates,
G = in-migration during n years,
L = out-migration during n years.

Urban analysts have introduced matrix methods into the solution of age-cohort-survival models because of the computational and conceptual advantages. One approach utilizes matrix multiplication to analyze the effects of fertility and mortality and then develops a *transition matrix* to account for the effects of migration on each age group.[4]

[4] Andrei Rogers, "Matrix Methods of Population Analysis," *Journal of the American Institute of Planners,* 32, no. 1 (Jan., 1966), 40-44; Nathan Keyfitz, "The Population Projection as a Matrix Operator," *Demography,* 1 (1964), 56-73.

The approach of Nathan Keyfitz, and the urban orientation given to Keyfitz's approach by Andrei Rogers, are interesting for our purposes. Mortality can be treated through matrix methods to show the effects upon a population which is divided into m age groups, assuming that the time period $n = 1$ for simplicity. In this case the matrix equation is

$$DP_t = P_{t+n}^{**},$$

where the two asterisks above P serve to indicate that the effects of fertility and net migration have not yet been examined. The matrix of death rates is expressed as

$$
\begin{matrix} D \\ m \times m \end{matrix} =
\begin{pmatrix}
0 & 0 & 0 & . & . & . & 0 \\
d_1 & 0 & 0 & . & . & . & 0 \\
0 & d_2 & 0 & . & . & . & 0 \\
0 & 0 & d_3 & . & . & . & 0 \\
. & . & . & & & & . \\
. & . & . & & & & . \\
. & . & . & & & & . \\
0 & 0 & 0 & . & . & d_{m-1} & 0
\end{pmatrix}.
$$

The only nonzero terms are on the subdiagonal, which has the effect of advancing each age group over the time period $n = 1$. In essence, since these rates are actually the probabilities that any person in the mth age group will survive to the next age group over the time period n, we have a probabilistic model composed of $n - 1$ probabilities. An example may clarify this. Assume a population of 4,000 that is evenly divided into four age groups: 0-14, 15-29, 30-44, 45 and over. Assume, for simplicity, that all age groups have the same probability of survival, where $d_m = .90$, which is another way of saying that 10 percent of each age group will not survive until the next age group. The matrix approach for finding P_{t+n}^{**} then becomes

$$
P_{t+n}^{**} =
\begin{pmatrix}
0 & 0 & 0 & 0 \\
.9 & 0 & 0 & 0 \\
0 & .9 & 0 & 0 \\
0 & 0 & .9 & 0
\end{pmatrix}
\begin{pmatrix}
1000 \\
1000 \\
1000 \\
1000
\end{pmatrix}
=
\begin{pmatrix}
0 \\
900 \\
900 \\
900
\end{pmatrix}
$$

The effects of fertility are examined in a similar manner. In ordinary approaches fertility rates are determined for women in the child-bearing age groups and a survival rate is applied to those children. In matrix terms a seemingly crude approach is undertaken where a birth rate is computed for each age group, regardless of sex, during a given time period, and these births are summed for total increases. The computation of these rates, however, can include adjustments for child survival; hence the absence of a sex breakdown (which is done for simplicity) does not interfere with the conceptual validity of the model. The fertility matrix B is computed in general:

$$
\begin{matrix} B \\ m \times m \end{matrix} =
\begin{pmatrix}
0 & 0 & . & . & . & 0 & b_1 & b_2 & b_3 & . & . & . & b_v & . & . & . & 0 & . & . & . & 0 \\
0 & 0 & & & & 0 & & . & . & . & & & . & & & & 0 & . & . & . & 0 \\
. & . & & & & . & . & . & . & . & & & . & & & & . & & & & . \\
. & . & & & & . & . & . & . & . & & & . & & & & . & & & & . \\
. & . & & & & . & . & . & . & . & & & . & & & & . & & & & . \\
. & . & & & & . & . & . & . & . & & & . & & & & . & & & & . \\
0 & 0 & . & . & . & 0 & 0 & 0 & 0 & . & . & . & 0 & . & . & . & 0 & . & . & . & 0
\end{pmatrix}.
$$

Note that only first-row elements which correspond to child-bearing age groups are greater than zero. Returning to our example, and assuming birth rates of .7 for the 15-29 age group and .5 for the 30-44 age group, we see that

$$
\begin{pmatrix}
0 & .7 & .5 & 0 \\
0 & 0 & 0 & 0 \\
0 & 0 & 0 & 0 \\
0 & 0 & 0 & 0
\end{pmatrix}
\begin{pmatrix}
1000 \\
1000 \\
1000 \\
1000
\end{pmatrix}
=
\begin{pmatrix}
1200 \\
0 \\
0 \\
0
\end{pmatrix}.
$$

We can determine a "survivorship" matrix S by adding B and D, where

$$
\begin{matrix} S \\ m \times m \end{matrix} = B + D =
\begin{pmatrix}
0 & 0 & 0 & . & . & . & b_1 & b_2 & . & . & . & b_v & 0 & . & . & . & 0 \\
d_1 & 0 & 0 & . & . & . & 0 & 0 & . & . & . & 0 & 0 & . & . & . & 0 \\
0 & d_2 & 0 & . & . & . & 0 & 0 & . & . & . & 0 & 0 & . & . & . & 0 \\
0 & 0 & d_3 & . & . & . & 0 & 0 & . & . & . & 0 & 0 & . & . & . & 0 \\
. & . & . & & & & . & . & & & & & & & & & . \\
. & . & . & & & & . & . & & & & & & & & & . \\
. & . & . & & & & . & . & & & & & & & & & . \\
0 & 0 & 0 & . & . & . & 0 & 0 & . & . & . & d_{m-1} & . & . & . & 0
\end{pmatrix}.
$$

Using our example,

$$
S =
\begin{pmatrix}
0 & .7 & .5 & 0 \\
.9 & 0 & 0 & 0 \\
0 & .9 & 0 & 0 \\
0 & 0 & .9 & 0
\end{pmatrix}.
$$

Since we account for fertility and mortality by S, we can find $P^*_{t+n} = SP_t$. In our example

$$
SP_t = P^*_{t+n} =
\begin{pmatrix}
0 & .7 & .5 & 0 \\
.9 & 0 & 0 & 0 \\
0 & .9 & 0 & 0 \\
0 & 0 & .9 & 0
\end{pmatrix}
\begin{pmatrix}
1000 \\
1000 \\
1000 \\
1000
\end{pmatrix}
=
\begin{pmatrix}
1200 \\
900 \\
900 \\
900
\end{pmatrix}.
$$

The asterisk above P serves to indicate that net migration has yet to be examined.

There are several scientific methods for estimating and predicting net migration. Rogers has used matrix methods to determine the net migration into an urban area from other urban areas in a California analysis.[5] This analysis, coupled with his theoretical approaches, offers a valid approach for a sophisticated application of matrix methods.[6] For less sophisticated approaches, dictated by time, money, or data constraints, any number of deterministic or probabilistic models can be employed to estimate and predict net migration. In our terminology the product of such efforts is a net migration vector (or matrix if several urban systems are being analyzed at the same time) which we call T, such that $T = G - L$. The vector T allows us to solve for P_{t+n}, where

$$P_{t+n} = SP_t + T_{t+n},$$

and allows us to estimate population by accounting for the effects of survivorship, fertility, and net migration. Assuming that

$$T = \begin{pmatrix} 100 \\ 200 \\ 150 \\ 110 \end{pmatrix}$$

in our example, we see that

$$P_{t+n} = \begin{pmatrix} 0 & .7 & .5 & 0 \\ .9 & 0 & 0 & 0 \\ 0 & .9 & 0 & 0 \\ 0 & 0 & .9 & 0 \end{pmatrix} \begin{pmatrix} 1000 \\ 1000 \\ 1000 \\ 1000 \end{pmatrix} + \begin{pmatrix} 100 \\ 200 \\ 150 \\ 110 \end{pmatrix} = \begin{pmatrix} 1300 \\ 1100 \\ 1050 \\ 1010 \end{pmatrix}.$$

Thus our hypothetical urban system is predicted to experience an increase of population in the amount of 460 persons by the time $t + n$, and more than 91 percent of that population will probably be less than 30 years old.

GOALS-ACHIEVEMENT MATRIX

Matrix methods have been used in less quantitative models for urban analysis. A good example of this type of application is the *goals-achieve-*

[5] Andrei Rogers, *Projected Population Growth in California Regions: 1960-1980* (Berkeley: University of California, 1966).

[6] Andrei Rogers, "A Markovian Policy Model of Migration," *Regional Science Association Papers,* 17 (1966), 205-224.

ment matrix developed by Morris Hill to test alternative solutions for solving urban problems or alternative plans for attaining urban goals.[7] Hill uses cost-benefit analysis, which is a method for computing the relevant direct and indirect costs and accrued benefits for each alternative plan and devising a ratio or other ranking computation, in a matrix approach. Various interest groups in the urban system are included in these computations through an analysis of the manner in which they perceive the costs and benefits for each goal and plan. Rather than limiting the measures of costs and benefits to the traditional resources of land, labor, and capital, Hill argues that the measure can vary depending on the particular goal. For example, time saved in travel, housing units retained, or other such measures may or may not be valid in a given application.

The goals-achievement matrix is developed by a vector which assigns weights to each group in a manner indicating the desired distribution of benefits. The costs and benefits are computed for each group by multiplying the group weight vector by the overall urban system benefit index. The plan or solution with the highest index would be ranked first. An example, using a modification of Hill's method, may be illustrative. Assume that plans A, B, and C purport to satisfy goal set S of n groups in an urban system. For each plan there is an associated benefit/cost index for the entire urban system, which can be expressed as scalars ub_a, ub_b, and ub_c. For each group there is an associated weight vector for each plan which shows desired benefit distribution. The goals-achievement matrix would take the general form represented in Table 2:1. Plans A, B, and C would

TABLE 2:1. Goals-achievement matrix.

	Goal Set S		
	Plan A	Plan B	Plan C
Group 1 Group 2 . . . Group n	$\begin{pmatrix} wa_1 \\ wa_2 \\ . \\ . \\ . \\ wa_n \end{pmatrix} ub_a$	$\begin{pmatrix} wb_1 \\ wb_2 \\ . \\ . \\ . \\ wb_n \end{pmatrix} ub_b$	$\begin{pmatrix} wc_1 \\ wc_2 \\ . \\ . \\ . \\ wc_n \end{pmatrix} ub_c$
	total benefit $= \sum_{i=1}^{n} (wa_i ub_a; \, wb_i ub_b; \, wc_i ub_c)$		

[7] Morris Hill, "A Goals Achievement Matrix for Evaluating Alternative Plans," *Journal of the American Institute of Planners*, 34, no. 1 (Jan., 1968), 19-29.

then be ranked in order of their respective total benefit. Note that there is much intuitive analysis in this model even though it is basically a deterministic matrix model.

TESTS OF MATRIX MODELS

Models should be tested in any application of scientific methods to urban analysis. It is especially important to test matrix models because they usually take many variations for given problems. Matrix models often involve input derived from intuitive analyses and informed judgment. While this does not lessen the utility of such models, it does give varying results for similar problem situations. The urban analyst should strive to develop the most efficient and reasonably accurate model that is possible through matrix methods.

Testing matrix models is largely an intuitive procedure based upon judgment with an assist from several measures of performance that are borrowed from applied mathematics or statistics (the science of data collection and classification in mathematical terms of their occurrence or relative number as a basis for inference). Three of these measures of performance are examined: (1) *graphic comparison,* (2) *root mean square,* and (3) *chi square.* It should be made clear, however, that these tests only provide verifications of intuitive analyses or an added factor for a judgment.

GRAPHIC COMPARISON

The simplest and most common test of matrix models is a mapping or graphic comparison of the results of the model and the real-world observations. Observations from the real-world problem are plotted in a mapping, and the corresponding estimates or predictions from the model are plotted. The differentials can be examined visually to determine how well the model compares to the real world; of course, this means in the eyes of the analyst.

Let us consider a well-known matrix model for illustrative purposes. Nobel Laureate Jan Tinbergen of the Netherlands School of Economics has been concerned with the distribution of people into urban centers and agricultural or rural areas as a function of their employment in various industries. In one of his models Tinbergen hypothesizes that the distribution of population into centers of various sizes (determined by the variety and number of industries and ranked in a hierarchy) can be estimated by a matrix model.[8] Tinbergen develops a series of matrix models which account for employment, demand for products of industries, income, and population distribution into centers in a rank order. He applies his models to modern-day France (making several simplifying assumptions) and arrives at the following results in Table 2:2. As can be seen, the urban centers

TABLE 2:2. Estimated and observed distribution of population.

Rank Order of Urban Centers	Number of Urban Centers in Rank Group	Estimated Total Population (thousands)	Observed Total Population (thousands)
7	1	5,100	7,813
6	4	3,575	2,626
5	20	10,040	4,725
4	69	9,335	5,317
3	203	5,507	4,615
2	599	1,959	3,671
1	2,257	1,314	5,174
0	–	10,722	13,613

are ranked from 7 to 0, with only one center (Paris) in the highest rank grouping and no centers in the lowest rank grouping (rural areas without urban centers).

The results of the model can be graphically compared to observations on the number of people living in each type of center in France (Fig. 2:3). This graphic comparison indicates something about the results from the model and the real-world corresponding observations. With the exception of Paris (rank group 7), the model tends to predict a higher concentration of people in the higher-ranked centers than has actually been observed. In the lowest-ranked groupings the model tends to underestimate the population distribution within the centers and rural areas. The question can then be raised about whether the model is conceptually adequate (in this case the model is based on a set of assumptions that tends to reflect optimal economic conditions, and the real world may not reflect these conditions). It is assumed, however, that the observations are accurate and that there are no computational errors (although this is always a possibility).

[8] Jan Tinbergen, "The Hierarchy Model of the Size Distribution of Centres," *Regional Science Association Papers,* 20 (1968), 61-68.

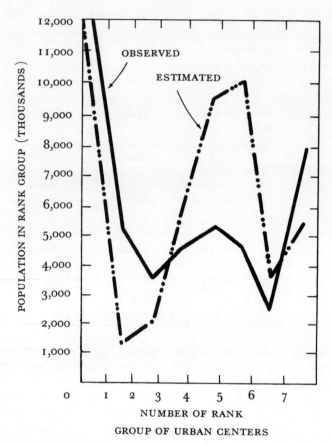

FIG. 2:3. Observed and estimated population by rank group
of urban centers.

ROOT MEAN SQUARE

The root-mean-square test is a way to determine how much error or
difference exists between the real world and the results of a model. The
root-mean-square test is well known and is often called the *standard deviation* or σ (the square of σ is called the variance). It is used to determine
the percentage of error by computing the root mean square as a percentage
of the mean of observed data from the real world — this is called the
coefficient of variance or V.

In order to compute the root mean square, which we can designate as *rms,* the following equation must be solved:

$$\sigma = rms = \sqrt{\frac{\Sigma\,(\text{observed} - \text{predicted})^2}{\text{number of observations}}},$$

or symbolically,

$$\sigma = rms = \sqrt{\frac{\Sigma(\chi - \chi_c)^2}{n}},$$

where

χ = observed data,

χ_c = estimated data,

n = number of observations.

The root-mean-square test computes the difference between a real-world data observation and its corresponding model estimate and squares this difference to attain all positive values, which are then averaged by dividing the summation by the number of observations; finally, the square root of the resultant is taken in order to determine the average or standard deviation from the real world. This can be expressed in terms of a percentage of the mean of data observed for the real world $(\bar{\chi})$ by

$$V = \left(\frac{rms}{\bar{\chi}}\right)\,100.00.$$

This test measures the relative difference or coefficient of variance between the model results and the real world.

The *rms* and *V* of Table 2:2 can be calculated for illustrative purposes. The result shows that the *rms* is 3,155, which, expressed as the coefficient of variance, is 53.0 percent. In either test an analyst would conclude, as Tinbergen did, that the model needs further experimentation and testing before more applications are made. The graphic comparison may indicate what areas need to be re-examined. While the *rms* and *V* may be interpreted differently by different analysts, the general rule is that a good model has the lowest *rms* and *V* possible — within reason and within the judgment of the analyst.

CHI SQUARE

The chi-square test is a measure of the difference between observed data and model results which can be used alone or with the root mean square as a further aid in judging the appropriateness of a matrix model. The

TABLE 2:3. Calculation of *rms* and *V* for Table 2:2.

χ	χ_c	$\chi - \chi_c$	$(\chi - \chi_c)^2$
7,813	5,100	2,713	7,360,369
2,626	3,575	−949	900,601
4,725	10,040	−5,315	28,249,225
5,317	9,335	−4,018	16,144,324
4,615	5,507	−892	795,664
3,671	1,959	1,712	2,930,944
5,174	1,314	3,860	14,899,600
13,613	10,722	2,891	8,357,881
−*	−	−	79,638,608

*$\bar{\chi}$ = 5,944

$$rms = \sqrt{\frac{79,638,608}{8}} = 3,155,$$

$$V = \left(\frac{3,155}{5,944}\right) 100 = 53.0 \text{ percent.}$$

chi square, χ^2, is computed by using the following equation for observed (χ) and expected or computed (χ_c) variables:

$$\chi^2 = \Sigma \left[\frac{(\chi - \chi_c)^2}{\chi_c}\right].$$

As can be seen, when actual observations and model results are the same, χ^2 will be zero — although in practice this can never occur because seemingly "perfect" models can be as invalid as "imperfect" models. After computing a χ^2, a standard table of chi-square values is consulted (see Appendix A). The chi-square standard table gives the probability P that there is no significant difference between observations and estimates or observed and theoretical data. This is done by computing the probability that the same theoretical observations could have been reached at random or by chance. Chi-square tables are presented by degrees of freedom (df) for a matrix, which means the number of opportunities in which values can be freely entered and removed from other cells of a matrix after an initial value has been entered.[9] The degree of freedom for $m \times n$ matrices is computed by

[9] For further discussion of degrees of freedom, see Frederick E. Croxton and Dudley J. Crowden, *Applied General Statistics* (Englewood Cliffs, N.J.: Prentice-Hall, 1955), pp. 681-691.

$$(m - 1)(n - 1) = df,$$

and for $m \times 1$ vectors by

$$(m - 1) = df.$$

An example of significance testing can be helpful. Assume that a rapid transit proposal referendum was approved in two neighborhoods, and we seek to determine whether there was a significant difference between the voting patterns in these two neighborhoods (which are different in size) (see Table 2:4).

TABLE 2:4. Rapid transit referendum.

	Neighborhood 1	Neighborhood 2	Total
Approved	160	440	600
Disapproved	100	180	280
Did Not Vote	40	80	120
Total	300	700	1,000

We can compute a theoretical value χ_c by assuming that each neighborhood would vote in the same proportion if there were no significant difference between them. For example, for disapproved votes in neighborhood 1, the theoretical vote would be $(280/1,000)300 = 84$, which is the proportion of disapprovals times the voters in neighborhood 1.

Summing from Tables 2:5 and 2:6, we get

$$\chi^2 = 5.71 + 2.44 = 8.15.$$

Since the matrix is 3×2, we see that there are two degrees of freedom. Looking up $\chi^2 = 8.15$ in a chi-square table for $df = 2$, we see that P is less than 0.05 and greater than 0.025. This means that the probability that there is no significant difference between neighborhoods 1 and 2 in their voting is between 5 and 2.5 percent. Since this is a very low probability, we could conclude that there is a significant difference in the voting on rapid transit between the two neighborhoods. As a general rule urban analysts consider data observations to be "significant" when the chi square indicates a P of less than 0.05 and "highly significant" when P is less than 0.01, but judgment may yield different conclusions.

A special use of χ^2 as a test of how well a matrix model estimates real-world observations is sometimes called a *goodness-of-fit* test. Table 2:7 represents the output of a 13×1 matrix model that estimates income by

TABLE 2:5. Neighborhood 1.

	x	x_c	$\dfrac{(x - x_c)^2}{x_c}$
Approved	160	180	2.22
Disapproved	100	84	3.05
Did Not Vote	40	36	.44
Total	300	300	5.71

TABLE 2:6. Neighborhood 2.

	x	x_c	$\dfrac{(x - x_c)^2}{x_c}$
Approved	440	420	.95
Disapproved	180	196	1.30
Did Not Vote	80	84	.19
Total	700	700	2.44

TABLE 2:7. Chi-square test of family income model.

Family Income Range (dollars)	Number of Families in Range[a]		$\dfrac{(x - x_c)^2}{x_c}$
	x	x_c	
Under $2,500	1	1.1	0.01
$ 2,500– 3,499	2	3.2	0.45
3,500– 4,499	7	9.1	0.48
4,500– 5,499	25	20.2	1.14
5,500– 6,499	33	35.0	0.11
6,500– 7,499	53	50.6	0.11
7,500– 8,499	64	57.4	0.76
8,500– 9,499	44	52.0	1.23
9,500–10,499	31	37.0	0.97
10,500–11,499	27	22.0	1.14
11,500–12,499	11	10.2	0.06
12,500–13,499	4	3.7	0.02
13,500 or more	1	1.5	0.17
Total	303	303.0	6.65

[a] This example is for illustrative purposes, and all frequencies of observations have been included in the x and x_c columns. In practice one is well advised to group ranges or intervals that have few observations, i.e., under $2,500 and $13,500 or more in our example, with the nearest range. This avoids errors in the computation of χ^2 and other measures.

number of families in a given neighborhood. The computed χ^2 is **6.65** and there are 12 degrees of freedom. The chi-square table indicates that P is less than 0.90 but greater than 0.80. This means that the probability that there is no difference between the observed data and the model results is high, and the model may be judged appropriate, since it so closely approximates the real world.

RECOMMENDED EXERCISES

1. Let

$$A = \begin{pmatrix} 11 & 22 & 33 & 14 \\ 15 & 61 & 21 & 18 \\ 19 & 10 & 11 & 32 \\ 18 & 44 & 15 & 26 \end{pmatrix}, \quad B = \begin{pmatrix} 11 & 25 & 19 & 20 \\ 22 & 36 & 10 & 33 \\ 18 & 17 & 11 & 49 \\ 34 & 28 & 13 & 50 \end{pmatrix}$$

Find

    (A) $A + B$ (B) $A - B$
    (C) $3A + 4B$ (D) AB

2. Let

$$A = \begin{pmatrix} 1 & 8 \\ 1 & 3 \end{pmatrix}, \quad x = \begin{pmatrix} x_1 \\ x_2 \end{pmatrix}, \quad y = \begin{pmatrix} 40 \\ 15 \end{pmatrix}.$$

Find χ for $A\chi = y$.

3. Develop an age-cohort-survival matrix model for any given city or part thereof. Use local vital statistics to determine the survivorship matrix, and use any readily available data for the net migration matrix (or estimate if no data are available). Using five-year age cohorts, project the population 20 years into the future, assuming that vital rates and net migration do not change.

4. Test the matrix model that you have developed in Exercise 3 by using the latest census data and finding the *rms*. Start your model with the nearest previous census for the area under study and conclude with the latest census year. Find the *rms* for the estimated and actual values for the latest census year.

5. Using the data presented for Exercise 1 in Chapter 1, use a chi-square test to determine if there is any significant difference between the response of students, teachers, and parents.

FURTHER READING

Lipschutz, Seymour. *Theory and Problems of Finite Mathematics*. New York: Schaum, 1966.

One of the well-known college outline series which treats matrix methods in an easily understandable manner and offers the student an opportunity to solve problems and verify his answers readily.

Perlis, Sam. *Theory of Matrices*. Reading, Mass.: Addison-Wesley, 1952.

A widely used textbook that treats matrix methods and related subjects in a mathematical manner at a higher level than other textbooks yet retains comprehension. The textbook also treats many subjects, such as determinants, that were not possible to examine in any detail in the present book.

A major use of the scientific method has been to estimate and predict the values of one variable by reference to the values of one or more associated variables. When a model can be developed which estimates and predicts variables through a pseudorelationship, based upon associated variables, the method is known as *correlation*. In this chapter we examine the most widely used form of correlation, which results in deterministic *linear models*.

Linear models are quite popular in all types of urban analysis because of their relative simplicity and accuracy. Linear models are by no means flawless, and they have been criticized on logical and mathematical grounds. There are pitfalls in the use of linear models which will be discussed. These pitfalls can be overcome or at least noted in the use of such models. Despite some recent philosophical arguments and lemmas, few scholars and analysts believe the real world to be linear; yet there is an appealing advantage in the application of linear models to urban analysis because of their inherent simplicity and comprehensibility. It is argued that since our knowledge of the real world of urban systems is imperfect, simplistic linear models are attractive predictors and estimators of imperfect variables.

Three applications of linear models are often found in urban analysis: (1) *trends,* (2) *relationships,* and (3) *explanations.* Linear models point out trends, usually over time, that may not be noted through intuitive or graphic analysis. Relationships can be determined by using the theory of correlation in conjunction with linear models. Linear models are used to explain occurrences (and predict the appearance and timing of occurrences) when nonscientific methods are inadequate or unsatisfactory.

Simple Linear Models

Simple linear models predict the values of a variable through its correlative functional association with *one* other variable raised to the first or zeroth power. Simple linear models are often called *trend lines, straight line projections,* or *regression lines.* The last term is derived from the computational process of correlation, which is called *regression* or *curve-*

CHAPTER 3

Linear Models

fitting. A simple linear model takes the mathematical form of a straight line, which is

$$Y = a + bX,$$

or for estimates and predictions,

$$y_c = a + bx_i,$$

where y_c stands for estimated or predicted $\hat{y}$. It is common to call the left-hand term (Y) the *dependent variable,* the right-hand term (X) the *in-* the *slope.* A mapping of this model assumes the familiar straight-line form of Fig. 3:1. As can be observed in Fig. 3:1, the point (vector) where the *dependent variable,* the constant (a) the *intercept,* and the constant (b) regression line touches the vertical or dependent variable axis is the intercept a. The slope of the regression line, which is the number of units that the dependent variable Y rises or falls for every unit of the independent

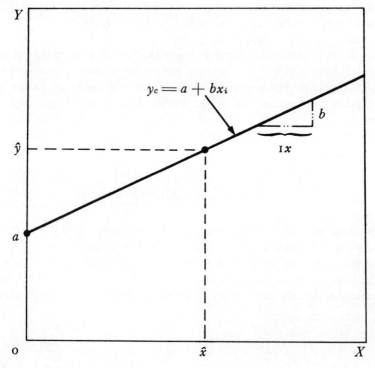

FIG. 3:1. Linear mapping.

variable X, is the constant b. The slope can be either positive or negative to indicate the nature of relationship of Y to X, and for every variable $\hat{x}_i$ (read as "x hat" and meaning a given value for x_i), there is a unique $\hat{y}_i$.

A good practice for urban analysts is to pretest the observations by graphic means. The plotting of observations of one variable for comparison with another is called a *scattergram*. For example, consider the scattergram shown as Fig. 3:2, which associates work-trip cost and work-trip distance

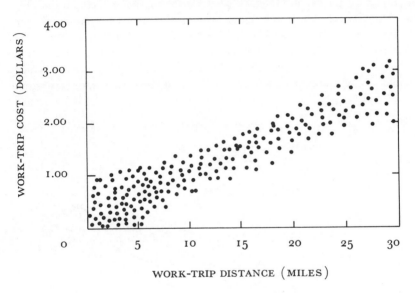

FIG. 3:2. Scattergram of work-trip distance and cost.

from national observations made by the Survey Research Center, University of Michigan. Solely by observation, we would suspect that a linear model could be developed, because the grouping of data has a steadily increasing slope and seems to follow a straight-line form. When observations do not reflect such a pattern, it may mean that nonlinear models are needed or that the data are too irregular to allow for any form of modeling. In special cases an observation of data may indicate that the nonlinear curves might approximate the trend of the clusters, but there are methods by which linear models could be used. For example, if we observe that clusters of data seem to resemble the curve of a squared function, such as $Y = X^2$, we could use a logarithmic base to form a linear relationship, such as $\log Y = 2 \log X$. This is called *transformation*.

SIMPLE REGRESSION COMPUTATIONS

The first step in fitting linear models is to plot a representative sample or selection of the observed data for the variables. This mapping is then examined for linear trends. The mapping is examined for variation by plotting bands that generally group the data. These bands should be equidistant in order to indicate that linearity exists. The third and final visual test should be an examination of whether the mapping seems to be normally distributed about the center line of the bands — that is, do the data between the bands seem to take a bell-shaped distribution about the center line of the bands? Those unfamiliar with the normal distribution may wish to refer to the section on the normal model in Chapter 5, which includes an introductory definition. These three visual tests are summarized in Fig. 3:3.

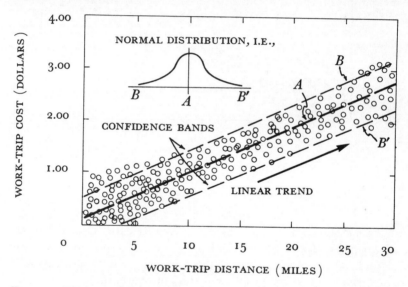

FIG. 3:3. Visual tests for linearity.

After having been reasonably convinced that the data would lend themselves to linear models through observation tests, the analyst can compute the values for a and b, which are called the model *parameters* (inherent characteristics). There are a number of computational rules or *algorithms* that can be used for finding parameters a and b. With the use of digital computers and library programs, the computational efforts can be minimal.

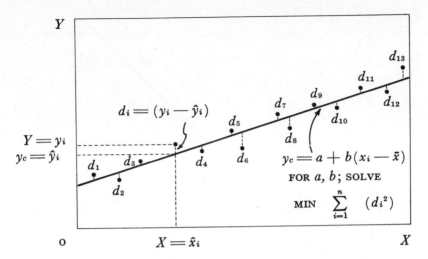

FIG. 3:4. Deviations from line of best fit.

For this reason it is valuable to discuss the algorithm most commonly found in library programs for finding a and b by use of digital computers.

The algorithm most commonly used for digital computer processing is called the *line of best fit*, as found by solving for the *least-squares* solution. The solution is called least squares because it minimizes the distance between observed data and the corresponding estimated values from a regression line. There are an infinite number of lines possible for approximating a set of observations, but only one will minimize the sum of the squared differences between observed and estimated values. Fig. 3:4 illustrates this concept.

For computational simplicity we can use the linear model form $y_c = a + b(x_i - \bar{x})$ (where $\bar{x}$ is the mean value for x) instead of the familiar $y_c = a + bx_i$.[1] The effect is to simplify interpretation and mathematically improve the accuracy of the line of best fit. We solve for the mean of the variables in the usual manner:

$$\bar{x} = \frac{1}{n} \sum_{i=1}^{n} x_i,$$

$$\bar{y} = \frac{1}{n} \sum_{i=1}^{n} y_i,$$

where n is the number of observations and both x and y have i vectors.

[1] These two forms are the same except that the intercept is a for $y_c = a + bx_i$; however, the intercept is $a - b\bar{x}$ for $y_c = a + b(x_i - \bar{x})$.

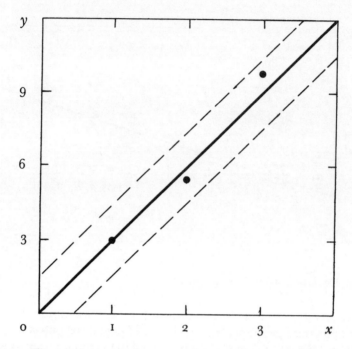

Fig. 3:5. Three-point example.

Using classical calculus, it can be proven that the minimization of d_i^2 can be accomplished by solving for a and b according to the following equations:

$$a = \frac{1}{n} \sum_{i=1}^{n} y_i,$$

$$b = \frac{\sum_{i=1}^{n} \left[(x_i - \bar{x})(y_i - \bar{y}) \right]}{\sum_{i=1}^{n} (x_i - \bar{x})^2}.$$

A simple example may be illustrative. Let

x_i	y_i
1.0	3.0
2.0	5.8
3.0	9.2

See Fig. 3:5 and Table 3:1.

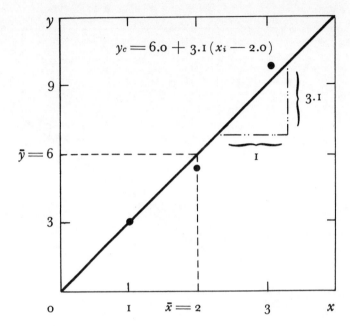

$$y_c = 6.0 + 3.1 (x_i - 2.0)$$

Fig. 3:6. Fitted three-point example.

Table 3:1. Three-point example computations.

x_i	y_i	$x_i - \bar{x}$	$(x_i - \bar{x})^2$	$y_i - \bar{y}$	$(y_i - \bar{y})^2$	$(x_i - \bar{x})(y_i - \bar{y})$
1.0	3.0	−1.0	1.0	−3.0	9.00	3.0
2.0	5.8	0.0	0.0	−0.2	0.04	0.0
3.0	9.2	1.0	1.0	3.2	10.24	3.2
$\sum_{i=1}^{3}$ 6.0	18.0	0.0	2.0	0.0	19.28	6.2
$\bar{x} = 2.0$ and $\bar{y} = 6.0$						

Therefore,

$$a = \frac{1}{3} \sum_{i=1}^{3} y_i = \frac{1}{3} 18.0 = 6.0,$$

$$b = \frac{\sum_{i=1}^{3} [(x_i - \bar{x})(y_i - \bar{y})]}{\sum_{i=1}^{3} (x_i - \bar{x})^2} = \frac{6.2}{2.0} = 3.1;$$

so

$$y_c = 6.0 + 3.1 (x_i - 2.0).$$

See Fig. 3:6.

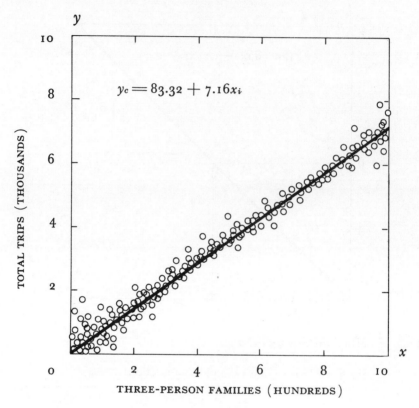

FIG. 3:7. Southeast Wisconsin linear model.

A real-world example of simple linear modeling was made by the Southeastern Wisconsin Regional Planning Commission (SEWRPC) for estimating and predicting the total number of trips (y_c) made by families of various sizes (see Fig. 3:7).

Let us examine only three-member families. In this case the form $Y = a + bX$ was desired, so this required another computational algorithm (often called the *raw data formula*) which is somewhat more cumbersome but mathematically the same as the previous:

$$b = \frac{\sum\limits_{i=1}^{n} (x_i y_i) - \left(\sum\limits_{i=1}^{n} x_i \right) \left(\sum\limits_{i=1}^{n} y_i \right)}{\sum\limits_{i=1}^{n} (x_i^2) - \left(\sum\limits_{i=1}^{n} x_i \right)^2},$$

$$a = \frac{\sum\limits_{i=1}^{n} y_i}{n} - b\,\frac{\sum\limits_{i=1}^{n} x_i}{n}.$$

The above algorithm yields a cleaner equation, it would seem, yet the use of $y_c = a + b(x_i - \bar{x})$ for computational purposes makes handling more easy.

TESTING SIMPLE LINEAR MODELS

If we return to the hypothetical example in which we fitted the simple linear model $y_c = 6.0 + 3.1(x_i - 2.0)$, we can examine the variance between the model results and the observed data. We can compute $y_i - y_c$ (where y_i is an observation and y_c is the *corresponding* estimated value as predicted from x_i), which is called the *residual* and shows the unexplained variation. It can be easily noticed in Table 3:2 that the sum of the residu-

TABLE 3:2. Residuals of hypothetical example.

	x_i	y_i	y_c	$y_i - y_c$
	1.0	3.0	2.9	+0.1
	2.0	5.8	6.0	−0.2
	3.0	9.2	9.1	+0.1
$\sum\limits_{i=1}^{3}$	6.0	18.0	18.0	0.0

als in our hypothetical example is zero — only errors due to rounding will change this situation. In any simple linear model where there is an a parameter which is not zero, the sum of the residuals will be zero except for errors due to rounding.

We know that an error exists every time we estimate or predict y_c which is either greater or less than zero by the amount of the standard error or root mean square. The commonly used test of the size of this error for simple regression is the *standard error of estimate* (SEE_s), which is found by computing

$$SEE_s = \sqrt{\frac{1}{n} \sum\limits_{i=1}^{n} (\hat{y}_i - \hat{y}_c)^2}.$$

This is similar in many aspects to the root mean square except that it is the standard error or deviation of y_i values around the estimating equation

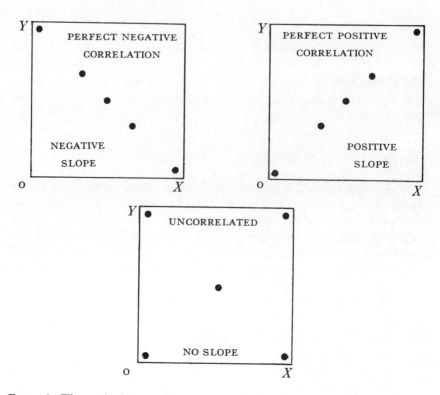

FIG. 3:8. Theoretical types of perfect correlation.

$y_c = a + bx_i$ or $y_c = a + b(x_i - \bar{x})$. The variance V can be computed by dividing SEE by $\bar{y}$ and multiplying by 100.00.

The most important test of simple linear models is the *simple correlation coefficient* (r). The interval in which r lies is always $-1.00 \leq r \leq +1.00$. In the theoretical case where r is $+1.00$, we have a *perfect positive correlation;* similarly, when $r = -1.00$, we have a *perfect negative correlation.* It is also theoretically possible to have a perfectly *uncorrelated* $r = 0.00$. The mappings of these theoretical possibilities are shown in Fig. 3:8.

The real world does not yield any of the three theoretical possibilities of perfect correlation or uncorrelation. We desire to test simple linear models by computing r and accepting those models where r is close to the extremes of the interval — values for r near zero would indicate that a simple linear model is not acceptable. The decision on how close r should be to $+1.00$ or -1.00 is a matter of intuitive analysis and judgment, as assisted by several tests. In many cases, however, intuitive judgment and analysis about given characteristics of a problem situation may be as important as quantitative tests.

One of the common tests of r is a determination of what the magnitude of r should be, for a given degree of freedom df, to indicate the probability that correlation is not due to chance. This is the so-called *null hypothesis test*, which requires that r have at least a magnitude r_s to prove that it is not due to chance. This is a test of *significance* which can be readily used by reference to a *standard r or R table* (see Appendix B). Like the chi-square test, significance levels of 0.01 and 0.05 are used commonly.

The value for r is closely associated with its square (r^2), which is called the *coefficient of determination* and is the ratio of explained variation to total variation. The coefficient of determination is the percentage of variation of y about its mean ($\bar{y}$) that can be accounted for by the simple linear model. The remaining variation is accounted for by the residuals and hence is associated with peculiarities of the real-world problem. For example, if $r^2 = 0.78$, then we can say that 78 percent of the variation is accounted for by the simple linear model and 22 percent cannot be accounted for by the model. The interval for r^2 is, of course, -1.00 to $+1.00$, so that r and r^2 tests should be complementary and expository. The value for r^2 is computed in the following manner:

$$r^2 = \frac{\left(\sum_{i=1}^{n} \left[(x_i - \bar{x})(y_i - \bar{y}) \right] \right)^2}{\left[\sum_{i=1}^{n} (x_i - \bar{x})^2 \right] \left[\sum_{i=1}^{n} (y_i - \bar{y})^2 \right]}.$$

The correlation coefficient (r) is found by taking the square root of r^2. Another approach sometimes favored when not using a digital computer is the raw data formula:

$$r = \frac{\left(n \sum_{i=1}^{n} x_i y_i \right) - \left(\sum_{i=1}^{n} x_i \sum_{i=1}^{n} y_i \right)}{\left[\sqrt{n \sum_{i=1}^{n} x_i^2 - \left(\sum_{i=1}^{n} x_i \right)^2} \right] \left[\sqrt{n \sum_{i=1}^{n} y_i^2 - \left(\sum_{i=1}^{n} y_i \right)^2} \right]}.$$

In this case the coefficient of determination (r^2) is found by squaring r.

At this point the urban analyst must decide whether he is satisfied with the simple linear model under examination. An insight can be gained by using the intuitive logic test, whereby the analyst examines the size of a and the sign of the slope of b. If a is unusually large in comparison to the mean of the dependent variable $\bar{y}$, an intuitive basis for rejection may exist. Accordingly, if the sign of b, which indicates the direction of slope as well as the sign of the correlation coefficient, does not seem intuitively logical, a basis for rejection may exist. For example, if we are predicting consumer spending by use of a family income variable, and if the model states that spending increases inversely with income, we would have several questions to pose, since this seems intuitively illogical.

A test of the efficiency of a simple linear model sometimes used is called the *index of predictive efficiency* (*IPE*). This test is a measure of whether the model predicts in the most efficacious manner:

$$IPE = 100.00 \, (1 - K),$$

where

$$K = \sqrt{1 - r^2}.$$

This tends to be a somewhat severe test in urban analysis because of the imperfection of our knowledge about real-world problems. For example, in order to say that the *IPE* shows an efficiency of more than 50 percent, we must have a correlation coefficient of 0.87 (which is quite high in many cases of urban problems).

There are many other tests of the reliability of simple linear models, all with varying degrees of relevance and necessity. For urban analysis the more proper direction to pursue in testing simple linear models — when coefficients of correlation and determination, standard error of estimate and variance, and intuitive logic tests are not convincing to an analyst — is to formulate a *confidence level*. Confidence levels can be computed for the fit of the model — that is, the parameters a and b — and the estimation and prediction values. Confidence levels have the effect of citing a level, such as 95 percent, whereby an urban analyst could conclude that "a model is fitted or predicts with 95 percent confidence." This is achieved by determining the range in which the hypothetical or true values of a, b, and y_c lie. This range is called a *confidence bounds* and is computed as follows:

for a
$$a - t\sqrt{\frac{s^2}{n}} \leq \text{true } a \leq a + t\sqrt{\frac{s^2}{n}},$$

for b
$$b - t\sqrt{\frac{s^2}{\sum\limits_{i=1}^{n}(x_i - \bar{x})^2}} \leq \text{true } b \leq b + t\sqrt{\frac{s^2}{\sum\limits_{i=1}^{n}(x_i - \bar{x})^2}},$$

for $\hat{y}_c$
$$[a + b(\hat{x}_i - \bar{x}) - p] \leq \text{true } y_c \leq [a + b(\hat{x}_i - \bar{x}) + p],$$

where

$$s^2 = \frac{1}{n-2}\left(\left[\sum_{i=1}^{n}(y_i - \bar{y})^2 - b^2\right]\left[\sum_{i=1}^{n}(x_i - \bar{x})^2\right]\right),$$

$t = t$-table value for confidence level at given percent and $n - 2$,

$$p = t \times s \sqrt{1 + \frac{1}{n} + \left[\frac{(\hat{x}_i - \bar{x})^2}{\sum_{i=1}^{n}(x_i - \bar{x})^2}\right]}.$$

The t-table is a standard table, included as Appendix C, which is a variation of the normal distribution, that specifies t-values for various confidence levels. In urban analysis confidence levels are usually specified from 75 percent to 95 percent, depending on the problem and the data.

Let us assume that we have computed the above confidence bounds at the 95 percent confidence level and find that for

$$y_c = 300 + 20(x_i - 60),$$

where

$$n = 62,$$
$$s^2 = 6,200,$$

that

$$280 \leq \text{true } a \leq 320,$$
$$18 \leq \text{true } b \leq 22,$$

and for $x_i = 160$ and $y_c = 2,300$,

$$1,985 \leq \text{true } y_c \leq 2,616.$$

Thus, since our values for a, b, and y_c all fall within the confidence bounds computed, we can conclude that this model is fitted and predicts with 95 percent confidence level.

COMPLEX LINEAR MODELS

The real world is far more complex than simple linear models would indicate *prima facie*. It often occurs that more than one independent variable is associated with a dependent variable. When more than two variables exist in a linear model, we call it a *complex linear model* or an example of *multivariate analysis*.

An interesting thing happens when one variable is associated with two others for estimation and prediction: a straight line is no longer adequate, and a plane must be fitted which best encompasses the vectors. Assuming

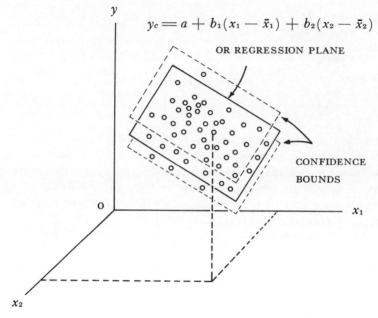

FIG. 3:9. Complex linear mapping.

that y is predicted by x_1 and x_2, this can be seen in Fig. 3:9. The equation for a plane is fitted by using

$$y_c = a + b_1(x_1 - \bar{x}_1) + b_2(x_2 - \bar{x}_2).$$

Complex linear models can include more than two associated or independent variables. In fact, they can include x_k associated variables, so that

$$y_c = a + b_1(x_1 - \bar{x}_1) + b_2(x_2 - \bar{x}_2) + \ldots + b_k(x_k - \bar{x}_k).$$

It is not possible to map such an equation in two dimensions, but these models can be mathematically formulated (they are still linear because none of the variables are raised to a power other than *one* or *zero*). As a practical matter, when the number of associated x_i variables becomes large, the cost and added difficulties (due to error compounding and data collection) often outweigh any analytical benefits, and it is better to delete unneeded and minor variables. As a *heuristic* (a kind of rule of thumb in mathematics), we seek to develop models that use no more than $k = 5$ associated variables and to avoid an excessive number of x_k variables. This rule of thumb holds that only the *key variables* which contribute the most to correlation are essential.

COMPLEX REGRESSION COMPUTATIONS

The concepts and previously stated assumptions of linearity, confidence bounds, and normally distributed error for regression and correlation are conceptually similar for both simple and complex linear models, although the form changes. The *plane of best fit* (when more than two associated variables are used, it is a *hyperplane*) is computed though the algorithm of least squares, except that a matrix notation is more efficient. The algorithm seeks

$$\text{Minimize} \sum_{i=1}^{n} (\hat{y}_i - \hat{y}_c)^2$$

or

$$\text{Minimize} \sum_{i=1}^{n} \left[\hat{y}_i - a - \sum_{k=1}^{m} b_k (\hat{x}_k - \bar{x}_k) \right]^2 = \text{Min} \sum_{i=1}^{n} (d_i^2).$$

For a two–independent variable model this is

$$\text{Minimize} \sum_{i=1}^{n} \left[y_i - a - b_1 (x_1 - \bar{x}_1) - (x_2 - \bar{x}_2) \right]^2.$$

The minimization of this two–independent variable model is accomplished by

$$\begin{bmatrix} d_{11} & d_{12} \\ d_{21} & d_{22} \end{bmatrix} \begin{bmatrix} b_1 \\ b_2 \end{bmatrix} = \begin{bmatrix} g_1 \\ g_2 \end{bmatrix}$$

and

$$D^{-1} = \begin{bmatrix} c_{11} & c_{12} \\ c_{21} & c_{22} \end{bmatrix},$$

where

$$d_{11} = \sum_{i=1}^{n} (x_{1i} - \bar{x}_1)^2,$$

$$d_{21} = d_{12} = \sum_{i=1}^{n} (x_{1i} - \bar{x}_1)(x_{2i} - \bar{x}_2),$$

$$d_{22} = \sum_{i=1}^{n} (x_{2i} - \bar{x}_2)^2,$$

$$g_1 = \sum_{i=1}^{n} (y_i - \bar{y})(x_{1i} - \bar{x}_1),$$

$$g_2 = \sum_{i=1}^{n} (y_i - \bar{y})(x_{2i} - \bar{x}_2).$$

This minimization is accomplished through a classical calculus method, and the matrix equation is solved for b_1 and b_2, given that $a = \bar{y}$.[2] Within the matrix equation the c_{ij} matrix comes from the inverse of the d_{ij} matrix, and the g_i vector comes from known values for x and y, so that

$$\begin{bmatrix} b_1 \\ b_2 \end{bmatrix} = \begin{bmatrix} g_1 \\ g_2 \end{bmatrix} \begin{bmatrix} c_{11} & c_{12} \\ c_{21} & c_{22} \end{bmatrix}.$$

Using a digital computer, this matrix equation is solved speedily and efficiently. When working manually, it is sometimes easier to use the raw data formula: for example, solve three normal equations for a, b_1, and b_2 which minimize the deviations in the same way as above, except use the form $y_c = a + b_1 x_1 + b_2 x_2$:

$$\sum_{i=1}^{n} y_i = an + b_1 \sum_{i=1}^{n} x_{1i} + b_2 \sum_{i=1}^{n} x_{2i},$$

$$\sum_{i=1}^{n} y_i x_{1i} = a \sum_{i=1}^{n} x_{1i} + b_1 \sum_{i=1}^{n} (x_{1i}^2) + b_2 \sum_{i=1}^{n} (x_{1i} x_{2i}),$$

$$\sum_{i=1}^{n} y_i x_{2i} = a \sum_{i=1}^{n} x_{2i} + b_1 \sum_{i=1}^{n} (x_{1i} x_{2i}) + b_2 \sum_{i=1}^{n} (x_{2i}^2).$$

Regardless of whether the matrix equation or normal equation algorithms are used, the same approach is used to calculate b_i for any x_i. In the matrix approach it can be seen that additional d's, b's, and g's are necessary so that the number of rows is the same as the number of x's. In the normal equation approach an additional equation must be added for every x added to the model. It is obvious that the volume of computations required to solve for a and b_i in complex linear models makes the use of available library programs for such purposes on digital computers a most enticing approach.

TESTING COMPLEX LINEAR MODELS

Tests of complex linear models are similar to the tests of simple linear models. Residuals are computed in the same manner and should total zero or very near zero. The SEE_c (standard error of estimate for complex models) is similar, although it must be corrected for additional loss in degrees of freedom. This is accomplished by solving

[2] Minimization is covered in Chapter 6. For a brief treatment, see C. O. Oakley, *The Calculus* (New York: Barnes and Noble, 1966), Chapter X.

$$SEE_c = \sqrt{\frac{1}{n-k-1} \sum_{i=1}^{n} (y_i - a - b_1 x_1 - \ldots - b_k x_k)^2},$$

noting that k is the number of x variables.

The most important test of complex linear models is the *complex correlation coefficient*, which is symbolized by R. The complex correlation coefficient is similar to the simple correlation coefficient, but additional variables contribute to the association. To further complicate matters, sometimes the independent or associated variables (x) are correlated with each other. For example, using income and education to predict miles of commuting is deceptive because income and education may be more correlated to each other than collectively or singly correlated to miles of commuting. The heuristic to be followed is that a complex linear model should not have a correlation between independent variables, called *intercorrelation* (or sometimes *multicollinearity*), that is higher than (or even close to) the total correlation R.

The total correlation is computed by

$$R = \sqrt{\frac{b_1 \left[\sum_{i=1}^{n} y_i (x_{1i} - \bar{x}_1)\right] + b_2 \left[\sum_{i=1}^{n} y_i (x_{2i} - \bar{x}_2)\right] + \ldots + b_k \left[\sum_{i=1}^{n} y_i (x_{ki} - \bar{x}_k)\right]}{\sum_{i=1}^{n} (y_i - \bar{y})^2}}.$$

The total correlation (R) is the result of the *partial correlation coefficients* between the specified variables as influenced (or controlled for influence) by the remaining variables. For our purposes we seek basically to insure that the simple coefficient of correlation (r) between the independent variables (x_i) is not greater for any pair than for the total (R). In the event that a pair of independent variables is highly intercorrelated, this may indicate a poor model because the x's may be more related to each other than to y. Model revision may be needed, or often a combinatorial variable representing the common areas should be developed (through such a method as *factor analysis*). Such a situation might also indicate that the dependent variable has been selected inappropriately, and alternative models should be sought.

Since the partial correlation coefficients each contribute to the complex correlation coefficient and its square, the complex coefficient of determination, independent variables can be selected for inclusion or deletion by the contribution that a specific independent variable makes to the equation — a process such as this is called *stepwise regression*. In most cases the independent variable with the highest partial correlation to the dependent variable will be added. The analyst determines at what point this is to be halted by determining how much contribution is being made to R^2 by adding more independent variables. There is some point at which the analyst is satisfied with the model or at least believes that no additional variables could further improve the model.

The tests for intuitive logic and related tests, such as the *IPE*, are the same for simple and complex linear models. Since complex linear models are sometimes deceptive, the intuitive logic tests are important. The urban analyst should examine complex linear models for logical signs of independent variables and correlation. Sometimes the addition of an independent variable has the effect of destroying the logical association of another independent variable — such a situation merits additional testing. The size of the *a* and *b* parameters also merits intuitive logic tests, since they may show peculiarities not readily detected through mathematical tests. A test that will assist the analyst in examining *b* parameters is to divide b_i by its standard deviation or rms_i. As a heuristic rule, a *b* parameter should be greater than its *rms* — this means that the absolute value of b_i/rms_i should be at least one. The higher the quotient and remainder, the better.

Having performed the *R* (and standard *R*-table), R^2, *IPE*, SEE_c, intercorrelation, intuitive logic, and b_i/rms_i tests, the urban analyst then has the option of whether to perform the confidence-level tests. Confidence bounds for a *b* parameter are computed by

$$b_k - t \cdot s_k \cdot \sqrt{c_{i1}} \leq \text{true } b_k \leq b_k + t \cdot s_k \cdot \sqrt{c_{i1}},$$

where

$$s = \sqrt{\frac{\sum\limits_{i=1}^{n} (y_i - y)^2 - \sum\limits_{k=1}^{m}\left[b_k \sum\limits_{i=1}^{n} y_i(x_{ki} - \bar{x}_{ki})\right]}{n - k - 1}}.$$

Confidence in a predicted $\hat{y}_c$ is computed from the bounds for a given predictor $\hat{x}_i$, where $x_1 = \hat{x}_1$, $x_2 = \hat{x}_2$, etc., by

$$\hat{y} - d \leq \text{true } \hat{y} \leq \hat{y} + d,$$

where

$$d = t \cdot s \cdot \sqrt{1 + \frac{1}{n} + \sum\limits_{i=1}^{k} (\hat{x}_i - \bar{x}_i)c_{ii} + 2 \sum\limits_{i=1}^{k-1}\left(\sum\limits_{j=i+1}^{k} (\hat{x}_1 - \bar{x}_i)(\hat{x}_j - \bar{x}_j)c_{ij}\right)}.$$

LINEAR MODEL APPLICATIONS

Examples of linear models applied to urban systems are far too numerous to adequately describe here. At best, we can present a few examples which are meant to be illustrative rather than exhaustive. To a certain degree the application of linear models to urban analysis is limited only by the imagination of the analyst and the proclivity for the real world to be described in linear terms.

WISCONSIN MIGRATION MODEL

Urban analysts in Wisconsin were concerned with the development of a model for estimating and predicting the way that families changed their residence both within the state and from without the state (on the part of new or returning residents). The analysts sought to use such a model for describing mobility among urban systems within the state. After several experiments a linear model using U.S. Census Bureau data was developed.

The key variables used were

$PMOV$ = percentage of population of a county that changed residences within the last ten years;

$UNEM$ = annual unemployment rate (percentage of total employed);

$EMAN$ = average annual employment in manufacturing jobs (thousands);

$EWCL$ = average annual employment in white-collar jobs (thousands).

The following model was developed. The first computation was the correlation matrix, as shown in Table 3:3. Note the so-called "mirror-image" effect in Table 3:3, in that the lower portion of the matrix is the same as the transpose of the upper portion.

TABLE 3:3. Correlation matrix for Wisconsin model.

	PMOV	UNEM	EMAN	EWCL
PMOV	1.0000	−0.3326	0.2377	0.5933
UNEM	−0.3326	1.0000	−0.3086	0.0416
EMAN	0.2377	−0.3086	1.0000	0.4166
EWCL	0.5933	0.0416	0.4166	1.0000

The following model was computed next:

$$PMOV = 104.5 - 0.7201\,UNEM - 0.0593\,EMAN + 0.3926\,EWCL \pm 0.7285.$$

The last term of the right-hand side is the SEE_c, sometimes shown in this manner to indicate that a small error is known to exist for the complex linear model. Since there were 71 counties in Wisconsin and, hence, 71 observations, correcting for four variables meant that there were 67 df for the model. The value for R was 0.7085 and R^2 was 0.5020. All tests discussed above were used.

1. *R Test.* The standard R-table showed that an R of at least 0.4010 was needed to be 99 percent significant. The computed R was well above this value.

2. *R^2 Test.* The R^2 indicated that 50.20 percent of the variation of *PMOV* about its mean could be accounted for in the model, while 49.80 percent could not be explained by the model. While there was much unexplained variation, using intuitive judgment, this was acceptable.

3. *IPE Test.* The *IPE* test indicated a 29.48 percent efficiency, which was somewhat disappointing.

4. *Intercorrelation Test.* The analysis of the correlation matrix showed that *EWCL* and *PMOV* had the highest association, yet neither *UNEM* or *EMAN* had a correlation with *EWCL* or with each other that was higher than R. This showed that no signs of intercorrelation were found.

5. *Intuitive Logic Test.* It seemed logical that families would change their residences more with increased *EWCL* and less with *UNEM* and *EMAN,* so the intuitive logic test was satisfactory.

6. *b_i/rms_i Test.* All quotients of b_i/rms_i were greater than one, so this test was satisfactory.

7. *Confidence Levels.* Computations showed that

$$0.6970 \leq \text{true } b_1 \leq 0.7310,$$
$$0.0490 \leq \text{true } b_2 \leq 0.0611,$$
$$0.3703 \leq \text{true } b_3 \leq 0.5113.$$

Since all b_i were within the confidence bounds, the linear model was satisfactory at the 95 percent level.

The complex linear model for *PMOV* in Wisconsin counties was satisfactory within the limitations set by available data and unexplained variation. While R, R^2, and *IPE* would have been more satisfactory if higher, the model seemed nonetheless adequate for the purposes intended. The model was satisfactory in terms of the tests used and of intuitive judgment, but it was not very efficient. Later examination of the partial correlation coefficients of the independent variables indicated that *EMAN* did not contribute very much to *PMOV* when the effects of *EWCL* and *UNEM* were held constant. The model could have been just as satisfactory, perhaps, without the additional complexity of the added variable *EMAN.*

The use of the stepwise regression algorithm is recommended for such situations. The stepwise regression algorithm seeks to develop the most efficient and economic model, but the level of satisfaction is left largely to the judgment of the analyst.

SEWRPC COMMUTING MODEL

We can review a linear model for the Milwaukee, Wisconsin, urban region in order to examine the efficiency and economy made possible by stepwise regression. The model mentioned was an attempt to estimate and predict the length in miles of the trip from home to work made by commuters in the Milwaukee urban region. Input data were observations of 14,554 commuters collected in a survey undertaken by the Southeast Wisconsin Regional Planning Commission. The dependent variable was home-work trip distance (HW); independent variables were the distance from the center of the city to the work place (CW), the distance from the center of the city to the home location (CH), and the family income of the commuter (I). The independent variables were determined to be the key variables, or those with the highest simple coefficient of correlation with HW, from a prerequisite analysis of 15 selected variables believed to be associated with HW. Using the Stepwise Regression Program of the BIOMED Library on a Control Data Corporation 3600 Computer, the very large input data file was processed step by step into a complex linear model. Independent variables were added to the linear model by the order in which they increased the value of R^2. The correlation matrix is shown as Table 3:4.

TABLE 3:4. Correlation matrix for SEWRPC model.

	HW	CW	CH	I
HW	1.0000	0.9521	0.6645	0.6134
CW	0.9521	1.0000	0.0996	0.3892
CH	0.6645	0.0996	1.0000	0.4332
I	0.6134	0.3892	0.4332	1.0000

Table 3:5 is a summary of the effect of adding independent variables. The tests for linear models were performed at each step, and each model at every step was held to be satisfactory. As can be seen, the values of R and R^2 increased slightly with the addition of CH and I, and the value of

TABLE 3:5. Stepwise regression summary for SEWRPC model.

Step	Variable Entered	A	b_1	b_2	b_3	R	R^2	SEE_c
1	CW	1.5200	0.9496	—	—	0.9522	0.9067	0.4632
2	CH	0.6315	0.9389	0.3841	—	0.9537	0.9089	0.4601
3	I	0.4917	0.8978	0.3965	0.0002	0.9540	0.9099	0.4573

SEE_c decreased slightly with the addition of CH and I. It was clear that all three independent variables were associated with HW, and each made the linear model slightly more reliable. The IPE showed that the simple linear model at step 1 was 68.82 percent efficient, and the IPE increased to 70.20 percent at step 2 and 70.44 percent at step 3. This means that the addition of CH to the simple linear model of HW associated with CW increased the efficiency of the model by only 1.38 percent, and the addition of I increased the efficiency of the complex linear model at step 2 by only 0.24 percent. In the judgment of the urban analysts the model was satisfactory at step 1, and the benefits of steps 2 and 3 were not sufficient in light of the increases possible in R, R^2, and IPE and the decrease in SEE_c. The most efficient and economic linear model in this case was the simple linear model of step 1:

$$HW = 1.5200 + 0.9496CW \pm 0.4632.$$

LOGICAL AND MATHEMATICAL CRITIQUE

We started this chapter by stating that linear models are not flawless even though they are most popular, efficient, and simple. Linear models are among the best scientific methods applicable to urban analysis, but the urban analyst should be aware of their weaknesses and pitfalls.

We have stressed that correlation is a pseudofunction that does not guarantee cause-and-effect relationships. A common pitfall in the application of linear models to urban analysis is to disregard this basic logical foundation. This can have serious implications if such a model is used for decision-making. The urban analyst should keep in mind that a linear model is for convenience in estimation and prediction, and it is not necessarily a true picture of functional relationships in urban systems.

The tendency to fall into a cause-and-effect posture with linear models can lead an urban analyst to a number of logical and mathematical pitfalls.

Variation in either the dependent or the independent variable may be caused by variation in the other. This is true in intercorrelation as well as in some examples with no intercorrelation, and the effect is that the urban analyst often cannot be certain about which of the variables is causing the others to change. In other cases variation in two or more variables in a linear model may be caused by a common force or forces which are not even considered in the model. For example, the latter case is often found when using linear models to estimate and predict nonwhite housing characteristics by such associated variables as income, education, etc. when such forces as racial discrimination and prejudice are causing variation by intervention.

The tests for linear models are effective and generally reliable, but there is always a possibility, however remote, that the linear model is deceptive. It is possible that the variation noted for variables in a linear model is due in large part to chance, even though significance tests show that the probability of a chance association is very small. It is largely a linear assumption that leads an analyst to use linear models. There is always the possibility that a nonlinear relationship better describes the real-world problem. Finally, there is also the problem of the assumption of normally distributed vectors in a scattergram about the line of best fit, and the same applies for planes of best fit. We must use a t distribution to solve and test linear models (because it works well), yet we still base our mathematical argument on a normal distribution that is not affected by degrees of freedom or nonnormal relationships. This is a mathematical problem which still merits attention.

These are the major criticisms that are often found when linear models are used. The pitfalls are to be noted and avoided by the urban analyst whenever possible. We still maintain, however, that linear models offer an interesting scientific method for many types of urban analysis. Their simplicity and comprehensibility are found in few other methods.

There is a significant amount of scientific and mathematical work being directed toward many of the criticisms of linear models. In the future many of these criticisms may be resolved. Presently, one method for reducing the possibility of pitfalls in the use of linear methods is *covariance analysis*. Covariance analysis, in its simplest terms, is a method which seeks to explain variance in associated variables by testing explanations of data groups through the introduction of factors often determined by intuitive analysis and judgment. For example, examining the four mappings in Fig. 3:10, we notice that the two-variable scattergrams all have the appearance of linear associations. In mapping A the line of best fit appears

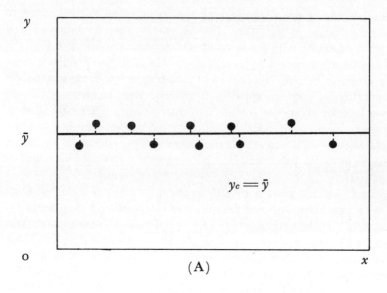

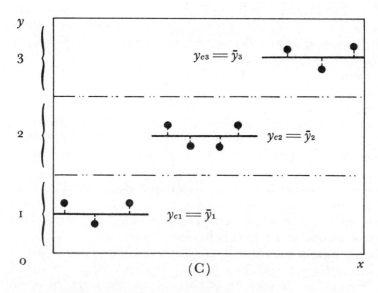

Fɪɢ. 3:10. Possible explanations of variance.

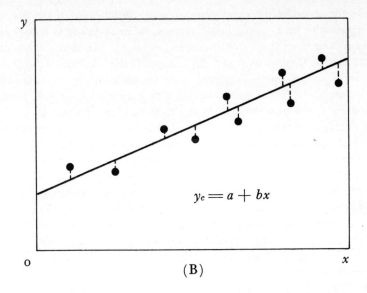

(B)

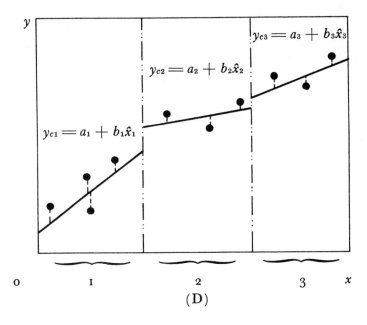

(D)

to be the mean of the dependent variable; in mapping B the line of best fit appears to be a simple linear regression; in mapping C it appears that lines representing three distinct means of subsets within the range of y are best; and in the last mapping, D, it appears that the values for y are best found by taking simple regression lines for three distinct subsets of the set of values for x. Thus linear relationships may exist in several forms, and there are many combinations of the cases mentioned above.

Covariance analysis does not specifically show what causes variation in a set of observations. This often requires intuitive judgment, logic, and a little luck. Guidelines for an intuitive search of data groupings, such as those shown in Fig. 3:10, can be effective. Geographical areas, such as the South, North, West, and Midwest, may cause data groupings. Data groupings may be caused by race, income, sex, age, partisan preferences, ethnic origin, education, personality traits and characteristics, and all those other difficult-to-quantify aspects of humans and their associations. Covariance analysis is helpful to the urban analyst as a scientific method to improve linear models and otherwise explain changes in associations between variables. The real challenge is for the urban analyst to explain the causes and effects not explained by linear models or covariance analysis and to use such explanations for the solution of problems in urban systems.

RECOMMENDED EXERCISES

1. Develop a simple linear model for any given city that estimates and predicts personal income by an association with education, say, measured by grades completed. Also attempt to develop supplementary simple linear models which predict and estimate personal income by associations with such variables as age, experience (years in profession or occupation), and mobility (years lived in city). Which model seems most satisfactory? Are there signs of intercorrelation between any of the independent variables? If so, how do you explain this?

2. Analyze the following complex linear model. Urban analysts sought to test the hypothesis that urbanization within a state, that is, the percentage of people living in urban areas, was an association that increased with increasing personal income and white-collar employment. The analysts selected a sample of 16 states throughout the United States.

y_c = percentage of urbanization in state, $\bar{y}$ = 0.3875,
x_1 = percentage of white-collar workers in state, $\bar{x}_1$ = 0.1121,
x_2 = percentage of personal incomes above \$10,000 in state, $\bar{x}_2$ = 0.6049.

Correlation Matrix			
	y	x_1	x_2
y	1.0000	0.8257	0.7805
x_1		1.0000	0.8266
x_2			1.0000

$R = 0.8446$
$R^2 = 0.7135$
$SEE_c = 0.1031$

$$y_c = -0.1110 + 1.1283x_1 + 2.4858x_2$$
$$(rms_i) \qquad (0.9645) \quad (1.1428)$$

3. Analyze the following complex linear model. Urban analysts sought to test the hypothesis that the area of the central business district (CBD) increased with the population and traffic of an urban system. The analysts selected a sample of 13 urban systems in the United States.

y_c = area of CBD in acres, $\bar{y}$ = 566,
x_1 = population of urban area around CBD, $\bar{x}_1$ = 1,510,860,
x_2 = person trips per day to CBD, $\bar{x}_2$ = 358,711.

Correlation Matrix			
	y	x_1	x_2
y	1.0000	0.6430	0.8631
x_1		1.0000	0.8913
x_2			1.0000

$R = 0.9267$
$R^2 = 0.8571$
$SEE_c = 101.7759$

$$y_c = 310 - 0.00007x_1 + 0.001x_2$$
$$(rms_i) \qquad (0.00037) \quad (0.00018)$$

Further Reading

IBM Technical Publications Department. *Concepts and Applications of Regression Analysis*. White Plains, N.Y.: International Business Machines Corp., 1966. A succinct and direct presentation of the major concepts of linear regression and suggested applications of these concepts. The report also examines the digital computer programs in the IBM library which compute linear model parameters and tests.

Draper, Norman, and Harry Smith. *Applied Regression Analysis*. New York: Wiley, 1966.
A detailed treatment of the concepts necessary for the application of regression to various problems. The authors go into much detail on the various aspects of regression and provide a most complete treatment. The mathematical concepts assume some previous experience in related branches of mathematics.

The concepts of correlation and regression, as well as least-squares fitting, are applicable to a large extent to urban problem situations which do not have linear characteristics. *Nonlinear models* can be developed from many of the same concepts for linear models through use of the methods of *curve-fitting,* and many of the tests of linear models can be used for non-linear models. There are a number of rules and tests that govern the use of nonlinear models in urban analysis, but there is such a large number of nonlinear models available that the urban analyst must use intuitive judgment and satisfaction, more so than with other types of models.

There are so many nonlinear models that this chapter can do no more than present the ones most commonly used in urban analysis. We will stress two-variable nonlinear models for simplicity and understanding. With a good foundation in such nonlinear models, the interested urban analyst can seek out other nonlinear models for possible application. Two-variable nonlinear models are especially well suited for the analysis of time-series data to uncover trends. Since trends do not always follow the neat linear-ity of the models in the preceding chapter, nonlinear models become inter-esting for both estimating and predicting values that are subject to variation of different orders at different times. Nonlinear models are by no means limited to time-series data, and they are often used to estimate and predict the values of dependent variables by an association with one or more inde-pendent variables.

There are two types of nonlinear models in terms of their inherent mathematical basis: (1) *inherently linear* and (2) *inherently nonlinear.* The distinction is that inherently linear models are nonlinear but can be transformed into linear models through a variety of methods. Inherently nonlinear models cannot be transformed into linear models and hence are more complicated and difficult to utilize.

Inherently Linear Models

Inherently linear models, which are formed by the transformation of non-linear models, are interesting to urban analysts. For simplicity we shall

CHAPTER 4

Nonlinear Models

define inherently linear models as transformed nonlinear models which do not have *asymptotes* (lower or upper limits) to the values that the dependent variable can take.

MULTIPLICATIVE MODELS

Multiplicative models are found in economic analysis of urban problems, especially with regard to such economic variables as productivity, consumption, and expenditures. The multiplicative model takes the general form

$$y_c = ax_1{}^b x_2{}^c.$$

The multiplicative model is inherently linear because it can be transformed into a complex linear model by expressing the equation in logarithms:

$$\log y_c = \log a + b(\log x_1) + c(\log x_2).$$

If we let the log variables be temporarily replaced by substitute variables, we see that this is a complex linear model.

Let

$$z_c = \log y_c,$$
$$v_1 = \log x_1,$$
$$v_2 = \log x_2,$$
$$d = \log a;$$

then

$$z_c = d + bv_1 + cv_2.$$

This model is developed in the same manner as the complex linear model, and it can be transformed back to the original multiplicative model by noting the substituted variables and replacing the original variables.

POWER FUNCTION MODELS

The *power function model* is the simplest form of the multiplicative model and takes the general form

$$y_c = ax^b.$$

The mapping of this model can take several shapes depending upon the b parameter value. Several examples are shown in Fig. 4:1. Taking the logarithms of both sides of the power function equation, we find that we have a simple linear function:

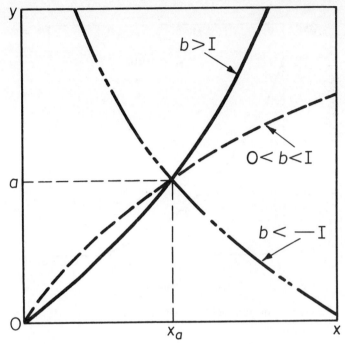

FIG. 4:1. Possible mappings of power function model.

$$\log y_c = \log a + b(\log x).$$

We can again use substitute variables for the log variables:

$$z_c = \log y_c,$$
$$c = \log a,$$
$$w = \log x.$$

This allows us to compute the simple linear model in the familiar manner for

$$z_c = c + bw.$$

We can either leave the model in its transformed linear form or transform back to the original variables.

The power function model is found frequently in urban analyses for transportation in its negative form because it describes the way that traffic variables decay with distance: these models are sometimes called *decay models*. An illustrative example is Ralph W. Pfouts's model for the way

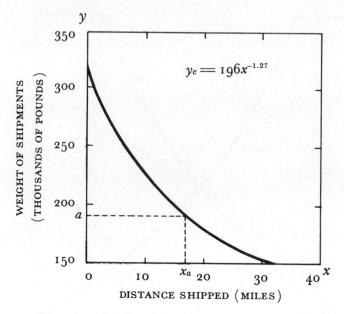

FIG. 4:2. Power function model for Piedmont Crescent goods shipments over distance in miles.

that distance is associated with the weight of goods shipped in the Piedmont Crescent Region of the Southeast, as shown in Fig. 4:2.[1]

EXPONENTIAL MODELS

The *exponential model* is quite similar to the multiplicative and power function models, except that the independent variable becomes a power:

$$y_c = ab^x.$$

Exponential models are used in urban analysis for time series and increasing growth factor variables. Exponential models have been used a great deal in transportation studies because traffic patterns often follow the mappings made possible by exponential models (see Fig. 4:3). The logarithms of both sides of the exponential model can be taken, so that we have a simple linear model:

[1] Ralph W. Pfouts, "Patterns of Economic Interaction in the Crescent," in F. Stuart Chapin and Shirley F. Weiss, eds., *Urban Growth Dynamics in a Regional Cluster of Cities* (New York: Wiley, 1966), pp. 31-58.

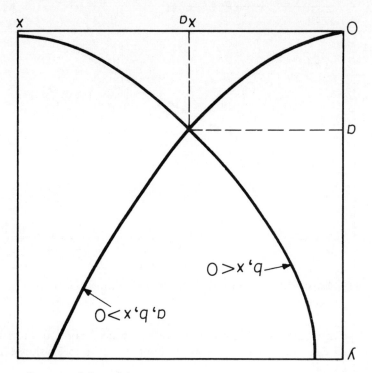

Fig. 4:3. Exponential model curves.

$$\log y_c = \log a + x(\log b),$$

and letting

$$z_c = \log y_c,$$
$$e = \log a,$$
$$d = \log b,$$

we can solve

$$z_c = e + xd.$$

We can solve for z_c in the usual manner and can either use the model in its logarithmic form or transform back to the original variables, which in this case would be

$$a = \text{antilog } e,$$
$$b = \text{antilog } d,$$
$$y_c = \text{antilog } z_c.$$

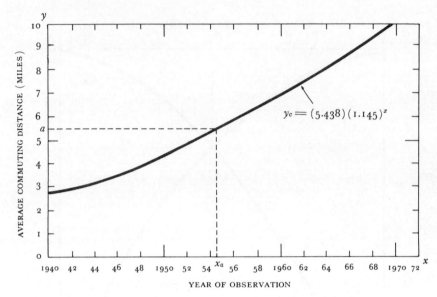

Fig. 4:4. Exponential model of average commuting distance over years.

As a point of interest, it can be noted that we need not transform log y_c to z_c and can solve for it in the same simple linear model fashion: this is called a semilog transformation.

If we plot the average distance that a person commutes over a period of years in the largest metropolitan areas in the United States, we find that an exponential model can be fitted to the data. This is shown in Fig. 4:4.[2]

INHERENTLY NONLINEAR MODELS

Many of the linear and nonlinear models we have and will discuss belong to the family of *polynomials* whose general form is

$$y_c = a + bx + cx^2 + dx^3 + \ldots + \text{etc.}$$

We have already discussed a group of these models, since the first-order polynomial is a straight line:

[2] See details in Anthony J. Catanese, "Separation of Home and Work Place in Urban Structure and Form" (Ann Arbor, Mich.: University Microfilms, 1969), Appendix B, pp. 77-79.

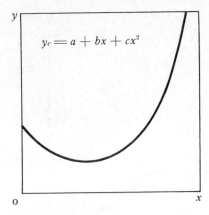
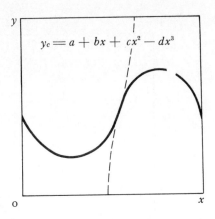

FIG. 4:5. Hypothetical second- and third-order polynomial models.

first order $y_c = a + bx$
second order $y_c = a + bx + cx^2$
third order $y_c = a + bx + cx^2 + dx^3$
fourth order $y_c = a + bx + cx^2 + dx^3 + ex^4$
fifth order $y_c = a + bx + cx^2 + dx^3 + ex^4 + fx^5$
etc. etc.

As can be seen, it is practical to express polynomials in this manner, since the degree or order is always known by observation of the power to which x is raised in the last term on the right-hand side of the equation.

The first-order polynomial model is a straight line and, of course, has no bends. The addition of a second-order term has the effect of creating a bend in the straight line, either positive or negative. The addition of a third-order term to a second-order polynomial model can result in two bends, and it is possible to have a mapping that changes direction. The addition of higher-order terms to third-order polynomial models can have the effect of adding bends, slope changes, and some rather strange-looking mappings. For practical purposes we have not seen any significant use of polynomial models beyond the third order in urban analysis, and we can limit our discussion to these second- and third-order polynomial models.

As can be seen in Fig. 4:5, the familiar mappings of polynomial models are *parabolas* for second-order models and sometimes reverse parabolas for third-order models. It is obvious that there are an infinite number of mappings and curves that can be fitted by polynomial models. The change of sign from $+$ to $-$ can in itself create an infinite number of mappings.

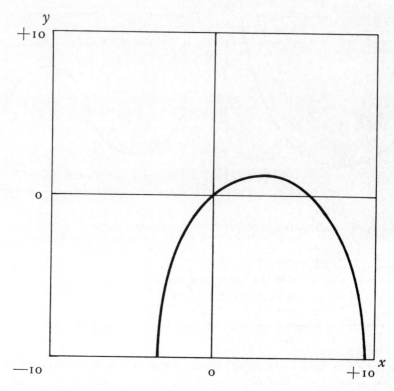

FIG. 4:6. Mapping of $y_c = -1 + 2x - 3x^2$.

This is why polynomial models are of interest to urban analysts: they are highly adaptive and flexible and are only slightly more difficult to use than simple linear models.

SECOND-ORDER POLYNOMIAL MODELS

Second-order polynomial models are similar to simple linear models: whereas a simple linear model indicates an association with a constantly increasing or decreasing line, a second-order polynomial indicates an association with increasing or decreasing amounts of increase or decrease. To be more specific, a second-order polynomial model is such that the second differences — the differences between the first differences of y_c — are constant (see Fig. 4:6 and Table 4:1).

Second-order polynomial models are fitted to data observations (which

TABLE 4:1. First and second differences of
second-order polynomial.

$y_c = -1 + 2x - 3x^2$			
x	y_c	First Difference	Second Difference
-3	-9.7	—	—
-2	-6.2	-3.5	—
-1	-3.3	-2.9	-0.6
0	-1.0	-2.3	-0.6
1	0.7	-1.7	-0.6
2	1.8	-1.1	-0.6
3	2.3	-0.5	-0.6
4	2.2	0.1	-0.6
5	1.5	0.7	-0.6
6	0.2	0.3	-0.6
Source: Croxton and Crowden.			

appear to be parabolic by observation) by the solution of three normal
equations for the parameters a, b, and c:

I. $\Sigma y = na + b\Sigma x + c\Sigma x^2$
II. $\Sigma xy = a\Sigma x + b\Sigma x^2 + c\Sigma x^3$
III. $\Sigma x^2 y = a\Sigma x^2 + b\Sigma x^3 + c\Sigma x^4$

When using times series or any other discrete variable, it is advisable to
substitute discrete numbers that allow the sums of the odd powers of x to
become zero; the general rules for treatment of time-series data are shown
in Table 4:2. When the middle of a time series is taken as origin in this
manner, and the odd powers of x sum to zero, then the three normal equations can be simplified to

I. $\Sigma y = na + c\Sigma x^2$
II. $\Sigma xy = b\Sigma x^2$
III. $\Sigma x^2 y = a\Sigma x^2 + c\Sigma x^4$

A little manipulation of these equations shows that

$$c = \frac{n\Sigma x^2 y - \Sigma x^2 \Sigma y}{n\Sigma x^4 - (\Sigma x^2)^2},$$

$$a = \frac{\Sigma y - c\Sigma x^2}{n},$$

$$b = \frac{\Sigma xy}{\Sigma x^2}.$$

TABLE 4:2. Discrete-variable substitutions for time series x.

	Odd n		Even n	
x	Discrete Substitute	x	Discrete Substitute
1960	−5	—	—
1961	−4	1961	−5
1962	−3	1962	−4
1963	−2	1963	−3
1964	−1	1964	−2
1965	0	1965	−1
1966	+1	1966	+1
1967	+2	1967	+2
1968	+3	1968	+3
1969	+4	1969	+4
1970	+5	1970	+5
	$\Sigma x = 0$		$\Sigma x = 0$

These equations can be readily solved by conveniently arranging the data in tabular form for Σx^2, Σx^4, Σy, Σxy, and $\Sigma x^2 y$. This computation can be further simplified by the use of library programs for digital computers which accomplish the same algorithm with breathtaking efficiency.

Urban analysts made use of the second-order polynomial model (and

TABLE 4:3. Long-run housing demand data for Atlanta urban system.

Year	Housing Demand (total population needing dwelling units)
1850	13,010
1860	14,427
1870	33,446
1880	49,137
1890	84,655
1900	117,363
1910	177,733
1920	232,606
1930	318,587
1940	392,886
1950	473,572
1960	556,326

several other nonlinear models) to attempt to estimate and predict housing demand for the long run in the Atlanta, Georgia, urban system. The data used are shown in Table 4:3. A second-order polynomial model was fitted to the data in Table 4:3, and the following equation resulted:

$$y_c = 1783.41 + 553.15x + 44.45x^2.$$

The estimates and predictions of this model are shown in Fig. 4:7 along with the observed data. From observation the model seems to account for observed data quite well, but it merits further evaluation of error. As would be suspected, the model shows that the growth rate in housing demand will continue at an increasing rate into the future.

THIRD-ORDER POLYNOMIAL MODELS

Third-order polynomial models are rarely used in urban analysis, although there have been some examples of its application in a few sophisticated studies of the costs of urban facilities. The reason is that there are few functions which lend themselves to the double slope of the third-order polynomial model other than the s-shaped curves of urban problems — for s-shaped curves, however, better models are available and will be discussed. For these reasons we will simply discuss the method for fitting third-order polynomial models and reserve further discussion for later subjects dealing with optimizing models.

Four normal equations are necessary to solve for parameters a, b, c, and d for the general form

$$y_c = a + bx + cx^2 + dx^3.$$

These four normal equations are

$$\text{I. } \Sigma y = na + b\Sigma x + c\Sigma x^2 + d\Sigma x^3$$
$$\text{II. } \Sigma xy = a\Sigma x + b\Sigma x^2 + c\Sigma x^3 + d\Sigma x^4$$
$$\text{III. } \Sigma x^2 y = a\Sigma x^2 + b\Sigma x^3 + c\Sigma x^4 + d\Sigma x^5$$
$$\text{IV. } \Sigma x^3 y = a\Sigma x^3 + b\Sigma x^4 + c\Sigma x^5 + d\Sigma x^6$$

Computations can be simplified by using discrete substitutes for x in time series in order to have odd powers of x sum to zero:

$$\text{I. } \Sigma y = na + c\Sigma x^2$$
$$\text{II. } \Sigma xy = b\Sigma x^2 + d\Sigma x^4$$
$$\text{III. } \Sigma x^2 y = a\Sigma x^2 + c\Sigma x^4$$
$$\text{IV. } \Sigma x^3 y = b\Sigma x^4 + d\Sigma x^6$$

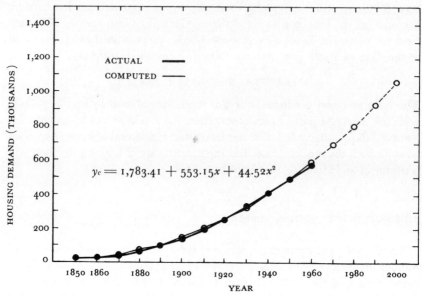

FIG. 4:7. Second-order polynomial model for housing demand, Atlanta urban system.

The observant analyst will notice a regular pattern of terms in the normal equations for solving both second- and third-order polynomial models and should be able to use these normal equations as guidelines for solving n-order polynomials if such a case is ever warranted.

ASYMPTOTIC MODELS

There are several nonlinear models that have asymptotes to the values that the y or dependent variable can take. The most interesting of these models for urban analysis are the so-called s-shaped models, although the s-shape is but one of several shapes that the mapping of the model can assume according to the parameters used.

Gompertz Model

One of the better-known asymptotic models is the *Gompertz model,* named for its discoverer, Benjamin Gompertz, a nineteenth-century mathematician. The Gompertz model describes a function in which growth incre-

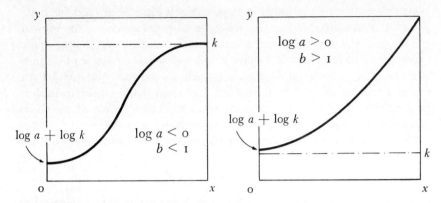

FIG. 4:8. Two forms of Gompertz model.

ments of the logarithms decline by a constant percentage change. In urban analysis the relevant forms are either an s-shaped curve with an upper asymptote or a curve with a lower asymptote, as shown in Fig. 4:8, which are the mappings of the general form of the Gompertz model:

$$y_c = ka^{b^x}.$$

The s-shaped curve is the most interesting of these two forms and actually has two asymptotes, upper and lower, although only the upper asymptote (k) need be defined for the curve-fitting.

Since the double curve of the Gompertz model requires a double superscript, it is most convenient to transform the equation to logarithmic form:

$$\log y_c = \log k + (\log a)\, b^x.$$

Computations for the parameters a, b, and k are more complicated than other models in this chapter. The observed data must be equally divided into three parts and various summations made of the forms: $\Sigma_1 \log y$, $\Sigma_2 \log y$, $\Sigma_3 \log y$, respectively, letting n stand for the number of y observations in each one-third summation. The parameters are computed by

$$b^n = \frac{\Sigma_3 \log y - \Sigma_2 \log y}{\Sigma_2 \log y - \Sigma_1 \log y},$$

$$\log a = (\Sigma_2 \log y - \Sigma_1 \log y)\,\frac{b - 1}{(b^n - 1)^2},$$

$$\log k = \frac{1}{n}\left[\Sigma_1 \log y - \left(\frac{b^n - 1}{b - 1}\right)\log a\right].$$

Gompertz models and other s-shaped curves have been used for many years in urban analysis because they describe an association of growth, change, and stability. Such a trend is common for economic, demographic, sociologic, and physical development variables. Late nineteenth-century German economists used Gompertz models to estimate and predict the size and spacing of cities in Europe and America. Early twentieth-century geographers and demographers in America extended the use of the Gompertz model to population, traffic, and physical development.

Using the data from Table 4:3, a Gompertz model was fitted with the following result:

$$\log y_c = 6.1671 + (-1.4778)\ 0.8554^x,$$

in which the parameters $\log k$, $\log a$, and b are defined. The mapping of this model and observed data is shown in Fig. 4:9, and as can been seen, the differences between the observed and estimated values appear to be small from visual inspection. The Gompertz estimation and prediction of housing demand can be interpreted to infer a four-stage development process: (1) beginning of demand for housing, (2) increasing growth and higher demands, (3) start of slowdown in rate of increase in demand, and (4) stabilization of housing demand. This four-stage process offers intriguing possibilities for many other urban problems and variables.

Logistic Model

The *logistic model* was developed by Raymond Pearl and Lowell J. Reed and is often referred to as the Pearl-Reed curve. It was developed for estimation and prediction of biological systems (albino rats, tadpoles, fruit flies, yeast cells, etc.) and was later extended to demography, anthropology, and sociology. It is based upon the theory that there is a law of growth in spatially limited environments such that the amount of growth of a system which occurs in any time period is proportional to the absolute size already obtained by the unit of time being considered, as observed, and the amount of resources needed for further growth in the environment.[3] The mathematical form of the logistic model is

$$y_c = \frac{k}{1 + 10^{a+bx}},$$

wherein a, b, and k are parameters to be computed. A very interesting

[3] Raymond Pearl, *Introduction to Medical Biometry and Statistics* (Philadelphia: W. B. Saunders, 1940), pp. 459-465.

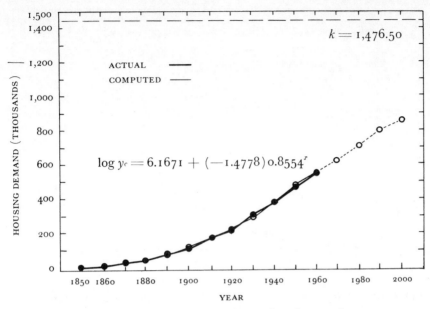

FIG. 4:9. Gompertz model for housing demand, Atlanta urban system.

algorithm that allows for simplistic computation of these parameters is called the *selected-points algorithm*. Three points are selected which are equidistant from each other, that is, y_0, y_1, y_2, such that y_0 is near the beginning of observations, y_1 is close to the middle, and y_2 is near the end. Obviously, this is a subjective approach. The parameters are then computed by solving

$$k = \frac{2y_0y_1y_2 - y_1^2 (y_0 + y_2)}{y_0y_2 - y_1^2},$$

$$a = \log \frac{k - y_0}{y_0},$$

$$b = \frac{1}{n} \left[\log \frac{y_0 (k - y_1)}{y_1 (k - y_0)} \right],$$

where n is the number of observations.

The logistic model is quite similar to the Gompertz model except that the Gompertz model describes a function with a constant ratio of successive first differences of y_c, while the logistic model describes a function with a constant ratio of first differences of $1/y_c$. This means that a mapping

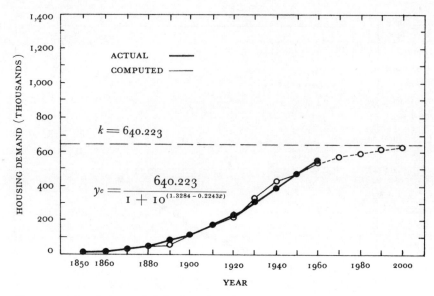

FIG. 4:10. Logistic model for housing demand, Atlanta urban system.

of y_c first differences would result in a left-skewed distribution for the Gompertz model and a normal distribution for the logistic model.

Fitted Gompertz models are similar to logistic models except that the latter will show a faster attainment of stability as the function approaches the asymptote k. This can be seen in Fig. 4:10, which is a logistic model fitted to the data from Table 4:3. The resultant model is

$$y_c = \frac{640.223}{1 + 10^{(1.3284-0.2243x)}}.$$

TESTING NONLINEAR MODELS

The neophyte urban analyst may be astounded at the results of y_c mapped against observed y values from Table 4:3 in Figs. 4:7, 9, and 10, which are from the corresponding second-order polynomial, Gompertz, and logistic models. Upon inspection and, in fact, upon computation of residuals of $y - y_c$, the errors of estimated y_c all appear to be acceptable. It is primarily in the predicted values of y_c that deviations appear among the three nonlinear models. Hence up to the year 1960 any of the three would seem to reasonably explain the housing demand, yet the three models show quite different predictions of future housing demand. As can be seen in Fig. 4:11, the second-order polynomial model predicts a relatively high housing demand, the logistic model predicts a relatively low housing demand, and the Gompertz model predicts a housing demand almost midway between the other two predictions (see Table 4:4). The urban analyst would seem to have his pick of predictions, or he could play it safe and present all three versions, indicating that these are the high, middle, and low predictions and that one of them should be close to what will actually happen.

TABLE 4:4. Comparison of nonlinear housing demand predictions, 1970-2000, Atlanta urban system.

Model	Year			
	1970	1980	1990	2000
Second-Order Polynomial	670,300	783,400	905,300	1,036,000
Gompertz	640,900	724,800	819,000	876,300
Logistic	572,000	597,000	614,000	625,000
Simple Linear	554,600	609,900	655,200	720,500

The cold truth of the matter is that there are no hard and fast tests that will replace the informed judgment and intuition of the urban analyst for selecting a nonlinear model. The urban analyst should formulate a hypothesis of the problem under consideration which describes the characteristics of change associated with the variables. The urban analyst can try to fit nonlinear models to the observed data in order to verify or refute the hypothesis. Obviously, some urban analysts will be luckier than others in such matters.

If our urban analyst is luckless, or if the real world proves too unwieldy for his informed judgment and intuition, there are a number of heuristics that can be applied to help in the selection of the appropriate model. A word of caution, however: it is always wise to examine relatively long time periods for time-series data — or small geographical areas for spatial analysis or many people for demographic and behavioral analysis, etc. — the basic point being that more data often help when the associations between variables are uncertain.

The heuristics to the selection of an appropriate nonlinear model begin simply. The urban analyst should plot his observations, or a reasonable

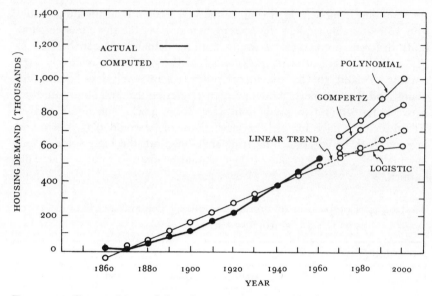

FIG. 4:11. Comparison of housing demand predictions, Atlanta urban system.

sample, on arithmetic grid paper. Excellent results can be obtained by such automated methods as digital computer library programs for cross tabulation, computer mapping for scattergrams, auxiliary machine mapping of data from punch cards, etc. The point is that a visual inspection of the observed data can be made, regardless of the method used for mapping, and, hopefully, a recognizable model will appear to the urban analyst. If the arithmetic grid mapping shows data clusters that appear to be always increasing or decreasing, the observations can be mapped on semilogarithmic grid paper to determine if linear transformations may be possible.

The urban analyst may still not be satisfied with the above tests of his judgment and intuition. In this case a hand-drawn curve should be mapped on the arithmetic or semilogarithmic mappings of the observed data. The curve should be smoothed as much as possible. There are several characteristics by which this smoothed curve can be tested, and these are summarized in Table 4:5. This should assist the urban analyst in selecting an appropriate linear or nonlinear model, and it should create some efficiencies.

The heuristic characteristics were compared with the nonlinear models fitted to the data from Table 4:3 in a *post facto* testing. The observed

TABLE 4:5. Heuristic characteristics for selecting linear and nonlinear models.

Test	Models and Characteristics				
	Linear	Exponential	Polynomial	Gompertz	Logistic
First Differences of y_c	Constant	Constant percentage	—	Skewed curve	Normal distribution curve
Second Differences of y_c	—	—	Constant	—	—
First Differences of Log y_c	—	Constant	—	Constant percentage	—
Second Differences of Log y_c	—	—	Constant	—	—
First Differences of $1/y_c$	—	—	—	—	Constant percentage
Arithmetic Grid Mapping	Straight line	—	—	—	Exponential curve when vertical scale $= 1/y_c$
Semi-logarithmic Grid Mapping	—	Straight line	—	Exponential curve	—

data plotted on the semilogarithmic grid looked very much like an exponential curve (with the appearance of an upper asymptote so that it could be a *modified exponential model*), which is the heuristic test for a Gompertz model. Yet the plotting of the same data on arithmetic grid paper with a reciprocal vertical scale resembled an exponential curve as well; thus it may satisfy the heuristic test for a logistic model. At any rate, these tests seemed to eliminate the second-order polynomial from consideration.

The familiar tests of correlation and regression are applicable to nonlinear models and in our example, from above, are necessary to make a final selection. The r, r^2, *IPE*, and SEE_{nl} (which we subscript to make clear that we are using it for nonlinear models) tests are quite similar to those used for simple and complex linear models.

Correlation coefficients can be computed for nonlinear models by using their generic foundation. The correlation coefficient is the square root of the coefficient of determination in which the ratio of the explained variation to the total variation is taken:

$$r^2 = \frac{\text{explained variation}}{\text{total variation}},$$

$$r^2 = \frac{\Sigma(y_c - \bar{y})^2}{\Sigma(y - \bar{y})^2}.$$

The coefficient of correlation and *IPE* can be computed from r^2. The SEE_{nl} can be computed by taking the square root of the total variation minus the explained variation divided by the number of observations:

$$SEE_{nl} = \sqrt{\frac{\text{total variation} - \text{explained variation}}{n}}.$$

The results of the Gompertz and logistic models were submitted to the r^2 and SEE_{nl} tests in order to help determine which was the more satisfactory model. The tests are shown as Table 4:6. As can be seen, both models

TABLE 4:6. Variation in Gompertz and logistic models of housing demand.

Source	Equation	Gompertz		Logistic	
		Amount (thousands)	Percentage	Amount (thousands)	Percentage
Unexplained	$\Sigma(y - y_c)^2$	25.09	9.5	41.70	17.9
Explained	$\Sigma(y_c - \bar{y})^2$	200.57	90.5	183.96	82.1
Total	$\Sigma(y - \bar{y})^2$	225.66	100.00	225.66	100.00

worked well, but the edge would seem to be in favor of the Gompertz model with its very satisfactory $r^2 = 0.905$. The SEE_{nl} were computed as 1,463 for the Gompertz model and 1,925 for the logistic model. While both are acceptable for prediction, the Gompertz model is slightly better because it has a slightly smaller amount of error.

Most testing for nonlinear models assumes that the urban analyst has already made a sound decision on what type of model to use. There is no alternative from scientific methods to this often unsatisfactory reliance upon judgment. The best that we can do for the present is to make a good guess about the type of nonlinear model to use, and then we can compute correlation coefficients and error terms to see how well we did.

Recommended Exercises

1. Verbally describe and evaluate each of the following models. In each of the models y_c represents the number of housing units occupied by black owners in various neighborhoods of a city. All data observations are from the period 1900 to 1960 with 1930 as the origin year(0) and ten-year units of time as x values.

$$\text{Neighborhood 1} \quad y_c = \frac{9,355}{1 + 10^{(1.4971-0.3233x)}}$$

Neighborhood 2 $\quad y_c = (4,531)(1.5711)^x$

Neighborhood 3 $\quad y_c = 1,101 + 2.51x$

Neighborhood 4 $\quad y_c = 3,316(53.21)^{0.67^x}$

Neighborhood 5 $\quad y_c = 3,200x^{-2.31}$

Neighborhood 6 $\quad y_c = 3,159 + 33.23x + 1.57x^2$

2. From the data shown in the table, plot the observations, pretest for model type, formulate a fitted model, and test for reliability. Having formulated a satisfactory model, predict the property tax for 1970, 1980, 1990, and 2000.

City of Atlantis: One Hundred Years of Property Taxation	
Year	Property Tax Revenues (ten thousands of dollars)
1860	16.3
1870	17.9
1880	19.1
1890	29.3
1900	43.8
1910	96.9
1920	150.3
1930	210.1
1940	241.3
1950	274.1
1960	295.9

3. Critique the various nonlinear models from an "intuitive judgment" point of view in light of your experience and insights into real-world urban systems and problems.

FURTHER READING

Wolfe, Henry Dean. *Business Forecasting Methods*. New York: Holt, Rinehart, and Winston, 1966.

A very good treatment of linear and nonlinear techniques for estimating and predicting cycles and trends that are relevant for urban analysis. There is also considerable detail on the nature of nonlinear models that is interesting to the reader desiring more information.

Croxton, Frederick E., and Dudley J. Crowden. *Applied General Statistics*. Englewood Cliffs, N.J.: Prentice-Hall, 1955.

This is perhaps the most famous textbook dealing with the applications of statistics to a variety of problems and conditions. It is particularly strong on nonlinear models for the analysis of time series and for applications of correlation and regression to nonlinear data observations.

Most of the models that have been examined so far are usually found with deterministic functional relationships. A group of models, that we shall call *probabilistic*, are those which are based on probabilistic functional relationships. These are special models which are always probabilistic and thus can be distinguished from matrix, linear, or nonlinear models that can be used sometimes with probabilistic variables.

Deterministic models estimate and predict with conditions of certainty. The real world of urban systems is often more complex and operates under conditions of uncertainty; hence probabilistic models are warranted. It is always comfortable for an urban analyst to use the simplest model, and since probabilistic models are more complicated than deterministic models, he may prefer to use the latter. This is a valid practice. Often it is not astute to use the simpler model because a probabilistic set of conditions occur that can be best understood and explained by probabilistic relationships of variables under uncertainty.

We shall examine the basic laws of probability to establish a minimum foundation for our examination of *discrete* and *continuous random-variable* probabilistic models. Several models of particular interest for urban analysis shall be discussed, illustrated by a number of examples.

FOUNDATIONS OF PROBABILITY

Probability theory arose obscurely from the gaming tables of seventeenth-century France. Games of chance were intriguing to early mathematicians and served as laboratories for formulating and testing laws of probability. Having established laws of probability theory, mathematicians began to expound upon applications to physical and social science as well as decision theory and philosophy.

The basis for probability theory is the performance of an act one or more times under specified conditions of uncertainty — this is called a *stochastic process*. Each performance of an act under these specified conditions is called a *trial*. For each trial there is a unique result which is often called an *outcome*. The total of the trials under specified conditions of uncer-

CHAPTER 5

Probabilistic Models

tainty is called an *experiment*. Sometimes an outcome is one or more *events*, which are elementary possibilities for each trial.

We can examine these foundations by considering the flipping of two coins, each coin having a head and tail. We can flip both coins at the same time, but we have no positive idea of what combination of heads and tails will result because flipping coins is rather uncertain. There are only four possible events, however: (1) two heads, (2) two tails, (3) a head for the first coin and a tail for the second, and (4) a tail for the first coin and a head for the second. We can then define our outcomes:

$$O_1 = \text{at least one head,}$$
$$O_2 = \text{at least one tail,}$$
$$O_3 = \text{at least one head and one tail.}$$

Thus we can see that the outcomes can contain more than one event. The outcomes defined as O_1, O_2, and O_3 include all possibilities of events.

Probability theory is conveniently noted in the symbols of *set theory*. For example, we can show that the set (usually enclosed in braces) of outcomes S for flipping two coins is

$$S = \{(O_1), (O_2), (O_3)\}.$$

Similarly, we can say that the set of events E is

$$E = \{(HH), (TT), (TH), (HT)\}.$$

Some standard notation is worth mentioning since it is used so often. If we want to express the probability that an *element* E of a set of events with j possibilities occurs, we write $P(E_j)$. This is read "the probability that E_j occurs." In order to express the probability that two or more events occur as the result of a trial, say, E_i and E_j, where we assume $i \neq j$, we write $P(E_i \cap E_j)$. This is read "the probability that E_i and E_j occur." We write $P(E_i \cup E_j)$ to read "the probability that E_i or E_j or both occur." If we desire to write in our shorthand the probability that an event does not occur, we write $P(\hat{E}_i)$, which is read "the probability that E_i does not occur."

There are three *laws of probability* that are the underlying foundation of probability theory:

1. $0 \leq P \leq 1$. The probability of an event occurring can be no less than zero or greater than one. Probabilities close to zero are quite unlikely to occur, and probabilities near one are most likely to occur.

2. $P(E_i \cup E_j) = P(E_i) + P(E_j) - P(E_i \cap E_j)$. The probability that E_i or E_j occurs is equal to the probability that E_i occurs plus the probability that E_j occurs minus the probability that E_i and E_j occur. In some trials E_i and E_j cannot occur together — this is called a *mutually exclusive event* — and hence

$P(E_i \cap E_j) = 0$. This means that in such cases — that is, only in cases where events are mutually exclusive — we can reduce the law to $P(E_i \cup E_j) = P(E_i) + P(E_j)$. To illustrate further, it is obvious that both E_i and $\hat{E}_i$ cannot occur at the same time by definition, yet either E_i or $\hat{E}_i$ must occur; hence $P(E_i \cup \hat{E}_i) = 1 = P(E_i) + P(\hat{E}_i)$.

3. $P(E_i \cap E_j) = P(E_i \mid E_j)P(E_j) = P(E_j \mid E_i)P(E_i)$. The notation $P(E_i \mid E_j)$ is used to denote a *conditional probability*. It means that E_i has a probability of occurring if we know that E_j has occurred. In some cases we will find that $P(E_i \cap E_j) = 0$ when $P(E_i)$ or $P(E_j) = 0$; thus we can compute the probability directly for $P(E_i \mid E_j)$ by definition. In some other cases we may find that $P(E_i \mid E_j) = P(E_i)$, which means that E_i is *independent* of E_j, and this reduces the law to $P(E_i \cap E_j) = P(E_i)P(E_j)$. This means that the probability of E_i and E_j occurring, when they are independent, is simply the product of their independent probabilities.

Sometimes it is useful to picture the elements of an outcome set as *Venn diagrams*. If we picture two sets, O_i and O_j, which represent possible outcomes, then Fig. 5:1 is a Venn diagram which may help make the laws of probability somewhat easier to visualize. If O_i and O_j are mutually exclusive, they will never intersect.

We can now return to our example of flipping two coins for illustrative purposes. Since we know there are only four events, and there is no reason that they cannot occur with equal probability, we can say that

Event	Probability
HH	.25
HT	.25
TH	.25
TT	.25

It is always best to break down outcomes into events and then examine the outcomes O_1, O_2, and O_3 as we have defined them above. Intuitively, we can see that the probability of outcomes is computed from the probability of events, and we can see that

Outcome	Probability
O_1	.75
O_2	.75
O_3	.50

The second law of probability can be examined for O_1 and O_2, that is, the probability that at least one head or one tail will result, and we see by substitution that

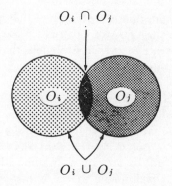

$$O_i \cap O_j$$

$$O_i \cup O_j$$

Fig. 5:1. Venn diagram.

$$P(O_1 \cup O_2) = .75 + .75 - .50 = 1.00.$$

This is intuitively obvious and serves as an informal proof of the law. Similarly, we can use the third law of probability to determine if O_1 and O_2 occur, that is, at least one head and at least one tail, and we see by substitution that

$$P(O_1 \cap O_2) = .66(.75) = .50.$$

For practical purposes we compute $P(E_i \,|\, E_j)$ by dividing $P(E_i \cap E_j)$ by $P(E_j)$, when $P(E_j) > 0$.

The foundations of probability theory are essential for the use of probabilistic models. There are two types of probabilistic models which are determined by the kinds of variables involved. *Discrete random-variable models* are those in which outcomes of experiments are usually expressed as positive integers. *Continuous random-variable models* are those in which outcomes of experiments are usually expressed within a range of values which need not be integers and can be any real numbers.

DISCRETE RANDOM-VARIABLE MODELS

Discrete random-variable models are quite interesting for urban analysis. One way of looking at these models is to consider an experiment where the outcomes are positive integer numbers. These outcomes arise one at a time as trials end, and they can be plotted according to the probabilities with which they have been observed, as seen in Fig. 5:2. We can generalize

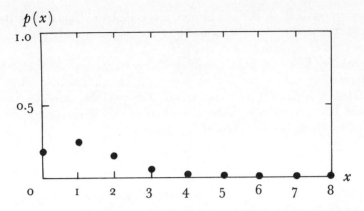

$p(x)$

1.0

0.5

0   1   2   3   4   5   6   7   8 x

FIG. 5:2. Discrete random-variable mapping.

the discrete random-variable model by considering an experiment in which there are n outcomes which can be given integer values. We know that the probability of all outcomes must be unity or one, and so we can state

$$p(0 \cup 1 \cup 2 \cup \ldots \cup n) = 1 = p(0) + p(1) + p(2) + \ldots + p(n) = \sum_{x=0}^{n} p(x).$$

This means that if the experiment is performed many times, the probability that x will reach a certain value approaches $p(x)$. Since there are $n + 1$ outcomes ($n + 1$ is used in order to account for $x = 0$), the probability of all being reached is one. The outcome of the experiment can be thought of as a model where x is the independent variable and $p(x)$ the dependent variable. In discrete random-variable models x can take only positive integer values, and it describes the outcome of an experiment; hence it is random.

In some cases we will not consider the whole of the n outcomes but will consider only n; hence $r \leq n$. The probability that x takes a value less than or equal to r, or $p(0 \cup 1 \cup 2 \ldots \cup r)$, is called the *cumulative probability*, $\hat{P}(r)$. It is defined by

$$\hat{P}(r) = p(0 \cup 1 \cup 2 \cup \ldots \cup r) = p(0) + p(1) + \ldots + p(r).$$

The cumulative probability function is considered the probability that an outcome of an experiment yields a value less than or equal to r.

A related probability density function which is often used is the *complementary cumulative function*. It is defined by

$$P(x) = 1 - \hat{P}(x - 1) = p(x) + p(x + 1) + \ldots + p(n).$$

The interpretation of the complementary cumulative function is that it gives the probability that the outcome of an experiment will yield a value greater than or equal to x.

Probability functions $p(x)$ are often characterized by two values for a given problem, called the *first moment* and *second moment* (there are also third, fourth, fifth, etc., moments). For practical purposes we can consider the first moment to be the mean of the observations, which is called the *expected value* in probability theory:

$$\bar{x} = E(x) = \sum_{i=1}^{n} x_i P(x_i) = \mu.$$

The second moment, for practical purposes also, can be considered the variance of the observations:

$$\text{Var}(x) = \sum_{i=1}^{n} x_i^2 P(x_i) - (\bar{x})^2.$$

This is simply the probability theory form of the familiar descriptive statistics variance, where

$$\sigma^2 = \frac{1}{n} \sum_{i=1}^{n} (x_i - \bar{x})^2.$$

Most probability models use moments to approximate model parameters, called the *method of moments*.

There are several important discrete random-variable models. Among the better known are the *binomial model, Poisson model, uniform model,* and *geometric model*. While all are important, we will examine only one which we feel to be relevant to urban analysis.

POISSON MODEL

The Poisson model is a significant discrete random-variable model because of its great flexibility and adaptability to complex random events in the real world. The Poisson model is named for its developer, S. D. Poisson (1781-1840), the great French mathematician. It is based on the concept that events which happen one at a time in a random order in time or space can be estimated and predicted if we consider a long period of time or many trials and can determine the average value of x for any given period of time or number of trials.

There are two basic assumptions incorporated in the Poisson model.

The first is that the probability of n occurrences in time or space (t) is exactly the same no matter where consideration of an interval of t begins and ends. The second assumption is that events which occur in any interval of time or space are independent of events that occur in other intervals of time or space.

These two basic assumptions (and several others related more to mathematical structure) are the foundations for the *Poisson series,* the general form of which constitutes the Poisson model:

$$p(x; \lambda t) = e^{-\lambda t} \frac{(\lambda t)^x}{x!},$$

where

$p(x; \lambda t)$ = functional notation of Poisson model,
e = Naperian log base = 2.7182,
λ = constant of proportionality,
t = time or space interval,
$x!$ = x factorial; e.g., if $x = 4$, then
$x! = 4 \cdot 3 \cdot 2 \cdot 1 = 24.$

Since the constant of proportionality λ times the interval t is the average occurrence of x, which is μ, and since it can be shown that $\mu = \text{Var}(x)$ in the Poisson model, then the more convenient form is to substitute $\mu = \lambda t$:

$$p(x; \mu) = e^{-\mu} \frac{\mu^x}{x!}.$$

This is the same as the mathematical model

$$\hat{P}(r; \mu) = \sum_{x=0}^{r} p(x; \mu),$$

which gives the probability of r or less occurrences. The cumulative probability function for the Poisson model is

$$\hat{P}(x; \mu) = \sum_{j=0}^{x} e^{-\mu} \frac{\mu^j}{j!}.$$

The complementary cumulative probability function for the Poisson model is

$$P(x; \mu) = \sum_{j=x}^{\infty} e^{-\mu} \frac{\mu^j}{j!}.$$

Consider a large city where the police find that they receive a mean rate of five phone calls for aid per minute, but these calls come at random. The Poisson model can be used to estimate the probability of a number of calls over some longer period of time, for example, one hour. The model would be

$$p(x;5) = e^{-5}\frac{5^x}{x!}.$$

The scheduling officer is interested in determining the slow periods. He realizes that the probability of no calls for any instant is infinitely small, but he attempts to find for an hour the probability of no calls per minute. Making the computations, he finds that $P_t(0) = 0.0067$ and concludes that a policeman's work is unlikely to ever be very slow. Similar computations can be made for any value for x and any mean rate of calls.

The cumulative probability of the Poisson model is used for questions about the probability that no more than r events (that is, r or less) will occur in a period t. For example, suppose our scheduling officer is curious about the probability that no more than two calls will occur during the next two minutes. We have the mean rate proportional to the time interval, $t = 2$ minutes, so we compute $\mu = 10$, and

$$\sum_{j=0}^{2} p(x;10) = \hat{P}(2;10) = 0.0027,$$

and he may decide that someone should not take a break, since it is doubtful that no more than two calls will come for the next two minutes. For convenience, an abstract of a table containing values for the cumulative probability for the Poisson model is included as Appendix D.

The Poisson model has a complementary cumulative probability associated with it as well. The table for cumulative Poisson probabilities (Appendix D) can also be used for complementary cumulative Poisson probabilities by reviewing the definitions. An example may clarify this. There is a city in the South that had, on the average, twelve racial disturbances every four months. The mayor asked his urban analyst to predict (1) the likelihood of one racial disturbance happening in the next month and (2) the likelihood of more than one racial disturbance during the next month. The urban analyst took the second question and developed a complementary cumulative Poisson model for $\mu = 3$ (that is, a mean rate of three racial disturbances per month):

$$\sum_{j=2}^{\infty} p(x;3) = 1 - \sum_{x=0}^{1} p(x;3)$$
$$= 1 - \hat{P}(1;3)$$
$$= 1 - 0.1991$$
$$= 0.8009.$$

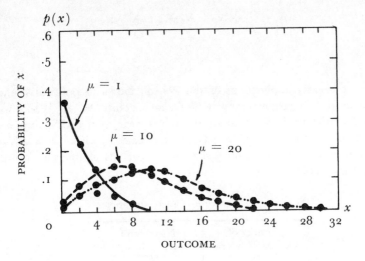

FIG. 5:3. Poisson model mappings for $\mu = 1, 10, 20$.

This meant that the probability of more than one racial disturbance in the next month was 0.8009, and the city could expect trouble. Using this same approach, the urban analyst predicted the probability that there would be exactly one racial disturbance in the following manner:

$$p(1;3) = \hat{P}(1;3) - \hat{P}(0;3)$$
$$= 0.1991 - 0.0497$$
$$= 0.1494.$$

Thus it seemed most likely that there would be more than just one racial disturbance.

The Poisson model takes a skewed form when mapped, but the shape varies, with skewness decreasing with the increase of μ. This can be seen in Fig. 5:3. The mean rate μ determines the characteristics of the Poisson model. When μ is not given, it is necessary to estimate it over a long period of time because of the random nature of events — this insures a somewhat more satisfactory estimate of the real world. A heuristic approach to computing a value for μ is to select an interval t and then observe a large number of intervals N of width t. For each integer value of x we let N_x denote the number of intervals in which the integer value of x has occurred, so that

$$T = 0(N_0) + 1(N_1) + 2(N_2) + \ldots + x(N_x),$$

where

$$N = N_0 + N_1 + N_2 + \ldots + N_x;$$

therefore,

$$\mu = \frac{T}{N}.$$

One of the early applications of the Poisson model to political science is a classic and illustrates many of the above points. W. A. Wallis was interested in the vacancies that occurred per year in the U.S. Supreme Court.[1] Wallis examined Supreme Court vacancies by virtue of death or resignation over a period of 96 years (or 96 periods of interval, $t = 1$). Table 5:1 shows his findings.

TABLE 5:1. Supreme Court vacancies.

Number of Vacancies in Year (x)	Number of Years x Occurred (N_x)
0	59
1	27
2	9
3	1
Over 3	0
Total	96

The computation for μ is reached by solving for T for $N = 96$, which is

$$T + 0(N_0) + 1(N_1) + 2(N_2) + 3(N_3) = 0 + 27 + 2(9) + 3(1) = 48;$$

therefore,

$$\mu = \frac{T}{N} = \frac{48}{96} = 0.5.$$

The Poisson model is calibrated as

$$p(x; 0.5) = e^{-0.5} \frac{(0.5)^x}{x!}.$$

By solving $p(x; 0.5)$ for $x = 0, 1, 2, 3$, we can compute the number of years in which similar x vacancies occur by multiplying by $N = 96$, as shown in Table 5:2.

The Poisson model of Supreme Court vacancies shows that they are

[1] W. A. Wallis, "The Poisson Distribution and Supreme Court," *Journal of the American Statistical Association*, 31 (1936), 326-380.

TABLE 5:2. Poisson model of Supreme Court vacancies for $\mu = 0.5$.

x	Probability of x Vacancies $p(x;0.5)$	Probable Number of Years in Which x Vacancies Occur $96(x;0.5)$	Residuals $(N_x - \hat{N}_x)$
0	0.6065	58.22	0.78
1	0.3033	29.12	−2.12
2	0.0758	7.28	1.72
3	0.0126	1.21	−0.21
Over 3	0.0018	0.17	−0.17
Totals	1.000	96.00	0.00

random variables which are discrete and are estimated satisfactorily by the method which assumes that a mean rate over a long period of time is useful for stochastic processes. Note that the probabilities for x as estimated by $p(x;0.5)$ in Table 5:2 total 1.000. The estimated or probable number of years expected for x to occur total $N = 96$, and the residuals for $N_x - \hat{N}_x$ (that is, observed minus estimated) total 0.00. By way of interpretation, Fig. 5:4 shows that the Supreme Court usually has no vacancies in a given year, but when they occur, it is most likely that there will be only one.

We have examined only the Poisson model for the reasons stated previously. It should be noted, however, that many discrete random-variable models are related to each other. A kind of hierarchy exists in that one model is a limit, and hence a higher form, of another model. For example, a limit of the geometric model is the binomial model, and a limit of the binomial model is the Poisson model; another is the normal model. Furthermore, under ideal conditions all probabilities of discrete random variables can be approximated by the normal distribution. We have not covered the discrete normal random-variable model here because it is widely known; but, more important, the ideal conditions needed or assumed for the normal distribution are not always found in urban systems applications. The Poisson model is well suited for discrete random-variable urban analysis in our experience.

CONTINUOUS RANDOM-VARIABLE MODELS

We have treated discrete random-variable models as random variables

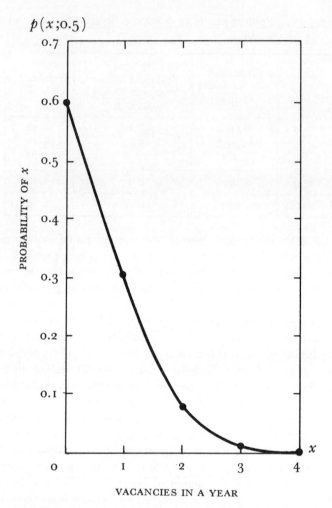

$p(x;0.5)$

FIG. 5:4. Mapping of $p(x;0.5)$ for Poisson model of Supreme Court vacancies.

with nonnegative integer values. Certain problems of urban analysis cannot be described in such terms, and it becomes necessary to consider random variables that can take any value between zero and ∞ (in some special cases $-\infty$ to $+\infty$), which are usually called *continuous random* or *stochastic variables*. Such a change requires some modification of the probabilistic description of random variables in probabilistic models.

Difficulty arises in the mathematical impossibility of having the proba-

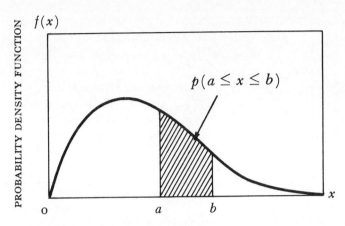

FIG. 5:5. Continuous random variable x in $[a,b]$.

bilities of all x values sum to unity, since x can be any real number (hence there are an infinite number of x values, even if we restrict x so that it lies in an interval $a \leq x \leq b$). In mathematical terms the probability of any specific value of x for a continuous random variable is zero. Mathematics does give us an escape hatch in that we can consider a continuous random variable x with a specific value lying in an interval $a \leq x \leq b$ (see Fig. 5:5). Our analysis of continuous random variables will be concerned with the probability that a specific x lies in some interval and not that it takes a specific value. When we say that x has a specific probability in a continuous random-variable model, we are citing an approximation.

Continuous random-variable models can be developed by a form-giving function, $f(x)$, called the *probability density function*. The probability density function should not be confused with the probability of x. The probability of x lying in an interval $a \leq x \leq b$ is found by computing the area under the curve formed by $f(x)$, i.e., the cross-hatched area in Fig. 5:5. The computational method is called *integration*. The probability for any specific value of x is the probability that x lies in a very small interval from x to $x + dx$, where dx, called the *differential* of x, is infinitesimally small (we shall consider its properties in the next chapter). The total area under $f(x)$ from $-\infty$ to $+\infty$ must equal unity, as shown in Fig. 5:6.

The probability of x in continuous random-variable models is somewhat abstract, and practitioners prefer to use the cumulative and complementary cumulative probabilities. The cumulative probability $\hat{F}(x)$ is the area under

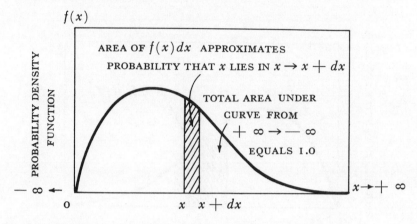

FIG. 5:6. Continuous random-variable probability.

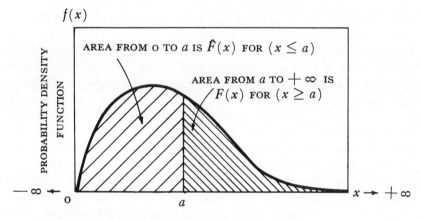

FIG. 5:7. $\hat{F}(x)$ and $F(x)$ for continuous random variable.

the curve of $f(x)$ from $-\infty$ to the specific value of x.[2] The complementary cumulative probability is $F(x) = 1 - \hat{F}(x)$.[3] The cumulative probability $\hat{F}(x)$ represents the probability that x will be less than or equal to a specific value for x; the complementary cumulative probability represents the

[2] The reader familiar with calculus will note that the derivative of $\hat{F}(x)$ is $f(x)$, in our terms.

[3] The reader familiar with calculus will note that the derivative of $F(x)$ is $-f(x)$, in our terms.

probability that x will be greater than or equal to a specific value for x, as can be seen in Fig. 5:7.

For continuous random variables the mean or expected value of x, μ, is defined as the area from $-\infty$ to $+\infty$ of $xf(x)dx$. The variance of x is defined as the area from $-\infty$ to $+\infty$ of $(x - \bar{x})^2 f(x)dx$. These terms are by way of definition, and computation is done in the more familiar manner in practice.

GAMMA MODEL

There are many continuous random-variable models that could be examined at this juncture. A variety of shapes and characteristics is available through the numerous continuous random-variable models that may be necessary and sufficient for specific problem statements. We have selected the *gamma model* as representative of these models. The gamma model has been used in traffic modeling on several occasions and has also been applied to problems concerning queues, inventories, and investments.

The gamma model has three parameters, a, b, and m, and it is closely related to several other models. The gamma model can be expressed, in a foreboding manner, by

$$f(x;a;b;m) = \frac{b^a \, (x - m)^{a-1} e^{-b(x-m)}}{\Gamma(a)},$$

where

$a =$ shape-giving parameter,
$b =$ scaling parameter,
$m =$ origin parameter,
$e =$ base of natural logarithms (2.7182).

For practical purposes the gamma function $\Gamma(a)$ can be approximated by $(a - 1)$! The value for m is usually zero in urban analysis. Urban analysts usually deal with the general form of the gamma model in which $a > 0$, $b > 0$, $m = 0$, $x \geq 0$, and hence $f(x;a;b;m) \geq 0$. The parameters a and b are often computed by the method of moments, so that

$$a = \frac{\mu^2}{\sigma^2},$$

$$b = \frac{\mu}{\sigma^2}.$$

The method of moments works well when the value of a is fairly large (say, $a \geq 10$). Our experience has shown that most urban analysis problems have rather small a values (say, $a \leq 5$) which result in the gamma model taking the shape of left-skewed curves when mapped. A practical method for dealing with this problem has been developed which facilitates the use of the gamma model.[4] An algorithm can be used in five steps:

1. Select the origin parameter such that $m = 0$.
2. Compute the expected value μ and the log of the geometric mean g, where

$$\log g = \frac{\Sigma \log x}{n}.$$

3. Solve the equation $y = \log \mu - \log g$.
4. Using a table of y and y_a values, as included in Appendix E, solve $a = y_a/y$.
5. Compute b from $b = a/\mu$.

This algorithm enables the urban analyst to employ the gamma model with efficacy and efficiency of computation for many urban problems.

An interesting example of the use of the gamma model in urban analysis is the estimation of the length of trips in the Toronto area.[5] The Toronto data are shown in Table 5:3. A similar model of Washington, D.C., is shown in Fig. 5:8.

As the value of the a parameter gets very small, the gamma curve becomes highly left-skewed, approaching a smoothness. If $a = 1$, a variation of the gamma model is the *probabilistic exponential model*. The probabilistic exponential model approximates the form of the gamma model in which $a = 1$, $b > 0$, $m = 0$, $x \geq 0$, and $f(x) \geq 0$ by using the expression

$$f(x;b) = be^{-bx}.$$

For such a case

$$b = \frac{1}{\mu}.$$

We can prove mathematically that the cumulative probability function is

$$\hat{F}(x) = 1 - e^{-bx}.$$

Similarly, the complementary cumulative function for the probabilistic exponential model is

---

[4] David Durand and J. Arthur Greenwood, "Aids for Fitting the Gamma Distribution by Maximum Likelihood," *Technometrics*, 2, no. 1 (Feb., 1960), 55-65.
[5] Alan M. Voorhees, *Factors and Trends in Trip Lengths* (Washington, D.C.: Highway Research Board, 1968).

$$F(x) = e^{-bx}.$$

Development and solution of the probabilistic exponential model is simplified using the above approach.

TABLE 5:3. Gamma model of trips, Toronto urban
system.

Length of Trip (x)	Observed Number of Trips (N_x)	Predicted Number of Trips
1	3,327	1,609
2	1,859	2,082
3	2,067	2,242
4	1,891	2,239
5	1,948	2,146
6	1,787	2,004
7	1,473	1,838
8	1,232	1,664
9	1,375	1,491
10	1,192	1,326
11	844	1,172
12	1,385	1,029
13	778	901
14	378	785
15	444	682
16	693	591
17	657	511
18	575	440
19	687	379
20	1,078	326
21	1,177	279
22	263	239
23	173	204
24	137	175
25	0	149
26	0	127
27	0	108
28	234	92

$\mu = 8.868$	$m = 0$
$\log \mu = 2.182$	$y = 0.366$
$\log g = 1.816$	$a = 1.638$
	$b = 0.185$

$$f(x;a;b;m) = \frac{0.185^{1.638} \, x^{0.638} \, e^{-0.185x}}{\Gamma(1.638)}$$

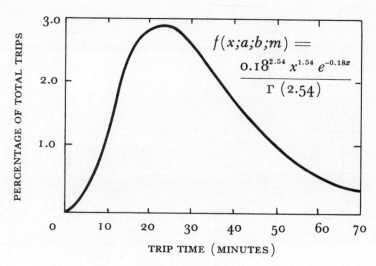

FIG. 5:8. Voorhees gamma model of Washington urban system trips, 1955, for percentage of total trips.

An interesting application of the probabilistic exponential model concerns the length of time that a computer center will operate effectively, measured by the mean value for its expected running without a breakdown.[6] If we know that $\mu = 360$ hours, and the probability density function is a probabilistic exponential function, we can compute various probabilities about the computer center's efficiency. For example, what is the probability that the computer center will run without breakdowns for 180 hours or less? We map the probability density function by

$$f(x;b) = \frac{1}{360} e^{-x/360}.$$

The cumulative probability function to answer the question is

$$\hat{F}(x) = 1 - e^{x/360}.$$
$$\text{For } x \geq 180$$
$$\hat{F}(180) = 1 - e^{180/360}$$
$$= 1 - e^{0.5}$$
$$= 0.3935.$$

This problem is shown in Fig. 5:9 (also see Appendix F).

[6] Problem from Ya-lun Chou, *Statistical Analysis with Business and Economic Applications* (New York: Holt, Rinehart, and Winston, 1969), pp. 216-217.

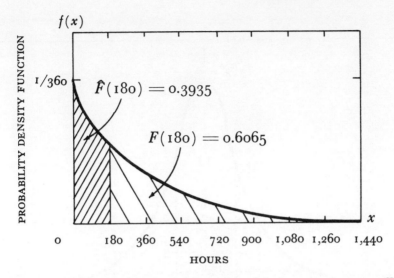

FIG. 5:9. Chou probabilistic exponential model of computer center efficacy.

NORMAL MODEL

Theoretically, a random variable, observed over a long period of time or a large number of trials, will approach the familiar normal distribution:

$$f(x) = f(\mu; \sigma) = \frac{1}{\sigma\sqrt{2\pi}} e^{-(x-\mu)^2/2\sigma^2}.$$

Since there are widely available tables that list values for the normal model, its forbidding mathematical form in actually quite simple to use. Its geometric characteristics are shown in Fig. 5:10, and these are probably familiar to the reader.

The normal model is often used in urban analysis for continuous random variables. The inherent problem is that the assumption of normally distributed sets of observations, according the normal probability law, is often difficult to apply in urban analysis, especially in urban behavior patterns. Nevertheless, it is useful and is sometimes the only practical approach to continuous-variable probability models.

It is possible to have a probabilistic model with two or more discrete or continuous random variables, but it is quite difficult to develop and

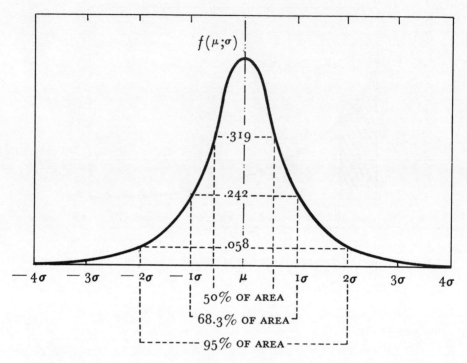

FIG. 5:10. Geometric characteristics of the normal model.

use such models. There have been some experimental attempts at modeling urban problems for two random continuous variables using a normal model. For example, assume that a person's commuting drive in miles (x_1) and home location from the center of the city (x_2) are random and normally distributed for a large number of observations (for persons working near the center city only and excluding reverse and intersuburban commuters). A probability density function $f(x_1,x_2)$ could be developed from the normal model, and it would take the three-dimensional bell shape shown in Fig. 5:11. The probability that x_1 lies in $x_1 + dx_1$ and x_2 lies in $x_2 + dx_2$ would be computed by finding the area under the surface for these intervals through a double integration of the function for the two intervals. The entire area below the bell-shaped surface and the plane formed by the two random variables would be equal to unity. Such models, as well as similar deterministic models, are quite interesting for the study of surfaces in urban analysis, such as urban form, densities, and abstractions.

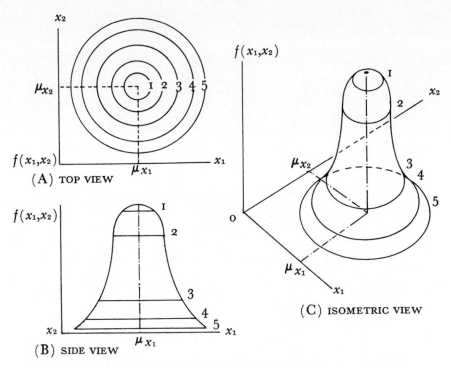

FIG. 5:11. Normal model with two random variables.

MARKOV CHAINS

A special group of models derived from probability theory is called *Markov chains* or *processes*. There has been growing interest in an application of these models in urban analysis over the last two decades. We shall look at the simplest of the Markov chains and suggest that the other types, which have been studied exhaustively in physics and mathematics, may hold potential utility for urban analysis.

The simplest of the Markov chains is discrete in time and space. It is used where a system can be described completely in terms of its *states,* and the discrete case means that it can be in only one state at a time. "Discrete in time" is a term used to mean that the system is examined at regular intervals, for example, every hour, every day, or every year. A typical example is to consider a toll booth at the end of a tunnel; one approach is shown in Fig. 5:12.

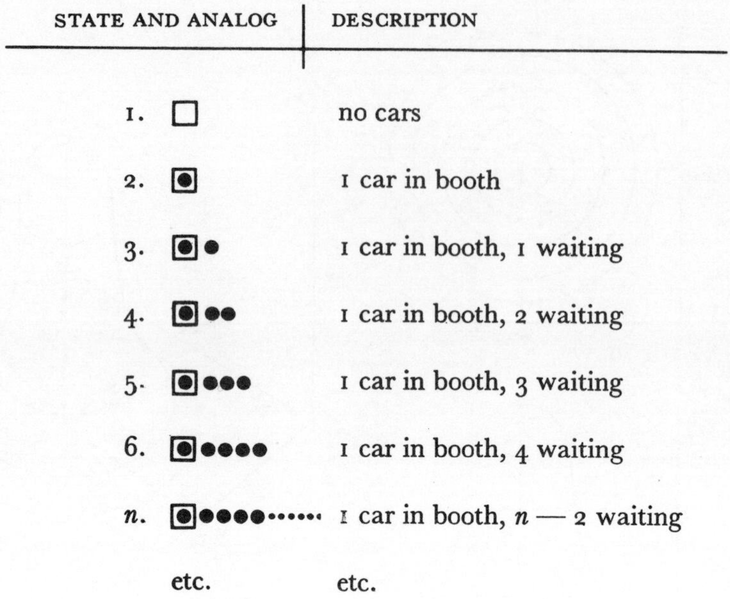

STATE AND ANALOG	DESCRIPTION
1. □	no cars
2. ◉	1 car in booth
3. ◉ •	1 car in booth, 1 waiting
4. ◉ ••	1 car in booth, 2 waiting
5. ◉ •••	1 car in booth, 3 waiting
6. ◉ ••••	1 car in booth, 4 waiting
n. ◉ ••••⋯⋯	1 car in booth, $n - 2$ waiting
etc.	etc.

FIG. 5:12. States of toll booth service system.

The general notation for a Markov model that is discrete in time and space is that the system can be in any of j states — called the *steady state* or *state space* — and is observed at any time t_r, where $r = (0, 1, 2, 3, \ldots, n)$. Markov chains with discrete space and continuous time for observations form a special category of mathematical analysis, often called *queuing theory*. When both time and space are continuous in a Markov chain, a complex type of mathematical analysis called a *diffusion process* is found. Examples of discrete time and continuous space in Markov chains are rare, but they are possible.

There are two important properties of Markov chains that are discrete in time and space:

1. The outcome of each experiment belongs to a finite set of outcomes $a_1, a_2, a_3, \ldots, a_m$.

2. The outcome of any trial depends most upon the outcome of the immediately preceding trial and not upon any other previous outcome; for any pair of states (a_i, a_j) there is a given probability p_{ij} that a_j occurs after a_i occurs.

The probabilities p_{ij} that represent the likelihood of a_j occurring after

a_i are called *transition probabilities,* and they are usually arranged in a matrix called a *transition matrix.* For example,

$$P = \begin{pmatrix} P_{11} & P_{12} & \cdots & P_{1m} \\ P_{21} & P_{22} & \cdots & P_{2m} \\ \cdot & \cdot & & \cdot \\ \cdot & \cdot & & \cdot \\ \cdot & \cdot & & \cdot \\ P_{m1} & P_{m2} & & P_{mm} \end{pmatrix}.$$

The transition matrix represents the set of probabilities that the system which was in state a_i at time t will be in state a_j at $t + 1$.

If we consider a system with three finite states, and we observe it at finite times t, then the corresponding transition matrix would be

$$P = \begin{pmatrix} P_{11} & P_{12} & P_{13} \\ P_{21} & P_{22} & P_{23} \\ P_{31} & P_{32} & P_{33} \end{pmatrix}.$$

This can be mapped, as shown in Fig. 5:13, allowing the respective transition probabilities to be better observed.

Transition matrices are *stochastic matrices.* This means that each row of the transition matrix represents the probabilities for the state a_i and hence must sum to unity, since the columns are the other possible finite states:

$$\sum_{j=1}^{m} P_{ij} = 1, \text{ where } i = 1, 2, \ldots, m.$$

Stochastic matrices must have nonnegative elements (with rows summing to unity) and are said to be *regular* if all elements of P^n are positive, $n = 1, 2, 3, \ldots, \infty$.

The entry P_{ij} in the transition matrix is the probability that the system will go from a_i to a_j in one step, $t + 1$. We can form the *n-step transition matrix* to determine the probabilities after n steps. The n-step transition matrix is the transition matrix P raised to the nth power:

$$P(n) = P^n.$$

An interesting application of Markov chains has been made in the analysis of attitudinal changes over time.[7] We can examine certain aspects

[7] T. W. Anderson, "Probability Models for Analyzing Time Changes in Attitude," in Paul F. Lazarsfeld, ed., *Mathematical Thinking in the Social Sciences* (Glencoe, Ill.: Free Press, 1954), pp. 17-66.

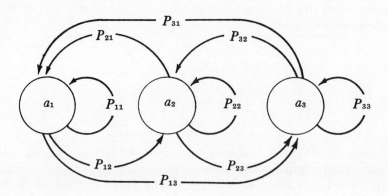

FIG. 5:13. Mapping of three-state Markov chain.

of this to clarify the above points. Assume a school bond issue in referendum during January, and we consider those who voted and examine yes and no votes. Given transition matrix P^1, which represents the probabilities that the attitudes will change in February for any individual, we can also compute additional transition matrices for March, April, etc.:

$$P(1) = P^1 = \begin{array}{c} \\ \text{Yes} \\ \text{No} \end{array} \begin{array}{cc} \text{Yes} & \text{No} \\ \begin{pmatrix} .9 & .1 \\ .2 & .8 \end{pmatrix} \end{array}, \text{January to February,}$$

$$P(2) = P^2 = \begin{array}{c} \\ \text{Yes} \\ \text{No} \end{array} \begin{array}{cc} \text{Yes} & \text{No} \\ \begin{pmatrix} .83 & .17 \\ .34 & .66 \end{pmatrix} \end{array}, \text{January to March,}$$

$$P(3) = P^3 = \begin{array}{c} \\ \text{Yes} \\ \text{No} \end{array} \begin{array}{cc} \text{Yes} & \text{No} \\ \begin{pmatrix} .781 & .219 \\ .438 & .562 \end{pmatrix} \end{array}, \text{January to April.}$$

As can be seen, the probability that an individual will change his attitude increases over time.

A limiting matrix T exists when a large number of time periods n are considered. This means that P^n can be approximated by T when n is sufficiently large. If we can consider every row of the transition matrix as a *probability distribution,* then we call the rows of the limiting matrix the *stationary distribution* of the Markov chain.

This can be seen by referring to the example discussed above. Let

$$P^1 = \begin{pmatrix} .9 & .1 \\ .2 & .8 \end{pmatrix}.$$

Find

$$P = \begin{pmatrix} P_1 \\ P_2 \end{pmatrix} \text{ or, in general, } P = \begin{pmatrix} P_1 \\ \cdot \\ \cdot \\ \cdot \\ P_m \end{pmatrix},$$

so that

$$pP = p$$

or

$$\sum_{i=1}^{m} P_i P_{ij} = P_i, \text{ where } j = (1, 2, \ldots, m).$$

Substituting, we have

$$(p_1, p_2) \begin{pmatrix} .9 & .1 \\ .2 & .8 \end{pmatrix} = (p_1, p_2).$$

Then

$$.9 p_1 + .2 p_2 = p_1,$$
$$.1 p_1 + .8 p_2 = p_2,$$

and since

$$p_1 + p_2 = 1,$$

then

$$p_1 = 2/3,$$
$$p_2 = 1/3,$$
$$p = \begin{pmatrix} .67 \\ .33 \end{pmatrix}.$$

This means that in the long run the probability is $p = .67$ that an individual will vote yes, regardless of his present opinion. In general, we find a fixed point p for the transition matrix P, which is square, by solving the matrix equations for $pP = p$.

There are some cases where a state a_i of a Markov chain is called an *absorbing state,* because the system remains in it once it has entered. An absorbing state exists if the ith row of the transition matrix P has a one on the main diagonal and zeros elsewhere in the row. For example,

$$P = \begin{array}{c} \\ a_1 \\ a_2 \\ a_3 \\ a_4 \end{array} \begin{array}{c} a_1 \quad\; a_2 \quad\; a_3 \quad\; a_4 \\ \begin{pmatrix} .25 & .25 & 0 & .50 \\ 0 & 1.00 & 0 & 0 \\ .25 & .25 & .25 & .25 \\ 0 & 1.00 & 0 & 0 \end{pmatrix}. \end{array}$$

The a_2 is an absorbing state by definition, but a_4 is not.

Testing Probability Models

The very concept of randomness in probability models (discrete random variable, continuous random variable, and Markov chains) makes testing difficult. If a variable has randomness inherent in its character, it cannot be estimated or predicted by deterministic models because the variance is unwieldy and error terms would be large for an individual case. This means that many of the tests for deterministic models are not applicable even though they are mathematically possible.

In practical terms the test of a probabilistic model is its performance. Performance is measured by comparing estimated and predicted values from probabilistic models against the observed values. For example, Fig. 5:14 compares the probability model results shown in Fig. 5:8 with the observed values. The interpretation of such a test is largely based on the informed judgment and intuition of the urban analyst as well as on the particular nature of the problem under consideration. As Fig. 5:14 shows, there is such a large range of variation among the observations that a probability model, such as the gamma model, may be the only scientific method by which form may be given to the problem.

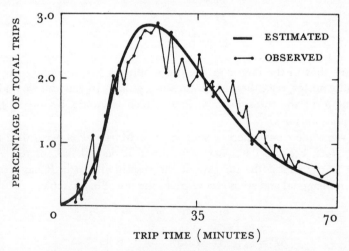

Fig. 5:14. Estimates from Voorhees gamma model and observed values of Washington urban system trips, 1955.

RECOMMENDED EXERCISES

1. Fire alarms come into the station house one at a time in a given precinct's terminal at the rate of one call every four hours over a 24-hour period. Assuming that these calls are Poisson-like in distribution, the fire chief asks you to find the probability that there will be (1) more than eight calls in the next two days and (2) exactly eight calls in the next two days. He has two men working the terminal that can each handle one call per hour maximum in a 12-hour shift. What is the probability that (3) these two men will be unable to answer some fire alarms?

2. A study by the traffic engineer of a western city shows that traffic lights in the city work well for an average of 200 days and then either burn out or lose phasing. His inspection crews examine and repair any given traffic light every 100 days. What is the probability that a given traffic light will be working when the inspection crew arrives?

3. The transition probabilities of Markov chains are often represented by *transition diagrams*. Formulate the transition probability matrix from the following transition diagrams:

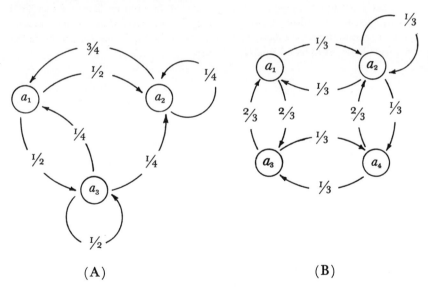

(A)   (B)

4. Formulate transition diagrams from the following Markov chain transition probability matrices:

$$P = \begin{pmatrix} 1/2 & 1/2 & 0 & 0 \\ 0 & 1/3 & 1/3 & 1/3 \\ 1/4 & 1/4 & 1/2 & 0 \\ 1/4 & 3/4 & 0 & 0 \end{pmatrix} \qquad P = \begin{pmatrix} 1/3 & 2/3 & 0 \\ 0 & 1/3 & 2/3 \\ 0 & 0 & 1 \end{pmatrix}$$

(A)   (B)

FURTHER READING

Chou, Ya-lun. *Statistical Analysis with Business and Economic Applications.* New York: Holt, Rinehart, and Winston, 1969.

A very good treatment of statistics in a general applied manner for business and economics with particular strength in probabilistic models. In addition to description and application, Chou uses probability theory to formulate and apply sampling and estimation theories.

Lazarsfeld, Paul F., ed. *Mathematical Thinking in the Social Sciences.* Glencoe, Ill.: Free Press, 1954.

An early attempt to apply probability theory to familiar problems of such fields of social science as politics, sociology, and decision theory. Many of the topics are quite interesting for urban analysts, and many of the mathematical problems that are raised have yet to be adequately resolved.

MASTER. *Wherefore in all great works are Clerks so much desired? Wherefore are Auditors so well fed? What causeth Geometricians so highly to be enhaunsed? Why are Astronomers so greatly advanced? Because that by number such things they finde, which else would farre excell mans minde.*

SCHOLAR. *Verily, sir, if it bee so, that these men by numbring, their cunning do attain, at whose great works most men do wonder, then I see well I was much deceived, and numbring is a more cunning thing then I took it to be.*

Robert Recorde, *The Declaration
of the Profit of Arithmeticke* (1540)

PART **III**

OPTIMIZING MODELS

Estimating and predicting models are used to describe urban systems so that we can understand them and predict characteristics of them in the future, or under various conditions, so that we can test them. *Optimization models* show what the best performance of urban systems could be under various conditions and at future times. In this sense optimization models are of interest to students of urban systems and are practical tools for those that plan and make decisions about urban systems.

We earlier discussed four types of optimal performance: (1) utopian, (2) optimal, (3) maximal, and (4) minimal. Utopian performance, for most practical purposes, is largely derived from intuitive analysis and has few if any constraints. Optimal performance is the best within the constraints established for the problem. In many cases an optimal performance could be either a maximal or a minimal performance, depending upon the characteristics of the problem and the constraints.

This chapter is concerned with *simple optimization models,* which quite often have maximal or minimal performance as the optimal performance. Simple optimization models are of the general form

$$\text{Opt } f(x),$$

subject to

$$g(x) = 0,$$
$$x \geq 0.$$

There is usually only one independent or decision variable in simple optimization models and usually only one constraint. The constraint often takes the form of a boundary for the domain of the function. For example, $g(x)$ could take the form $a \leq x \leq b$, where a, $b \geq 0$. Similarly, as a general rule in urban analysis, we deal primarily with nonnegative values for independent or decision variables (and consequently for dependent or nondecision variables). The techniques most often used are classical and have been borrowed from *calculus.* Calculus is used within a procedure that will be developed for an optimal search.

The succeeding chapters are concerned with *complex optimization models,* which often have several independent or decision variables and

CHAPTER 6

Classical Calculus and Optimization

a number of stages to be optimized owing to many constraints. The general form of such models is

$$\text{Opt} f(x_1, x_2, \ldots, x_n),$$

subject to

$$g_1 (x_1, x_2, \ldots, x_n) \leq 0,$$
$$g_2 (x_1, x_2, \ldots, x_n) \leq 0,$$

$$\cdot \qquad\qquad \cdot$$
$$\cdot \qquad\qquad \cdot$$
$$\cdot \qquad\qquad \cdot$$

$$g_m(x_1, x_2, \ldots, x_n) \leq 0,$$
$$x_i \geq 0.$$

As with simple optimization models, we generally deal with nonnegative independent or decision variables in urban analysis. The optimization by stage of complex optimization models requires mathematical programming techniques, such as *linear programming, nonlinear programming, dynamic programming,* and *stochastic programming.*

Conditions for Optimization

A set of conditions is necessary for an optimal solution to exist for a simple optimization model (while we shall discuss simple optimization models, the same set of conditions must exist for complex optimization models in

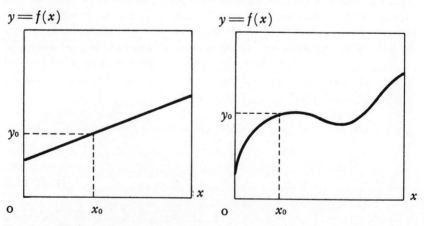

FIG. 6:1. Unique value functions.

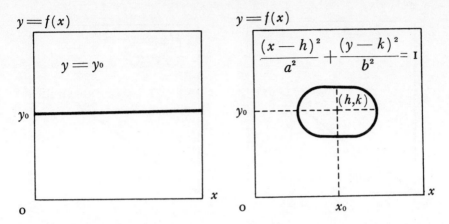

$y = f(x)$

$y = y_0$

y_0

x

O

$y = f(x)$

$$\frac{(x-h)^2}{a^2} + \frac{(y-k)^2}{b^2} = 1$$

y_0

(h,k)

O $\quad x_0 \quad x$

FIG. 6:2. Trivial and non-unique value functions.

a modified form). These conditions we shall call *sufficient* and *necessary conditions* for optimal solutions.

Only functions that have one and only one value for the dependent variable for each value of the independent variable will be considered. By this we mean that we use models that have unique values for the decision variable over the domain of the function (see Fig. 6:1). We may consider functions where there are several values of the decision variable for a given nondecision value, but these are usually trivial. We will not consider non-unique value functions for mathematical reasons and for practical purposes in that they are quite unrealistic and are usually only mathematical toys (see Fig. 6:2). We shall place an asterisk by the values for optimal solutions, for example, x^*, y^*.

BOUNDEDNESS

The domain of the function, or at least the range of the decision variable, must be bounded in order for an optimal solution to exist. In most cases of simple optimization models this entails setting a closed interval for the decision variable in which either a maximum or a minimum can be found. Without a closed interval it is mathematically impossible to determine if a maximum or minimum exists; there is no way of knowing such a value because there are an infinite number of possibilities (see Fig. 6:3). A closed interval insures that a maximal or minimal value can be found,

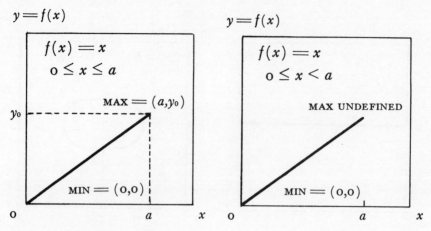

FIG. 6:3. Closed and open intervals.

especially if it exists at the end-points of the interval, and further assuming that a maximal or minimal value exists for the given function.

CONTINUITY

Urban analysis almost always involves continuous functions. A *continuous function* is one in which there is an existing value for the dependent variable for every possible value of the independent variable — in most functions where the domain is a set of real numbers, this could be an infinite number of places. In heuristic parlance the rule of thumb holds that if it is possible to map a function without raising the pen from the paper within the domain, it is a continuous function (see Fig. 6:4). Discontinuous functions are sometimes found in urban analysis and can be solved for optimal solutions, if such exist, in certain cases. The mathematical difficulty is that it is often hard to prove that an optimal solution exists where there are discontinuous points within the function.

EXTREME VALUE THEORY

We can find optimal solutions to problems by using the well-known *extreme value theory*, which incorporates many of the above concepts. The extreme value theory holds that if a function is bounded, continuous, and has real-number values, at least one maximum and minimum value

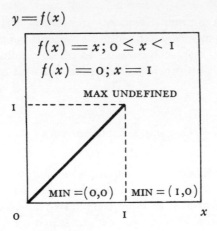

FIG. 6:4. Discontinuous function.

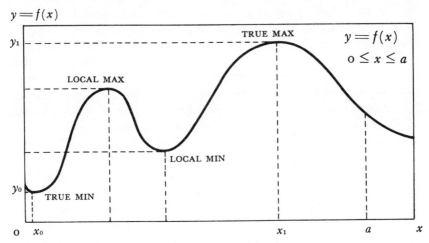

FIG. 6:5. True and local maxima and minima.

must exist. The proof of this theory is beyond the mathematical scope of this book and is left to the interested reader to pursue independently. It should be noted that the extreme value theory provides at least one maximal and minimal value, but often there are several intervening values which appear to be maximal or minimal within a smaller interval for the function, as can be seen in Fig. 6:5.

The concepts of boundedness, continuity, and real-number values, as incorporated in the extreme value theory, hold for complex optimization models where there are multiconstraints and several decision or independent variables. It is necessary to modify the concepts to fit such conditions, and it is difficult to map such concepts for these conditions, but the extreme value theory does provide a theoretical basis for optimal solutions.

OPTIMAL SEARCH ROUTINE

Many simple optimization models require little more than a search of the end-points for maximum and minimum values, especially where the function is linear or linear-like. In more complicated functions, however, we must develop a routine to narrow down our search for optimal solutions.

One alternative is a complete enumeration of all possible values for $f(x)$ and x. We could then rank these values from highest to lowest and select the extreme values as maximum and minimum. This might be possible if we had a model with only integer values for x and $f(x)$ and if the domain of the function was quite small and finite. Even such a simple problem can be tedious, however. In most models we consider all real-number values (both integer and noninteger), and a complete enumeration is mathematically impossible because there are an infinite number of values for x and $f(x)$. Even where x and $f(x)$ have an infinite number of values, however, an optimal solution exists if the extreme value theory holds.

A far more sensible alternative in seeking optimal solutions for simple optimization models is to use an *optimal search routine*. Our optimal search routine is based on the extreme value theory and some of its implications. In essence, we will use the theory to the extent that it points out three types of places to look for optimal solutions. The first place is the end-points of the interval for the decision variable. The second place is the local maxima and minima if they exist. The third place is where local maxima and minima appear intuitively yet may not exist mathematically.

The optimal search routine can be expressed in more formal terms in order to allow generalization. Let us consider the optimal value for the decision variable x^* as belonging to a set of possible values S:

$$x^* \varepsilon S = S_1 \cup S_2 \cup S_3,$$

where

$$S_1 = \{a, b\},$$
$$S_2 = \{\text{local maxima and minima}\},$$
$$S_3 = \{\text{apparent maxima and minima or discontinuities}\}.$$

The values for S_1 are straightforward and are obtained by substitution. Values for S_2 are best obtained by using calculus. Values for S_3 can be obtained by using observation and calculus: sometimes maxima and minima exist when calculus does not reveal them (usually at points of discontinuity or intersecting straight lines), but these maxima and minima can be observed.

CLASSICAL CALCULUS

Since classical calculus offers us assistance in finding values for two of the three sets in our optimal search routine, we should spend some time reviewing the basic principles. The calculus, developed almost simultaneously by Sir Isaac Newton (1642-1727) and Gottfried Wilhelm von Liebniz (1646-1716), is most useful for our purposes in that it allows the computation of the rate of change in a function. This is accomplished by computing the places where the *first derivative* is zero, $f'(x) = 0$, with respect to x.

A familiar analog is to consider a boy throwing a ball into the air. When the ball reaches its highest point, its rate of change (velocity) will be zero.

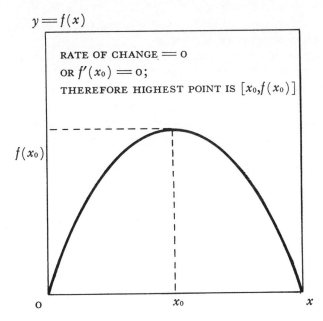

FIG. 6:6. Path of ball and highest point.

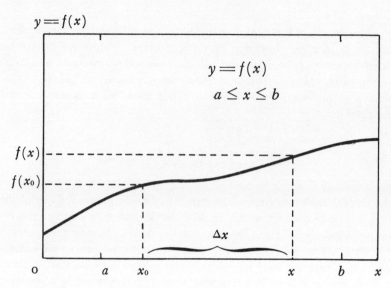

$y = f(x)$

FIG. 6:7. Mapping of general function $y = f(x)$.

We can compute the highest point reached if we know precisely when the rate of change in the velocity of the ball was zero (see Fig. 6:6). For this problem we can say that when $f'(x_0) = 0$, then at x_0 we can compute $f(x^*)$, the highest point the ball reaches.

We can extend these concepts for a general function $y = f(x)$, as shown in Fig. 6:7. The rate of change is called the *slope* of the function and represents the increase in y for every unit of increase in x. The slope of a function can be approximated by its *difference quotient:*

$$\frac{f(x) - f(x_0)}{x - x_0}.$$

We can substitute $x_0 + \Delta x$ for x in the difference quotient and assume that $x \neq x_0$ and that Δx is very small. This gives us

$$\frac{f(x_0 + \Delta x) - f(x_0)}{(x_0 + \Delta x) - x_0}$$

and

$$\frac{f(x_0 + \Delta x) - f(x_0)}{\Delta x}.$$

We assume that as Δx gets smaller and smaller, a stable value, or *limit* in mathematical terms, can be found. The limit of $f(x)$ as $\Delta x \to 0$ is called the *derivative*. It is expressed by $f'(x)$, where

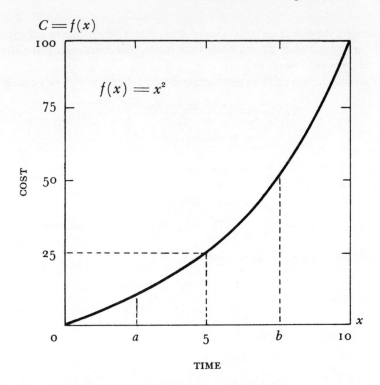

$C = f(x)$

$f(x) = x^2$

COST

TIME

FIG. 6:8. Mapping of planning study cost function.

$$f'(x) = \lim_{x \to x_0} \frac{f(x) - f(x_0)}{x - x_0},$$

or, by substitution,

$$f'(x_0) = \lim_{\Delta x \to 0} \frac{f(x_0 + \Delta x) - f(x_0)}{\Delta x}.$$

We will use the above expression as the definition of the derivative. For practical purposes we can consider the derivative to the equation which expresses the rate of change or the slope of the function for various values of x.

We can illustrate the derivative with a simple example. Let us consider the costs of a planning study (C), which we know to be the square of the time spent on it (x); hence $C = f(x) = x^2$. If we consider an interval, such that $a \leq x \leq b$, what is the rate of change in the cost function as mapped in Fig. 6:8? Assume that the value $x_0 = 5$ lies within $[a, b]$. The derivative of $f(x)$ at $x_0 = 5$ can be computed by making various substitutions for Δx.

For example, $\Delta x = 0.5$, $\Delta x = 0.1$, $\Delta x = 0.01$, etc. The process of substitution, if carried out over a sufficiently long series, will eventually show that a limit of ten exists for $x_0 = 5$.

We can demonstrate this in more general terms. Let $C = f(x) = x^2$; then

$$
\begin{aligned}
f'(x_0) &= \lim_{\Delta x \to 0} \frac{(x_0 + \Delta x)^2 - (x_0)^2}{\Delta x} \\
&= \frac{x_0^2 + 2x_0\Delta x + \Delta x^2 - x_0^2}{\Delta x} \\
&= \frac{2x_0\Delta x + \Delta x^2}{\Delta x} \\
&= \frac{\Delta x(2x_0 + \Delta x)}{\Delta x} \\
&= 2x_0 + \Delta x.
\end{aligned}
$$

As $\Delta x \to 0$, we can assume Δx is negligible:

$$f'(x_0) = 2x_0.$$

For $x_0 = 5$, then

$$f'(5) = 10.$$

Let us take another example:

$$f(x) = ax - bx^2.$$

Solve for $f'(x_0)$, where

$$
\begin{aligned}
f(x_0) &= ax_0 - bx_0^2, \\
f(x_0 + \Delta x) &= a(x_0 + \Delta x) - b(x_0 + \Delta x)^2.
\end{aligned}
$$

Thus

$$
\begin{aligned}
f'(x_0) &= \frac{[a(x_0 + \Delta x) - b(x_0 + \Delta x)^2] - (ax_0 - bx_0^2)}{\Delta x} \\
&= \frac{ax_0 + a\Delta x - (bx_0^2 + 2b\Delta x x_0 + b\Delta x^2) - ax_0 + bx_0^2}{\Delta x} \\
&= \frac{a\Delta x - 2b\Delta x x_0 - b\Delta x^2}{\Delta x} \\
&= \frac{\Delta x(a - 2bx_0 - b\Delta x)}{\Delta x} \\
&= a - 2bx_0 - b\Delta x.
\end{aligned}
$$

As $\Delta x \to 0$, its value is negligible, so that

$$f'(x_0) = a - 2bx_0.$$

The astute reader may have noticed that a pattern exists for a general solution of $f'(x)$ for $f(x)$. For simple functions, such as

$$f(x) = x^c,$$

this pattern can be generalized as

$$f'(x_0) = cx_0^{c-1}.$$

The first derivative of a constant is always zero, of course, since in practical terms a constant has no rate of change. Using this general rule, we can see that if

$$f(x) = x^3 + x^2,$$

then

$$f'(x_0) = 3x_0^2 + 2x_0.$$

Similarly, when we see

$$f(x) = x^2 + x + 5,$$

we can compute

$$f'(x_0) = 2x_0 + 1.$$

The four general rules for finding derivatives of simple functions can be summarized:

1. If $f(x) = x^c$, where c is a real number, then $f'(x) = cx^{c-1}$.
2. The derivative of a constant is zero.
3. If $f(x) = e^{g(x)}$, then $f'(x) = g'(x)e^{g(x)}$.
4. If $f(x) = \log_e g(x)$, then $f'(x) = g'(x)/g(x)$.

These general rules are time-savers and are most useful for eliminating tediousness when computing derivatives of simple functions. There are many other rules for computing the derivatives of more complex functions, and most calculus books have extensive lists of these rules. For example, the four basic rules for finding derivatives of complex functions are:

1. The derivative of the sum is the sum of the derivatives; if a and b are constants, and if $F(x) = af(x) + bg(x)$, then $F'(x) = af'(x) + bg'(x)$.

2. The derivative of a product of two functions is first times derivative of second and second times derivative of first; if $F(x) = f(x) \cdot g(x)$, then $F'(x) = f'(x) \cdot g(x) + g'(x) \cdot f(x)$.

3. The derivative of a quotient is the quotient of the derivatives, provided that the derivative of the denominator is not zero; if $F(x) = f(x)/g(x)$, then

$$F'(x) = \frac{f'(x) \cdot g(x) - g'(x) \cdot f(x)}{[g(x)]^2}.$$

4. The derivative of a composite function is found through the *composite function rule;* if u is a variable which is expressed as $u = g(x)$, and if $f(u)$ is a function of u such that $F(x) = f[g(x)]$, then $F'(x) = f'(u) \cdot g'(x)$.

$y = f(x)$

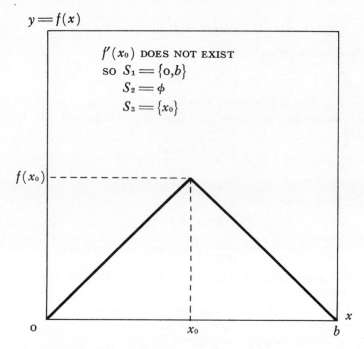

Fig. 6:9. Complex function where $f'(x_0)$ does not exist.

There may be points on complex functions where the first derivative does not exist. For example, as seen in Fig. 6:9, the intersection of two straight lines appears to be a maximum, but it can be shown through calculus that the first derivative does not exist at x_0. The nonexistence of a first derivative for a function is a clue that a maximum or minimum may exist, and the optimal search routine set S_3 may include the optimal solution. Lack of first derivatives also may indicate discontinuous functions, which may or may not be analyzed for maxima and minima. There is a special case in which setting $f'(x_0) = 0$ may yield values for x_0, $f(x_0)$ which are not maxima or minima. Such a case is called an *inflection point*, as shown in Fig. 6:10. An inflection point is a change in slope for a mapping which results in an instantaneous interval of no rate of change. Inflection points should be distinguished from local maxima or minima when using the optimal search routine.

It is obviously useful to our purposes if we can employ some technique which helps us to determine whether we have a maximum, minimum, or inflection point when we compute $f(x_0) = 0$ for x_0. Calculus is helpful for

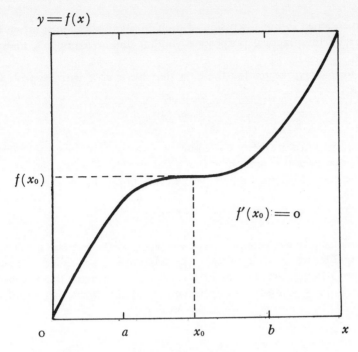

$y = f(x)$

$f(x_0)$

$f'(x_0) = 0$

O a x_0 b x

FIG. 6:10. Mapping of function with inflection point.

this problem. The *second derivative* of a function expresses the rate of change of the rate of change (acceleration). It is computed by taking the derivative of $f'(x_0)$ and is denoted as $f''(x_0)$. If the rate of change of the rate of change is always greater than zero, or $f''(x) > 0$, then a function is said to be *strictly convex* and $f'(x_0) = 0$ denotes a minimum. If the rate of change of the rate of change is always less than zero, or $f''(x) < 0$, then a function is said to be *strictly concave* and $f'(x_0) = 0$ denotes a maximum.

We can extend the above technique to test for the inflection point. We can take any number n of derivatives for a function. Let $f^n(x) = 0$ and $f^{n+1}(x) \neq 0$; then we have two possible cases. If n is odd:

1. If $f^{n+1}(x_0) > 0$, then $\{x_0, f(x_0)\}$ is a minimum.
2. If $f^{n+1}(x_0) < 0$, then $\{x_0, f(x_0)\}$ is a maximum.

If n is even, then $\{x_0, f(x_0)\}$ is neither maximum nor minimum and is an inflection point.

Although somewhat peripheral to our present discussion, if we call the above technique of taking derivatives *differentiation,* then the inverse of differentiation, *integration,* is interesting and useful for certain problems.

As we mentioned in our discussion of probabilistic models, integration can be regarded for practical purposes as finding the area under a mapped function.

The formal expression for the first derivative of x with respect to y $= f(x)$ is

$$\frac{dx}{dy} = f'(x),$$

which is a first-order differential equation (where dx and dy are *differentials*). Let us write the same thing in a different way. The first derivative of x with respect to y, where $y = y(x)$, we can call simply $f(x)$, so that

$$\frac{dx}{dy} = f(x).$$

The solution of this equation would be $y = \phi(x) = y_1(x) + c$, and hence $y_1(x)$ is any function where $y'_1(x) = f(x)$. The solution $y'_1(x)$ is called a *primitive function* or *antiderivative*. The more formal way to express this inverse of differentiation is to form an expression called the *definite integral* of the function $f(t)$ from a to b for the function $F(x)$:

$$F(x) = \int_a^x f(t)dt.$$

The function $F(x)$ then is also an *indefinite integral* because $F'(x) = f(x)$.

We can clarify this somewhat in the following equation:

$$y = \phi(x) = y'_1(x) + c = F(x) + c = \int_a^x f(t)dt + c.$$

This is simply the general solution to the differential equation we discussed above.

A further note of interest is the so-called fundamental theory of calculus, where a function $F(t)$ whose derivative is $f(t)$ is continuous and then

$$\int_{T_1}^{T_2} f(t)dt = F(T_2) - F(T_1).$$

This theory is fundamental because it links differential and integral calculus. The importance of the theory is that it reduces the problem of finding the definite integral defined from T_1 to T_2 to finding a function $F(t)$ whose derivative is $f(t)$. This is not easily computed, and standard tables of integrals are most useful.

One of the most practical applications of integration of functions in urban analysis is the computation of the area under a curve generated by a function. The most common example is the computation of the probability that a continuous random variable x lies in some interval $a \leq x \leq b$, for which the reader may review the chapter on probabilistic models. When we discussed areas under probability density functions, we implied that integration was the technique most useful for computation. It may be clearer to the reader now if we restate that the area under a probability density function $f(x)$ is

$$\int_{-\infty}^{+\infty} f(x)dx = 1.$$

APPLICATION OF SIMPLE OPTIMIZATION

There has been a significant application of simple optimization models in urban analysis. The usual procedure is to formulate an estimating and predicting model of the problem situation and satisfactorily test it. Having been satisfied that the problem has been explained and can be predicted, the urban analyst can use simple optimization techniques, especially calculus, to determine if optimal values exist. The urban analyst can use optimization models as a test of predetermined or intuitive optimization values as well. Alternative solutions to urban problems are sometimes tested by use of simple optimization models to determine if theoretical and analytical values are similar.

LINCOLN TUNNEL PROBLEM

A classic application of simple optimization models is the Lincoln Tunnel problem, in which many of the concepts that we have been discussing were applied. The problem derived its name from the case of the Lincoln Tunnel, which connects northern New Jersey suburbs to mid-Manhattan. The operating and planning agency for the Lincoln Tunnel is the Port of New York Authority (PONYA), a quasi-public organization established by the states of New York, New Jersey, and Connecticut.

By the early 1950s it had become clear that the tunnel was near capacity, largely owing to the growth of postwar automobile ownership and use. The PONYA planners authorized a series of studies to determine ways to get the most out of the facility within its existing limitations. The problem was to optimize the flow of traffic through the tunnel as constrained by its physical capacity.

The flow of traffic through the tunnel is a function of the capacity of the tunnel and the speed and density of vehicles. The following variables were formulated:

s = speed of vehicles in miles per hour,
d = density of vehicles in vehicles per mile,
v = flow in vehicles per hour.

The flow v is simply the speed times the density, so that

$$v = sd.$$

The analysts assigned to the problem studied the speed and density of vehicles moving through the tunnel and recorded many observations over a long period of time. Using a simple linear model, the analysts hypothesized that speed decreases with the density of vehicles in the tunnel, and they fitted the following model:

$$s = 42.1 - 0.324d.$$

The simple linear model was satisfactorily tested. Implicit in the model were many factors, the most important of which was an implicit effect of physical capacity. Specifically, it can be noted that physical capacity affects the linear relationship by imposing a constraint:

$$0 \leq d \leq 42.1/0.324.$$

This means that if $d \geq 42.1/0.324$, the tunnel will be overflowed and traffic will come to a halt ($s = 0$, a real-life fact familiar to many commuters in the area).

The Lincoln Tunnel problem can be formally stated with the above considerations in mind:

$$\text{Opt } v = sd,$$

subject to

$$0 \leq d \leq 42.1/0.324.$$

By substitution we see that

$$v(d) = (42.1 - 0.324d)d$$

and

$$v(d) = 42.1d - 0.324d^2.$$

We compute the first derivative of this function and set it equal to zero to determine whether there exists a local maximum or minimum:

$$v'(d_0) = 42.1 - 0.648d_0 = 0,$$

so that

$$0.648d_0 = 42.1,$$

$$d_0 = 64.9 \cong 65 \text{ vehicles per mile.}$$

The second derivative of the function is

$$v''(d_0) = -0.648,$$

which is a constant that is always less than zero; hence the value $x = 65$ is at least a local maximum, since the function is strictly concave.

The optimal search routine can be used to define the three sets where we can find the optimal values for d in the problem. This results in

$$S_1 = \{0, 42.1/0.324\},$$
$$S_2 = \{65\},$$
$$S_3 = \phi,$$

and thus

$$S = \{0, 65, 42.1/.324\}.$$

The next step is to substitute the possible values for d^* in the equation $v = 42.1d - 0.324d^2$:

$$v = 0 \text{ when } d = 0,$$
$$v = 1,362.9 \cong 1,363 \text{ when } d = 65,$$
$$v = 0 \text{ when } d = 42.1/0.324.$$

Therefore, it is obvious that

$$d^* = 65,$$
$$v^* = 1,363,$$

and, by substitution,

$$s^* = 21.0.$$

One other interesting quantity is the optimal spacing between vehicles (f), which can be measured in feet by

$$f^* = 5,280/d^*,$$

so that

$$f^* = 81.$$

The interpretation of this solution is that given the relationship between s and d as a fixed constraint, the PONYA can optimize traffic flow to 1,363 vehicles per hour per lane of traffic by setting the speed limit so that most vehicles are traveling at about 21.0 (say a limit of 25) miles per hour, and there is a space of 81 feet between vehicles in each lane of traffic (and, consequently, there are 65 vehicles per mile), as shown in Fig. 6:11.

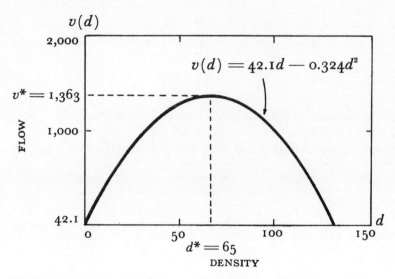

FIG. 6:11. Mapping of solution to Lincoln Tunnel problem.

MINIMUM-COSTS MODELS

Objectives established for urban systems often conflict with each other; hence one objective must be selected in preference to other objectives. The basis for selection of one objective over another depends upon many forces and factors. In many problems of administration and capital construction for urban systems, a basic tenet of engineering economy is often used. The basic tenet is that the best compromise among conflicting objectives for public funds is to provide the facilities that will cost the least to build and use over a period of time. This is usually a politically and economically acceptable approach, since taxpayers do not like to see elaborate public facilities requiring tax increases in urban systems. This is obviously not a perfect objective, however, since many social forces demand that facilities be built which are not the least expensive: the social benefits of such facilities outweigh the political and economic benefits of minimum costs. Such a difficult conflict requires the urban analyst to use a great deal of care when selecting minimum-costs optimization models for evaluating plans. When the use of the minimum-costs model is valid, there are several interesting techniques that we can examine.

Administrative-Costs Minimization Problem

A well-accepted goal among public administrators (as well as business-men) in urban systems is to minimize the costs of operations. The classical analytical model, which is a simple optimization model, is called the *economic lot-size model*. This is a relatively simple model that has been used in business for several years and is finding more and more application in public administration of urban systems. For example, when public administrators order goods by lots that are depleted over a period of time, such as school lunch supplies, public service reports and publications, equipment and parts which are expendable, and other kinds of stocks that are depletable, the economic lot-size model is useful.

The economic lot-size model is based on a number of simplified assumptions and variables. The key variables are

c_1 = cost of purchasing one unit of goods,

c_2 = fixed costs of placing one order, assumed to be independent of actual number of goods ordered,

c_3 = costs of holding or storing one unit of goods per unit of time,

d = rate of utilization or demand for goods required per unit of time,

x = size of lots ordered or number of units of goods constituting one order,

n = number of orders placed per unit of time,

$\bar{i}$ = average number of units of goods in stock,

t = total costs per unit of time.

The objective of the public administrator is to minimize the total costs of his operations; he requires an optimal lot size x^* that will minimize total costs: $t(x^*)$.

Several of these variables are interrelated. As can be seen, x and n are related through the rate of utilization of goods (d). If we assume that n is an integer, such as $n = 1, 2, \ldots, m$ for days, weeks, months, years, etc., then we can use x as the key decision variable and attempt to express x as a function of n wherever possible. The basic relationship is

$$x = \frac{d}{n},$$

assuming that the total demand will be met over some period of time.

The average number of units of goods in stock during a period of time is essential if we are to compute the costs of holding or storing the goods. For practical purposes we can simplify this computation by assuming a perfect operation in which orders are so placed that when a previous order

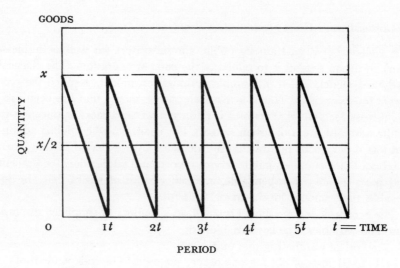

FIG. 6:12. Depletion and storage of goods over time in a perfect operation.

is exhausted, a new order arrives for distribution. Intuitively, we can assume that the average number of goods in stock is half the number of units ordered:

$$\bar{\imath} = \frac{x}{2}.$$

This may be clearer intuitively by considering Fig. 6:12.

Using these simplifying assumptions, we can formulate the total-costs model by its components. The first component is the purchasing cost, c_1d, or the cost of purchasing one unit times the demand per unit of time. The second component is the cost of ordering, c_2n, or the cost of placing one order times the number of orders placed per unit of time. Through substitution we see that

$$c_2n = \frac{c_2d}{x}.$$

The third and final component of cost is the holding or storage cost, $c_3\bar{\imath}$, or the cost of holding one unit times the average number of units in stock. Again through substitution we see that

$$c_3\bar{\imath} = \frac{c_3x}{2}.$$

These components are additive, so that our total costs are

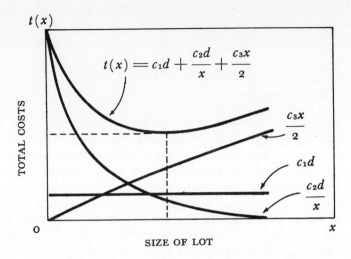

$$t(x)$$

$$t(x) = c_1 d + \frac{c_2 d}{x} + \frac{c_3 x}{2}$$

TOTAL COSTS

$$\frac{c_3 x}{2}$$

$$c_1 d$$

$$\frac{c_2 d}{x}$$

O   x

SIZE OF LOT

FIG. 6:13. Mapping of cost components and total-costs function.

$$t = t(x) = c_1 d + \frac{c_2 d}{x} + \frac{c_3 x}{2},$$

shown in Fig. 6:13.

Using the optimal search routine, we can see that the minimum costs of the total-costs function $t(x)$ is the local minimum for the function and can be found by using the first derivative:

$$t'(x_0) = (-1)c_2 d x_0^{-2} + \frac{c_3}{2} = 0,$$

$$\frac{c_2 d}{x_0^2} = \frac{c_3}{2},$$

$$x_0^2 = \frac{2c_2 d}{c_3},$$

$$x_0 = \sqrt{\frac{2c_2 d}{c_3}}.$$

Two constraints are possible for optimization:

1. If $d > 2c_2/c_3$, then $x^* = x_0$:

$$x^* = \sqrt{\frac{2c_2 d}{c_3}},$$

and

$$t''(x_0) = \frac{2c_2 d}{x_0^3}$$

is strictly convex, so a minimum exists at $t(x^*)$.

2. If $d \leq 2c_2/c_3$, then $x^* = d$ and

$$t(x^*) = c_1 d + c_2 + \frac{c_3 d}{2}.$$

Plan Evaluation Problem

A relatively simple extension of the minimum-costs problem has been made for the evaluation of competing plans, the most common area of which has been in transportation facilities, especially highway planning. The transportation planning approach has been to compare alternative plans by their respective system and travel costs. System costs are measured or estimated for a period of time for the principal components of capital costs amortized over a period of time at a given rate of return; maintenance and operating costs of the transportation system are measured or estimated for a comparable period of time. The travel costs are usually those which are borne by users: travel time cost, user operating cost, and cost of accidents. The sum of the system and travel costs is called the total costs for a period of time.

When a number of plans are being considered, a rank order comparison can be made by increasing travel and system costs, as shown in Fig. 6:14. In the case shown, seven alternative plans are compared, and the minimum-costs plan appears by inspection to be plan 4 (a specific determination is made by computation and comparison of costs for each alternative plan).

The total-costs curve often takes the form of a second-order polynomial, since the additive system and travel costs are parabolic for a large number of plans. When many alternative plans are being compared, it may be useful to formulate a second-order polynomial model of the total costs. The decision variables are integers, however, and a pseudofunction must be used to imply a continuous real-number variable. There are i plans to be considered, and the total costs can be approximated by $\phi(i)$, where

$$\phi(i) = ai^2 - bi + c.$$

We can use a pseudo real-number variable x such that

$$f(x) = ax^2 - bx + c,$$

subject to

$$0 \leq x \leq i.$$

The function $f(x)$ can be used to approximate the discontinuous integer

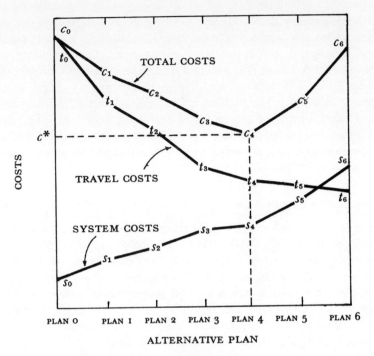

FIG. 6:14. Plan evaluation by minimum costs.

function $\phi(i)$, and the optimal search routine can be used. Taking the first derivative of $f(x)$,

$$f'(x_0) = 2ax_0 - b = 0,$$
$$2ax_0 = b,$$
$$x_0 = \frac{b}{2a}.$$

Hence we compute our solution sets for x:

$$S_1 = \{0, i\},$$
$$S_2 = \{b/2a\},$$
$$S_3 = \{\phi\},$$

and

$$S = \{0, b/2a, i\}.$$

Since we know that the total-costs curve is parabolic, it is likely that $x^* = b/2a$; yet it is possible that x^* could be found in S_1 owing to an arbitrary selection of the end-points for our closed interval. Thus all possible optimal values should be considered. Having determined an optimal solution for $f(x)$, we can use it to approximate the optimal solution for $\phi(i)$. It should be noted, however, that this approach is not foolproof: the possibility exists that the optimal values of $f(x)$ may not be sufficient for determining optimal values for $\phi(i)$ if the value for x^* is found to be midway between two neighboring values of i. The problem can be resolved simply by testing both values of i and comparing the results of $\phi(i)$ for a minimum. The possibility may arise in some cases that the total-costs curve cannot be satisfactorily approximated by a second-order polynomial, and hence other linear and nonlinear models should be explored.

Expressway Spacing Problem

One of the most sophisticated applications of the minimum-costs model was made by the Chicago Area Transportation Study (CATS) for the spacing of expressways in an urban system.[1] The basic policy of the urban analysts was to plan additional public investment in new expressways as long as it led to overall decreases in total transportation costs — in other words, new expressways were planned if the savings in total transportation costs were greater than the investment costs. The key variable in such a computation emerged as the spacing between expressways.

The expressway spacing problem can be stated succinctly. Given a particular network of expressways, other types of highways in the area, and a particular pattern of trips by length, what is the optimal spacing policy for a regular grid network of expressways? The Chicago urban system is easy to make such a mathematical statement about because of its flat topography and relatively regularized population and development density. There are two components of the total-costs function. The first component is the cost of expressway construction as a function of expressway spacing. The second component is the cost of operating and using the expressways as a function of expressway spacing, which can be called the travel cost. Hence the total costs are

$$TC = C_1 + C_2,$$

where

TC = total costs of construction and travel,
C_1 = construction cost,
C_2 = travel cost.

The simple optimization problem is

[1] Chicago Area Transportation Study, *Final Report*, vol. 3 (Chicago, 1962).

$$\text{Opt} f(C_1, C_2) = TC = C_1 + C_2,$$

subject to

$$x \leq z \leq y,$$
$$z \geq 0,$$

where

$$z = \text{spacing of expressways.}$$

The Chicago urban system was found to have a uniform density of trip origins and characteristics, so that expressways were relatively similar in design for various parts of the area. Construction costs were proportional to the linear miles of expressways, and the linear miles of expressways were determined by the expressway spacing. For practical reasons the urban system was hypothesized as being square and the expressway network as a grid. This yielded the following construction-cost function:

$$C_1 = 2c \frac{l^2}{z},$$

where

$c = \text{construction cost per mile,}$
$l = \text{a constant describing the size of the region.}$

The travel costs were more complicated because it was necessary to consider trips of varying lengths. Trips of a short length (a) were computed and assigned to local streets other than expressways in the area. These short trips, from zero to a miles, had a travel cost which was the sum of their lengths times the cost per mile for traveling on local streets. This was stated by

$$pl^2 \int_0^a K_a r F dr \text{ for } 0 \rightarrow a,$$

where

$p = \text{density of trip origins in region,}$
$K_a = \text{cost per vehicle mile on local streets,}$
$F = \text{distribution of trips with respect to length, such that } F = dn/dr.$

The travel cost of trips longer than a, but still not long enough to use expressways, is similar, except that a part of the trip length may be spent on local streets and the remainder on arterial highways. This can be expressed in the form

$$pl^2 \int_a^b [K_a a + K_b (r - a) F dr] \text{ for } a \rightarrow b.$$

The remaining trips and costs are those which are long enough to assign to expressways (that is, they are longer than b). Their computation is similar to the above and yields C_2:

$$C_2 = pl^2 \left[\int_0^a K_a r F dr + \int_a^b [K_a a + K_b (r - a)] F dr \right.$$
$$\left. + \int_b^\infty [K_a a + K_b (b - a) + K_c (r - b)] F dr \right] \text{ for } b \to \infty.$$

Since we are interested only in expressway spacing, we can ignore all terms not containing b (that is, all trips less than the average distance used for access to the expressway system). Using the following definitions,

$$\int r F dr = R \text{ and } \int F dr = G,$$

the equation for C can be simplified to

$$C = 2c \frac{l^2}{2} + pl^2 (K_b - K_c) [R(b) + bG(\infty) - bG(b)].$$

The first derivative of C with respect to z is

$$C'(z_0) = \frac{dC}{dz} = pl^2 \frac{db}{dz} (K_b - K_c) P(b) - 2l^2 \frac{c}{z^2} = 0,$$

where $P(b)$ stands for the proportion $[G(\infty) - G(b)]$; so

$$z^* = \sqrt{\frac{2c}{p(K_b - K_c) \frac{db}{dz} P(b)}}.$$

Empirical computation of db/dz, $P(b)$, c, and p makes the equation for z^* simpler. In the Chicago case

$$\frac{db}{dz} = 0.40,$$
$$P(b) = 0.89e^{-.057},$$
$$p = 20,000 \text{ trips per day per square mile},$$
$$c = \$6,000,000 \text{ per square mile}.$$

This simplifies the equation for z^* to

$$z^* = 2.78e^{.0285z},$$

where $K_b - K_c = \$0.06$ and an interest rate of 10 percent is assumed (depreciation is neglected). For practical purposes $z^* = 3$ miles was found to be optimal (minimum costs) for Chicago. The results are mapped in Fig. 6:15. Urban analysts at CATS used the model for predictive purposes to 1980 for various rings (i) around the central city. As can be seen in

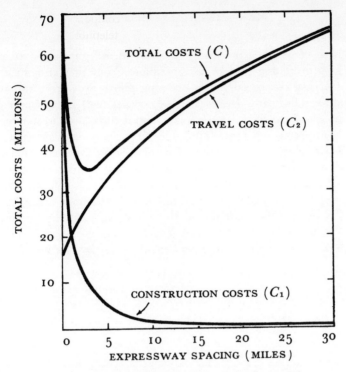

FIG. 6:15. Mapping of CATS expressway spacing model.

Table 6:1, there is variation in p, c, and z in the various rings; hence several z^* exist, depending upon the ring, $i = \{0, 1, 2, 3, 4, 5, 6, 7\}$.

TABLE 6:1. Estimated z_i^* for 1980, CATS.

Ring i	1980 p	Current c (millions)	z_i^* (miles)
2[a]	28,700	$14	3
3	25,300	12	3
4	19,600	8	3
5	13,400	6	4
6	10,000	4	6
7	7,700	2	6

[a] 0 and 1 (the Loop and CBD) were unique and were not computed.

Recommended Exercises

1. The head of the data processing department in a medium-sized city asks your help in cutting costs of his operations. Your first assignment is to reduce the costs of operations for ordering punchcards. You find that the demand for punchcards (which come 2,000 per box) is 125 boxes per month. One box of punchcards costs \$2.00, and it costs \$1.00 to store each box in the data processing center. The largest cost component is for placing an order, however, since the process of invoices, telephone bids, and administrative matters in the city comes to \$50.00 per order of boxes of punchcards, regardless of the number of boxes ordered. Set up an appropriate minimum-costs model and optimize the model to determine the number of boxes of cards that should be ordered to yield the minimum total costs (try the economic lot-size problem).

2. Given the following $f(x)$, find $f'(x)$ and solve $f'(x_0) = 0$ for x_0:

(A) $f(x) = 4x^4$　　　　　　　　(B) $f(x) = 7 + x - x^3$

(C) $f(x) = 2x^2 - 3x + 4$　　　(D) $f(x) = \dfrac{2x}{2 + x}$

(E) $f(x) = e^{3z^2}$　　　　　　　(F) $\log f(x) = \log a + b(\log x)$

Further Reading

Carr, Charles R., and Charles W. Howe. *Quantitative Decision Procedures in Management and Economics: Deterministic Theory and Applications.* New York: McGraw-Hill, 1964.

One of the best textbooks on deterministic optimization theory and application for both simple and complex optimization models. The theoretical foundations are very good, and applications for business and economics provide interesting possibilities for urban analysis. There is an especially good coverage of the economic lot-size problem at various levels of complexity.

Taylor, Angus E. *Calculus with Analytic Geometry.* Englewood Cliffs, N.J.: Prentice-Hall, 1959.

Classic among calculus textbooks, this is one of the most detailed treatments. While the urban analyst would not usually need to be familiar with the advanced topics in the later parts of the book, it is advantageous to have such a ready reference source ranging from the fundamental to the advanced topics of calculus. The incorporation of analytic geometry is especially relevant to many spatial problems in urban analysis.

The most popular of the complex optimization models is *linear programming*. While the mathematical foundations of linear programming (matrix algebra, vector analysis, analytical geometry, and algebra) are found in works several centuries old, the first solved linear program was not developed until 1947 by George B. Dantzig. Dantzig developed an algorithm for solving linear programming problems and, with the collaboration of Marshall Wood and Alex Orden, made several applications for the U.S. Air Force concerning such military problems as optimal bombing patterns, search and destroy tactics, and others as part of Project SCOOP (Scientific Computation of Optimum Programs). Its first major testing ground was the Berlin Airlift in 1949. A host of mathematicians, such famous names as A. W. Tucker, John von Neumann, and T. C. Koopmans, had advanced the theory of linear programming to mathematical sophistication by 1955. The paramount use of linear programming was not in the military but in business. Sophisticated linear programming models have been developed and solved for fuel blending, airline scheduling, job assignment, transportation and distribution, maintenance, and a host of other problems.

Linear programming has been applied to urban systems in recent years with interesting results. The most important applications to urban systems have been made to problems of transportation and land use. Increasingly, we are seeing linear programming applied to urban administration, management, and economic development. Many abstract problems in urban systems have been proposed for modeling and optimization through the linear programming approach, but the results have been unconvincing.

Linear programming can be defined as a mathematical algorithm and theory for optimizing problems stated in linear terms and subjected to linear constraints. In many cases simple and complex linear models must be fitted to the problem and constraints prior to use of the linear programming approach. If the problem and constraints cannot be modeled in linear terms, then linear programming is an inappropriate approach to optimization.

The general expression for linear programming can be expressed as follows:

$$\text{Opt}\,[f(x_1, x_2, \ldots, x_n) = c_1x_1 + c_2x_2 + \ldots + c_nx_n],$$

CHAPTER 7

Linear Programming

subject to

$$a_{11}x_1 + a_{12}x_2 + \ldots + a_{1n}x_n \leq b_1,$$
$$a_{21}x_1 + a_{22}x_2 + \ldots + a_{2n}x_n \leq b_2,$$

$$a_{m1}x_1 + a_{m2}x_2 + \ldots + a_{mn}x_n \leq b_m,$$
$$x_1 \geq 0,\ x_2 \geq 0,\ \ldots,\ x_m \geq 0.$$

The linear function describing the problem is called the *objective function,* and the linear inequalities describing the limits are the familiar constraints. The general linear programming expression is a variation of the general complex optimization problem. This variation is made for flexibility in objective function and constraint description as well as for certain computational advantages.

The principal formulation of the linear programming problem under consideration, whether it be maximization or minimization, is called the *primal problem.* For every maximization problem there exists a minimization problem corresponding to it, and for every minimization problem there exists a corresponding maximization problem. This ancillary problem corresponding to the primal problem is called the *dual problem.* The dual problem can be expressed by transposing the A matrix elements (a_{ij}), B vector elements (b_i), and C vector elements (c_j), and forming a new function (g), using dual variables (u_i), such that

$$\text{Dual Opt } [g(u_1, u_2, \ldots, u_m) = b_i u_i + b_2 u_2 + \ldots + b_m u_m)],$$

subject to

$$a_{11}u_1 + a_{21}u_2 + \ldots \quad a_{m1}u_m \geq c_1,$$
$$a_{12}u_1 + a_{22}u_2 + \ldots \quad a_{m2}u_m \geq c_2,$$

$$a_{1n}u_1 + a_{2n}u_2 + \ldots \quad a_{mn}u_m \geq c_n,$$
$$u_1 \geq 0,\ u_2 \geq 0,\ \ldots,\ u_m \geq 0.$$

We will evaluate the dual problem at a later point, but it is interesting to note here that Max f = Min g, or vice versa depending on the given problem. In formal terms:

Primal	*Dual*
Max/Min$\{f(X) = C'X\}$	Min/Max$\{g(U) = B'U\}$
Subject to $AX \leq B,\ X \geq 0$	Subject to $A'U \geq C,\ U \geq 0$

$$\text{Max } C'X = \text{Min } B'U \text{ or Min } C'X = \text{Max } B'U.$$

The concept of linearity merits further discussion. Linear programming uses a special case of the linear model which omits constants by moving the origin point of the variables to correspond to the origin of the function. This means that the simple linear model $f(x) = a + bx$ would have to be adjusted to $f(x) = bx$ by moving the $f(x)$ axis from zero to a. The mathematical reason is that linearity must be strict; in formal terms

$$f(ax_1 + bx_2) = af(x_1) + bf(x_2).$$

The addition of a constant to this strict definition of linearity would make the above relationship only an approximation. This is not a serious problem to deal with in practical terms.

GEOMETRIC INTERPRETATION

The mathematical algorithm and theory of linear programming have their roots in analytical geometry. Embedded in analytical geometry is the analogy to vector analysis and matrix algebra which lies at the heart of linear programming. A geometric interpretation of linear programming can serve as a simplifying and suggestive benchmark.

A few principles of analytical geometry are relevant to linear programming. The essential notion of the additive nature of vectors, let us say in two-dimensional space (2-space) for simplicity, is most important. Consider two vectors, $X_1 = (x_1, y_1)$ and $X_2 = (x_2, y_2)$, which can be added, so that

$$X_1 + X_2 = (x_1 + x_2, y_1 + y_2).$$

This same algebraic principle has its complementary geometric equivalent, as shown in Fig. 7:1.

We first noticed in our discussion of matrix models that a constant or scalar k, multiplied by a vector, resulted in a new vector. This can be expressed by the multiplication of scalar k by vector $X = (x_1, x_2)$:

$$kX = (kx_1, kx_2).$$

The concepts of vector additivity and multiplication of a vector by a scalar can be combined; the resultant is called a *linear combination*. For example, let us say that there exists a set of vectors $X_1, X_2, \ldots, X_m$ and a set of corresponding scalars $k_1, k_2, \ldots, k_m$; the resulting linear combination is a vector we can call $\hat{X}$, so that

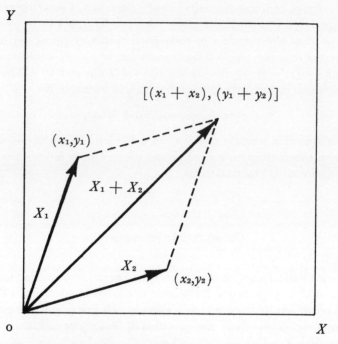

FIG. 7:1. Additivity of vectors in 2-space.

$$\hat{X} = k_1 X_1 + k_2 X_2 + \ldots + k_m X_m.$$

Some special cases merit mention. If the $k_i \geq 0$, then we have a *nonnegative linear combination*. If the k_i are nonnegative and

$$\sum_{i=1}^{m} k_i = 1,$$

it is called a *convex linear combination*.

A few examples of the above concepts may be illustrative. Consider $X_1 = (3,7)$ and $X_2 = (6,2)$, so that all nonnegative linear combinations of the form $X = k_1 X_1 + k_2 X_2$ will form a set of infinite vectors within the shaded area called a *cone* (see Fig. 7:2). The convex linear combination formed when

$$\sum_{i=1}^{2} k_i = 1$$

is a set of infinite vectors along a line joining X_1 and X_2 (see Fig. 7:3).

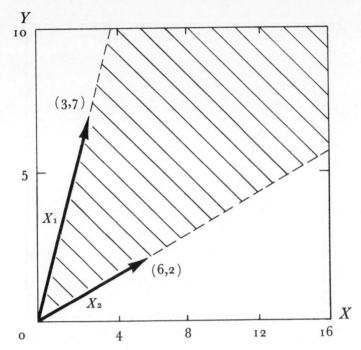

Fig. 7:2. Cone formed by nonnegative linear combination for X_1, X_2.

A most interesting thing happens when we add another vector to our consideration of convex linear combinations. Assume that we add $X_3 =$ (7,6) to our above convex linear combination. All vectors that can be generated from various values of k_i are no longer along a line but within an enclosed area called a *convex set* (see Fig. 7:4). The convex set is important to linear programming in that it helps define an area in which solutions to a problem can be sought. In our example for X_1, X_2, and X_3 all values for the convex linear combination lie within the convex set or along the lines forming the borders and nowhere else. Hence, if any X_i = o, and the remaining two vectors are not zero, then the values for the convex linear combination lie along the line joining the positive vectors.

A convex set can be defined in geometric terms for practical purposes as a set of vectors such that given any two vectors belonging to the set, a line can be drawn to connect them which will lie entirely within the set. The most common examples of convex sets are shown in Fig. 7:5. The example shown as A results from a convex linear combination of X_i vec-

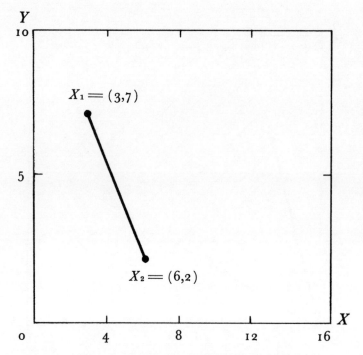

FIG. 7:3. Set formed by convex linear combination for X_1, X_2.

tors. The vectors along the boundary line which are unique and are not formed by the convex linear combination of any two vectors are called *extreme points*. The example shown as B is the result of an infinite number of convex linear combinations of an infinite number of X_i; hence there are an infinite number of extreme points along the quasi circumference as well as an infinite number of vectors in the interior. The example shown as C is a nonconvex set which does not have any extreme points but does have an infinite number of vectors within its interior — it is not possible to form a nonconvex set with linear constraints.

This geometric interpretation provides an intuitive key to understanding the linear programming model as well as providing the mathematical basis for solution. The practical approach is to express linear programming problems such that the answers lie at the extreme points of the convex set. This means that we have only to search the extreme points for a solution which is optimal.

The geometrical interpretation can be used to solve elementary linear

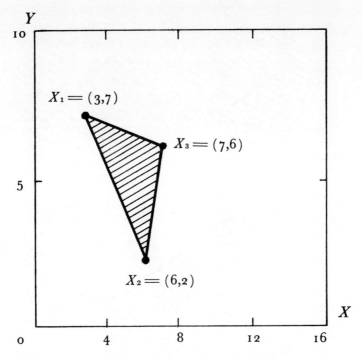

$X_1 = (3,7)$

$X_3 = (7,6)$

$X_2 = (6,2)$

FIG. 7:4. Convex set formed by convex linear combination for X_1, X_2, X_3.

programming problems. Consider the simple linear programming problem:

$$\text{Max } f(x_1, x_2) = x_1 + 2x_2,$$

subject to

$$7x_1 + 5x_2 \leq 35,$$
$$5x_1 + 8x_2 \leq 40,$$
$$x_1 \geq 0,$$
$$x_2 \geq 0.$$

We can begin our solution of this problem by examining the nature of the constraints. In general, constraints of the form

$$a_{11}x_1 + \ldots + a_{1m}x_m \leq b$$

are called *half spaces* when rendered as geometric expressions on a grid coordinate mapping. Our first constraint forms a half space when mapped; similarly, another half space is formed when the second constraint is mapped. Since we have restricted our $x_i \geq 0$, then we need consider only

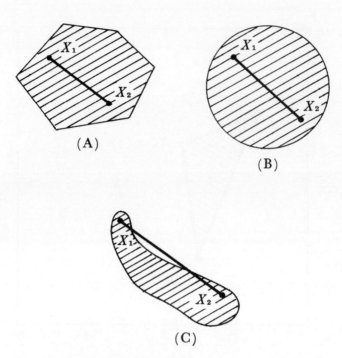

FIG. 7:5. Convex sets and a nonconvex set.

the first or positive quadrant of our mapping. All values for x_1 and x_2 lie along the boundary lines or within the interior of the convex set formed by the intersection of the half spaces that satisfy the four constraints, as shown in Fig. 7:6. It is obvious from inspection that maximum and minimum values must exist at the four extreme points. Since we have specified a maximization for the objective function, we need only to evaluate each of the extreme points to determine which yields a maximum $f(x_1,x_2)$. The reader may recall that this is analogous to the boundary search (S_1) discussed as part of the simple optimization model's optimal search routine.

There are two approaches to searching for the extreme point that maximizes the objective function. The first approach is to map the objective function by setting it equal to certain arbitrary values and mapping the resulting lines over our convex set (or hyperplanes where more than two x_i are used). Intuitively, one can imagine that, done carefully enough, the line drawn closest to the extreme point that has the highest arbitrary value is an approximate maximum. An example of this approach is shown in Fig. 7:7, and it appears that Max $f(x_1^*, x_2^*) = 10$, for $x_1^* = 0$ and $x_2^* = 5$.

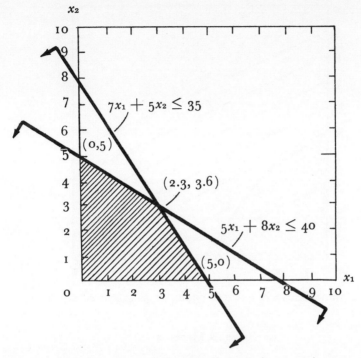

FIG. 7:6. Convex set formed by two half spaces for x_1, $x_2 \geq 0$.

A more rigorous search can be made by the substitution of the four extreme-point values in the objective function, a determination of which yields a maximum:

(x_1, x_2)	$f(x_1, x_2) = x_1 + 2x_2$
(0,0)	0
(5,0)	5
(2.3,3.6)	9.5
(0,5)	10

This complete enumeration of possible extreme-point values verifies our geometric solution, and we can state that $x_1^* = 0$, $x_2^* = 5$, and $f(x_1^*, x_2^*) = 10$, with the aforementioned knowledge of the heuristic rule that the optimal solution is always found among the extreme points. While this example may be trivial, the theoretical and mathematical foundation underlies all linear programming algorithms and concepts.

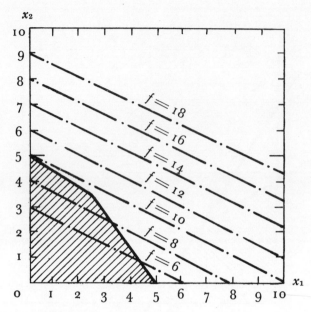

F<small>IG.</small> 7:7. Optimal search of extreme points by geometric substitution.

S<small>IMPLEX</small> M<small>ETHOD</small>

It would be delightful if urban system problems were as simple as our above example so that we could use geometric approaches to solutions. Unfortunately, the real world is rarely so simple. Most linear programming applications to urban systems involve several x_i and many constraints. Rather than our simple 2-space mapping, we must deal with n-space configurations, often impossible to visualize or draw. For example, when we have multiple x variables and multiple constraints, the area in which the solution lies, called the *solution space,* takes a multifaceted, diamondlike form. There are often very many extreme points to consider, eliminating a complete enumeration for practical purposes.

Fortunately, George B. Dantzig developed a mathematical algorithm to minimize our efforts when dealing with a linear programming problem in which the constraints generate a solution space which is a convex set. The algorithm is called the *simplex method.* The simplex method has four basic steps:

1. Select an extreme point at a corner of the convex set or solution space as a starting place.

2. Select an edge (or line) that goes through this extreme point such

that f increases in value along the edge (or decreases in minimization problems).

3. Proceed along the selected edge to the next extreme point which lies at a corner.

4. Repeat steps 2 and 3 until an extreme point is found at a corner of the convex set such that f no longer increases in value (or no longer decreases for minimization), and consider this point the optimal values for the problem.

There are a number of special mathematical problems that create special cases in linear programming. For the purpose of clarity we shall omit special cases by adhering to two assumptions. The first assumption is that we have a *positive condition* whereby all constants to the right of the inequality signs in constraints, that is, the b variables, are nonnegative, and that each row of the matrix of coefficients A has at least one positive value. The second assumption is that we deal with *nondegenerate conditions*, which means that the c and b constants are not linear combinations of fewer rows and columns than shown in the initial problem statement.

The four basic steps of the simplex method have mathematical complements. We shall examine the simplex method by restating the four basic steps in terms of the mathematical concepts associated with each.[1]

STEP I. THE INITIAL TABLE

Having expressed the problem in the proper linear programming format, we must remove the inequality signs from the constraints by establishing the *equivalent problem;* we use artificial variables, called *slack variables,* to achieve this. We can rewrite the general expression as

$$\text{Max } c_1 x_1 + c_2 x_2 + \ldots + c_n x_n + 0 x_{n+1} + 0 x_{n+2} + \ldots + 0 x_{n+m},$$

subject to

$$a_{11} x_1 + a_{12} x_2 + \ldots + a_{1n} x_n + x_{n+1} + 0 x_{n+2} + \ldots + 0 x_{n+m} = b_1,$$
$$a_{21} x_1 + a_{22} x_2 + \ldots + a_{2n} x_n + 0 x_{n+1} + x_{n+2} + \ldots + 0 x_{n+m} = b_2,$$
$$\cdot$$
$$\cdot$$
$$\cdot$$
$$a_{m1} x_1 + a_{m2} x_2 + \ldots + a_{mn} x_n + 0 x_{n+1} + 0 x_{n+2} + \ldots + x_{n+m} = b_m,$$
$$x_1 \geq 0, \, x_2 \geq 0, \, \ldots, \, x_n \geq 0, \, x_{n+1} \geq 0, \, x_{n+2} \geq 0, \, \ldots, \, x_{n+m} \geq 0.$$

[1] This approach is the clearest we have found and is developed fully in Seymour Lipschutz, *Theory and Problems of Finite Mathematics* (New York: Schaum, 1966).

For simplicity and clarity we shall assume a maximization problem but note that the simplex method is the same for minimization problems. The reader may notice that the equivalent problem is solely the initial problem augmented by an identity matrix of coefficients for the slack variables.

The *initial table* of the simplex method is obtained by regarding the columns of coefficients of the constraints as vectors (P_n) and the slack-variable coefficients as an identity matrix and then placing the b and c elements as follows in Table 7:1. The last row of the initial table is called

TABLE 7:1. Initial table of simplex method.

P_1	P_2	. . .	P_n						
a_{11}	a_{12}	. . .	a_{1n}	1	0	. . .	0	b_1
a_{21}	a_{22}	. . .	a_{2n}	0	1	. . .	0	b_2
.	.		.	.	.		.	.
.	.		.	.	.		.	.
.	.		.	.	.		.	.
a_{m1}	a_{m2}		a_{mn}	0	0	. . .	1	b_m
$-c_1$	$-c_2$	. . .	$-c_n$	0	0	. .	0	0

the *indicator row* and is simply the negative values of the objective function coefficients. The last entry of the indicator row is called the *criterion* and represents the value of the objective function, in this case the value of the objective function at origin.

Returning to the problem that we solved geometrically in Fig. 7:7, we can express the initial table of the problem in the following way:

P_1	P_2			
7	5	1	0	35
5	8	0	1	40
-1	-2	0	0	0

STEP 2. THE PIVOT POINT

The *pivot point* is an element of the initial table that is computed in three substeps:

1. Select any column which has a negative element in the indicator row.

2. Divide each positive entry in the corresponding column into the corresponding element in the last column.

3. Determine the entry that results in the smallest quotient from substep 2 and consider it the pivot point. In the remote case that a problem does not have any negative elements in the indicator row, it has no pivot point and can be regarded as an optimal solution to the problem with the proper interpretation of the simplex method.

Considering our example, we can select either P_1 or P_2 and complete all three substeps. If we select P_1, then 7 is the pivot point; whereas if we select P_2, then 8 is the pivot point. We shall select P_2:

P_1	P_2				
7	5	I	O	35	
5	⑧	O	I	40	
-1	-2	O	O	O	

STEP 3. COMPUTING THE NEW TABLE

The third step requires a set of computations which eventually results in a solution to the problem. In essence, the pivot point is used as a starting place for performing computations on the row in which it exists; then use row operations to manipulate the other rows so that zeros result in the same column as the pivot point.

The computation is performed in three substeps. Let the prescripted term $_1S$ be the simplex initial table with rows R_i, whose pivot point is the rth row and cth column — that is, if $_1S$ has elements s_{ij}, then $\hat{s}_{rc}$ is the pivot point. One must compute a new simplex table $_2S$, with rows $_2R_i$, using the initial table, and repeat this procedure until a *terminal table* $_tS$ is found wherein all elements of the indicator row are nonnegative. This means that k different tables for S may exist such that $k = 1, 2, \ldots,$ $t, \ldots, m$, of which only t is important to us. The substeps are described below.

1. Divide each element of the pivot row $_1R_r$ of $_1S$ by the pivot point $\hat{s}_{rc}$ to obtain the new row $_2R_r$ of $_2S$ by using

$$_2R_r = \frac{_1R_r}{\hat{s}_{rc}}.$$

If the pivot column c is labeled P_n, where $n = 1, 2, \ldots, q$, then label the corresponding pivot row r as P_n. It can be observed that this substep always results in $_2s_{rc} = 1$.

2. All other rows of $_2R_i$, where $i \neq r$, are computed by row operations

which involve adding the proper multiples of $_2R_r$ to the remaining rows $_1R_i$ of $_1S$ such that all elements of the pivot column c are zero, except that $_2s_{rc} = 1$. This is accomplished by

$$_2R_i = \pm (s_{ic})_2R_r + {}_1R_i.$$

3. Substeps 1 and 2 are repeated until all elements of the indicator row are nonnegative, and if any row of a new table $_{k-1}S$ has rows labeled P_n, then these rows are correspondingly labeled in $_kS$ and especially in $_tS$.

Considering our previous example, we can rewrite the initial table and circled pivot point as

initial table $= {}_1S =$

	P_1	P_2			
$_1R_1$	7	5	1	0	35
$_1R_2$	5	⑧	0	1	40
$_1R_3$	-1	-2	0	0	0

where the pivot point $= \hat{s}_{22} = 8$.

The new table $_2S$ is computed and the result is

new table $= {}_2S =$

		P_1	P_2			
	$_2R_1$	29/8	0	1	$-5/8$	10
$P_2 = {}_2R_2$		5/8	1	0	1/8	5
	$_2R_3$	1/4	0	0	1/4	10

As can be noted, this new table $_2S$ was obtained by dividing $_1R_2$ by $\hat{s}_{rc}$ $= 8$, multiplying $_2R_2$ by -5 and adding it to $_1R_1$ to yield $_2R_1$, and then multiplying $_2R_2$ by 2 and adding it to $_1R_3$ to yield $_2R_3$.

Our example is relatively simple in that only one new table must be computed to find all elements of the indicator row to be nonnegative. Hence in our simple problem $_2S = {}_tS$, or the new table computed from the initial table is a terminal table.

STEP 4. INTERPRETING THE TERMINAL TABLE

The terminal table is the optimal solution to the linear programming problem and has some interesting things about it to consider. The criterion of the terminal table is the maximum value of the primal problem and minimum value of the dual problem (if the problem is reversed, then the maximum and minimum values are reversed). Considering our example above, we note that the criterion of the terminal table is 10; hence

$$\text{Max } f(x_1^*, x_2^*) = \text{Min } g(u_1^*, u_2^*) = 10,$$

which confirms our geometric solution.

The values resulting in the last column that have a corresponding row vector P_n represent the optimal values for the decision variables x_1^*, x_2^*, $\ldots$, x_n^*. In our example only P_2 exists as a row vector in the terminal table, so we know that $x_1^* = 0$, $x_2^* = 5$, which also confirms our geometric solution.

The resulting elements of the indicator row corresponding to columns with no P_n (these are the slack-variable columns) of the terminal table are the values for the dual problem optimization. In our example $U = \{u_1, u_2\}$, $u_1^* = 0$, and $u_2^* = 1/4$. This can be easily seen if we rewrite the original problem to form the dual problem:

$$\text{Min } g(u_1, u_2) = 35u_1 + 40u_2,$$

subject to

$$7u_1 + 5u_2 \geq 1,$$
$$5u_1 + 8u_2 \geq 2,$$
$$u_1 \geq 0,$$
$$u_2 \geq 0.$$

We can interpret the terminal table such that

$$g(u_1^*, u_2^*) = 10 = f(x_1^*, x_2^*),$$

where

$$u_1^* = 0, \qquad x_1^* = 0,$$
$$u_2^* = 1/4, \qquad x_2^* = 5.$$

There are quite a few versions of the simplex method in terms of the kinds of matrices or tables developed. We have presented the most elementary algorithm that could be found. In practice the urban analyst normally uses a computer and any of several library programs to solve linear programming problems. However, the urban analyst should be at least as familiar with what the computer is doing as would be entailed in a basic understanding of the above discussion. To use an analogy, the above discussion is conceptually similar to explaining to a reasonable person the steps in starting a car engine, shifting to drive, controlling the moving car, and turning off the engine when one reaches the desired destination. This would work well for most drivers, but one would be reluctant to enter the Sebring 500 with only this knowledge and experience.

MEANING OF THE DUAL SOLUTION

The dual solution holds some interesting implications for planning and management of urban systems. The dual variables are *resource* or *shadow prices* in an economic sense. The linear programming problem corresponds to the economic problem of allocating scarce resources in the best manner in order to achieve some goal (maximization or minimization of an objective function). The dual solution represents the prices that should be paid for the resources in economic terms of *marginal prices*.

The planning implication is that the dual solution represents the increase (or decrease) in the value of the optimal objective function of the primal solution that can be gained by relaxing constraints on the corresponding resource by one unit. Again returning to our example, $u_2^* = \frac{1}{4}$ means that Max $f(x_1^*, x_2^*)$ can be increased by $\frac{1}{4}$ by relaxing the constraints on x_2 by one unit. There is a limit as to how far this can be taken before an entirely new linear programming problem must be formulated, and this can be determined by several types of analysis, often called *sensitivity analysis*. The salient point is that the primal solution tells the planner and manager what the best solution to the problem is within the given constraints; the dual solution tells the planner and manager what they can gain for the urban system by easing the constraints for resources. Planning and management of urban systems require change in constraints in many cases, and this is where the urban analyst can specify the dimensions of change.

SPECIAL LINEAR PROGRAMMING TOPICS

We have examined the basic linear programming problem with the inherent assumption that the optimal values could be any real numbers. Especially in urban systems such an assumption is not always possible. Use of linear programming for problems of equipment replacement or use, facility location, capital improvements, batch order sizes, transportation scheduling, and many "go–no go" problems requires integer values for optimal solutions. Similarly, when using the linear programming approach to choose among different alternatives, an integer solution is essential.

Consider the following general linear programming problem:

$$\text{Opt} f(x_j) = \sum_{j=1}^{n} c_j x_j,$$

subject to

$$\sum_{j=1}^{n} a_{ij} x_j \leq b_i,$$

$$x_j \geq 0,$$

where

$$j = 1, 2, \ldots, n,$$
$$i = 1, 2, \ldots, m.$$

If all x_j must be integers, we have what is often called a *pure-integer programming problem*. If some x_j must be integers and the remainder can have real-number values, we have a *mixed-integer programming problem*.

A variation of the pure-integer programming problem is the *combinatorial problem*. The combinatorial problem seeks to find the best alternative to solving a problem when there are any number of alternatives n that will solve the problem. For example, the classic example is the traveling salesman who must visit n cities and return to his starting point. There are $(n - 1)!$ possible routes or tours that he can take, but only one of them is the cheapest, shortest, and most efficient. While this may not seem to be a mathematical problem, consider a candidate for governor of a state who asks an urban analyst to find the shortest tour he can make of the ten largest cities in the state. The urban analyst would find that there are $(10 - 1)! = 9 \cdot 8 \cdot 7 \cdot 6 \cdot 5 \cdot 4 \cdot 3 \cdot 2 \cdot 1 = 362,880$ possible tours — which one should he recommend as the shortest?

One of those little ironies of mathematics is that the easiest problems to visualize, such as integer problems, are the hardest to solve. The pure- and mixed-integer programming problems are among the most difficult to solve and often cannot be solved. The alert reader may suggest formulation of a general linear programming problem and rounding the solutions to the nearest integers. Unfortunately, this does not work for any but the most elementary problems because there are so many extreme points in many problems that rounding the solution will almost guarantee an error. When any elements a_{ij} of the A matrix are negative, rounding is not possible in most cases. Similarly, in both integer and combinatorial problems a search of all extreme points or possible solutions is obviously beyond the capability of urban analysts. In fact, for most problems a complete enumeration and search of all possible solutions is beyond the capability of even the largest computers.

A kind of compromise must be used to find solutions to integer and combinatorial programming problems. There are many algorithms which in some cases guarantee little more than an approximation, often unable to be proved optimal. Nonetheless, there are three classes of algorithms into which most examples fall.

1. *Cutting-Plane Algorithms.* These algorithms start with a general linear programming approach but add a condition, usually an additional constraint, that satisfies an integer solution. After a distressingly large number of attempts (*iterations*) some signs appear that indicate *convergence* (coming together) of non-integer and integer solutions. These algorithms require a great amount of time, both human and machine, and tend to be very tedious.

2. *Back-Track Algorithms.* The back-track class of algorithms rely more on partial enumeration of possible solutions than on convergence of non-integer and integer solutions. The basic approach usually involves generating a family of separate linear programming problems which essentially find a solution piece by piece. The back-track notion appears in that a possible solution usually points to other possible solutions which one must go backward to compute. The most common examples of back-track algorithms are the *branch-and-bound algorithm,* which is used to stratify mixed-integer programming problems into integer and real-number variables, and the *partial-enumeration algorithm,* which separates partial solutions from the variables until a full solution is found.

3. *Heuristic Programming.* A most popular and interesting class of algorithms is the extension of the heuristic or rule-of-thumb idea into a programming context. Sophisticated and simple heuristics are generated for the particular problem under consideration which limit the number of possible solutions. For example, in our traveling candidate scenario it may be that a rule of thumb is to visit a particular city always before visiting another city for any of a variety of reasons (but probably partisan in nature). This would substantially restrict the number of possible tours. The basic tool of the heuristic programming approach is trial and error.

In all of the classes of algorithms for integer and combinatorial programming problems, it is almost essential to use a computer and any one or group of library programs available. Heuristic programming almost always requires assistance from computer programmers to develop the software for computer solutions.

A special topic that one should also consider is optimization of networks by linear programming techniques. *Networks* are closed systems of *nodes* and *paths* to represent flows in problem conditions. Networks have been used in urban analysis for several years for work programming (critical path and program evaluation review techniques), division sequencing, communications, and transportation.[2]

The classical problem of optimization in networks is the *transportation problem*. The transportation problem involves the minimization of time, cost, and effort in travel, subject to the constraints that all goods must be delivered to all places where demanded or all origins must have destinations. In economic terms the transportation problem requires minimization of the cost of distribution, subject to the constraint that supply must equal demand. The transportation problem is usually expressed as follows:

$$\text{Min} \sum_{i=1}^{m} \sum_{j=1}^{n} c_{ij} x_{ij},$$

subject to

$$\sum_{j=1}^{n} x_{ij} \leq S_i \quad \text{(supply or origins)},$$

$$\sum_{i=1}^{m} x_{ij} \geq D_j \quad \text{(demand or destinations)}.$$

Thus

$$\sum_{i=1}^{m} S_i = \sum_{j=1}^{n} D_j \quad \begin{pmatrix} \text{supply} = \text{demand} \\ \text{origins} = \text{destinations} \end{pmatrix},$$

where

$$i = 1, 2, \ldots, m,$$
$$j = 1, 2, \ldots, n,$$
$$x_{ij} \geq 0.$$

The network in the transportation problem can be depicted as shown in Fig. 7:8. One must establish a stated time interval in which to consider the constraints, often called the *planning period* in urban analysis.

The computational difficulty with the transportation problem is that S_i and D_j are nonnegative integers; consequently, $x_{ij} = 1, 2, \ldots, q$. Further, the equality constraint requires that a factor, called a *dummy variable*, be employed to create an inequality for the proper linear programming format. Fortunately, there are several approaches to solution

[2] See Anthony J. Catanese and Alan W. Steiss, *Systemic Planning: Theory and Application* (Boston: D. C. Heath, 1970), especially Parts 2 and 3.

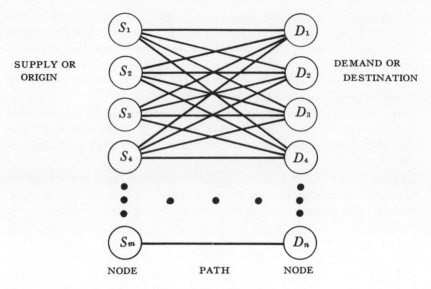

FIG. 7:8. Network for transportation problem.

of the transportation problem that have been developed because of its extensive use. Some approaches salvage the simplex algorithm by deleting one of the redundant supply or demand constraints. Other algorithms modify simplex and integer programming techniques; a fine example of this is the *Dennis transportation code.*

APPLICATION OF LINEAR PROGRAMMING

There have been much interest in and work on linear programming applications in urban systems, much of which was fostered by the considerable success of these optimization models in business and defense applications. It is difficult to present an adequate coverage of the applications of linear programming in urban analysis because the applications are being continually modified, revised, and restructured. The most sensible approach seems to be to evaluate the linear programming applications that have met with enough success that the applications are well known. Within this perspective, we can examine linear programming models as formulated in economic development, transportation, and land use and development.

ECONOMIC DEVELOPMENT

Urban analysts are often called upon to evaluate and assist in the solution of economic problems of urban systems revolving around such matters as income distribution, economic base and structure, and labor problems. A distinct field of study exists for the analysis of economic development problems at the regional level that uses highly sophisticated scientific techniques — it is called *regional science*. Regional science is a hybrid of economics and urban systems planning. The classic work describing the scientific techniques of regional science is by Walter Isard.[3]

Linear programming is applied in problems of economic development of urban systems for the optimal use of scarce resources, as constrained by limitations on availability and consumption. Resources are defined in traditional economic terms of land, labor, capital, and natural resources. Linear programming has been applied to such problems as firm and industry location, production scheduling, commodity flows and distribution, and various special industry problems in such areas as petrochemicals, fluid milk, airline routes, and coal mining.

Isard describes the general linear programming problem in economic development terms, and we can profit from examining it.[4] If we consider economic activities that can be undertaken in an urban system, in terms of unit levels of operation that result in one new dollar of income, then we know that resources, say land, labor, capital, and water, are required for each unit level of operation. Consider two economic activities, x_1 and x_2; using an arbitrary measure of resource availability MM, it is known that the urban system has available for consumption $6MM$ units of water, $1.8MM$ units of land, $3MM$ units of labor, and $24MM$ units of capital.

TABLE 7:2. Resource requirements per dollar of new income in MM units.

Required Units	Activity 1	Activity 2
Water	0.5	0.6
Land	0.2	0.15
Labor	0.4	0.2
Capital	3.0	2.0

[3] Walter Isard, *Methods of Regional Analysis: An Introduction to Regional Science* (Cambridge, Mass.: M.I.T. Press, 1960).

[4] Ibid., pp. 413-492.

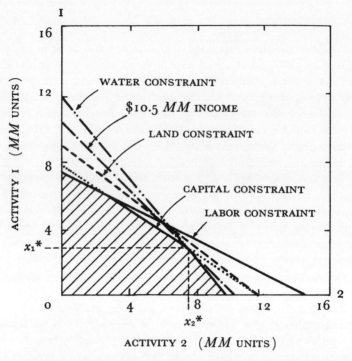

FIG. 7:9. Geometric solution of linear program for economic development by Isard.

The resource requirements for each unit level of operation are shown in Table 7:2. Hence the linear programming problem can be expressed as

$$\text{Max } f(x_1, x_2) = x_1 + x_2 \qquad \text{(new income objective function)},$$

subject to

$$0.5x_1 + 0.6x_2 \leq 6 \qquad \text{(water constraint)},$$
$$0.2x_1 + 0.15x_2 \leq 1.8 \qquad \text{(land constraint)},$$
$$0.4x_1 + 0.2x_2 \leq 3 \qquad \text{(labor constraint)},$$
$$3.0x_1 + 2.0x_2 \leq 24 \qquad \text{(capital constraint)},$$
$$x_1 \geq 0 \qquad \text{(nonnegativity constraint)},$$
$$x_2 \geq 0 \qquad \text{(nonnegativity constraint)}.$$

Since this is a simple problem, we can use a geometric solution, as shown in Fig. 7:9. Using the familiar geometric solution approach, we find that $x_1^* = 3MM$ units and $x_2^* = 7.5MM$ units; hence $f(x_1^*, x_2^*) = \$10.5MM$

units. The same and similar problems can be solved by the simplex algorithm with equal efficiency.

There have been highly sophisticated applications of linear programming to such complex problems of regional science as interregional flows of goods and services. Economic analysis in general has used the linear programming model extensively.[5] It is beyond the scope of our discussion to go into these applications, but the interested reader will find individual study to be rewarding in these areas. Economic development and regional science, as well as economics per se, have used linear programming to a higher degree than any other social science discipline.

TRANSPORTATION

Notable applications of linear programming to the form of the transportation problem have been undertaken in urban analysis. The usual concern is the determination of the optimal distribution of origin and destination places in the urban system such that time, cost, or effort is minimized. One of the more interesting of these attempts was undertaken in the Buffalo, New York, urban system as part of the Niagara Frontier Transportation Study.[6] The project involved computation of the optimal time for commuting, that is, the minimum time spent in commuting, and comparison of the optimal time against the actual time.

The minimum time spent in commuting was computed by use of the transportation problem:

$$\text{Min } T_m = \sum_{i=1}^{m} \sum_{j=1}^{n} a_{ij} x_{ij} \quad \text{(objective cost function)},$$

subject to

$$\sum_{j=1}^{n} x_{ij} = J_i \quad \text{(destination constraint)},$$

$$\sum_{i=1}^{m} x_{ij} = H_j \quad \text{(origin constraint)},$$

$$\sum_{i=1}^{m} x_{ij} \geq 0 \quad \text{(nonnegativity constraint)},$$

[5] The classic work in the field is Robert Dorfman, Paul A. Samuelson, and Robert M. Solow, *Linear Programming and Economic Analysis* (New York: McGraw-Hill, 1958).

[6] John R. Hamburg et al., *A Linear Programming Test of Journey to Work Minimization* (Albany: New York State Department of Public Works, 1966).

where

$$T_m = \text{minimum total travel time,}$$
$$a_{ij} = \text{travel time from zone } i \text{ to zone } j,$$
$$x_{ij} = \text{trips from zone } i \text{ to zone } j,$$
$$m = \text{number of work zones,}$$
$$n = \text{number of home zones,}$$
$$J_i = \text{work places in zone } i,$$
$$H_j = \text{homes in zone } j.$$

The solution of this problem was accomplished by using the Dennis transportation code.

In order to compare the optimal time spent in commuting with the real world, the urban analysts developed an *index of indifference,* expressed by

$$I_s = \frac{T_a - T_m}{T_p - T_m},$$

where

$$I_s = \text{index of indifference for group } s,$$
$$T_a = \text{actual travel time,}$$
$$T_p = \text{probable travel time for complete indifference.}$$

The actual travel time T_a was computed by

$$T_a = \sum_{i=1}^{m} \sum_{j=1}^{n} a_{ij} x_{ij}.$$

The probable travel time, if commuters were completely indifferent to time, was found by assuming that workers were allocated to homes on a proportional basis. The equation for T_p was the same as T_a except that

$$x_{ij} = \frac{J_i H_j}{\sum_{j=1}^{n} H_j}.$$

The index can be interpreted by taking heed of values for I close to zero as reflecting patterns approaching the optimal; values for I close to one reflect complete indifference to time spent in commuting to work.

The data from the Buffalo urban system were grouped according to income, race, and driver status. As can be seen in Table 7:3, lower- and middle-income groups are more sensitive to travel time than the high-income group. It also can be noted that nonwhite nondrivers are the group most indifferent toward time spent in commuting. There were many extensions and ramifications of the findings, but urban analysts believed that the most important result was an explicit proof that commuters were not

TABLE 7:3. Index of indifference for income, race, and driver status groups, Buffalo urban system.

Group s	Number of Commuters	Total Travel Time (hours)			Average Travel Time (minutes)			Index of Indifference I_s
		T_p	T_a	T_m	$\bar{T}_p$	$\bar{T}_a$	$\bar{T}_m$	
1. Less than $4,999	51,242	21,820.9	9,973.8	3,223.0	25.5	11.7	3.8	0.36
2. $5,000–$7,999	108,696	50,806.6	25,358.0	9,059.3	28.0	14.0	5.0	0.39
3. More than $8,000	92,750	32,595.4	24,498.8	10,709.1	21.1	15.8	6.9	0.63
4. White Driver	247,099	87,140.2	45,827.9	18,954.9	21.1	11.1	4.6	0.39
5. White Non-driver	45,536	12,846.1	6,625.8	2,545.6	16.9	8.7	3.3	0.40
6. Non-white Driver	10,616	2,565.2	1,839.1	1,341.0	14.4	10.3	7.6	0.41
7. Non-white Non-driver	6,919	3,254.7	1,716.9	755.6	11.8	9.1	6.6	0.65
All Commuters	252,688	117,379.4	59,830.6	22,411.0	27.9	14.2	5.3	0.39

indifferent to the time spent in commuting (as some theorists have proposed). Several avenues for further application of this approach exist and should be traveled in the near future in urban analysis.

LAND USE AND DEVELOPMENT

Considerable interest and research in the mathematical modeling of land use and development of urban systems have been generated since the early 1950s. Linear programming has been used in several of the successful models with varying degrees of complexity and utility.[7]

One of the earliest attempts at modeling land use and development used linear programming to distribute residential activities within an urban system (Philadelphia).[8] The original problem used a variation of the transportation problem of optimization in a network to assign families to residential locations in order to optimize (maximize) their price- or rent-paying ability (sometimes referred to simply as *bid rent*). The proposed approach was to predict the optimal price- or rent-paying ability of the family. For various reasons, not denying lack of sufficient data, the model was not operational until the bid-rent concept was revised to reflect actual, rather than optimal, family price- or rent-paying patterns.[9]

It is somewhat difficult to describe the operational version of the model, which is sometimes referred to as the *Penn-Jersey model,* because of the very large number of variables and constraints.[10] Suffice it to say that the objective function describes the preference of families for price or rent for various-sized dwellings according to their incomes. The assumption is made that socioeconomic factors are explained by the actual patterns, and it is not necessary to evaluate each specific factor upon preference for dwelling size for families of varying income — this is sometimes called *averaging out.* The resultant optimal solution is a matrix which can be interpreted to represent a three-dimensional *spatial distribution surface* around the central city (where bid rent is the highest) and into the suburbs (where bid rent becomes lower). Homogeneity is implicit in the model, and critics have argued that it tends to distribute families within space in an urban system in a manner which is quite unlike the real world. Nonetheless, this pioneering effort has received considerable notice and emulation.

A more pragmatic model was developed for the Milwaukee urban system which assumed that the best plan for the area was that which minimized

[7] The only major integration of these models into a unified context that has reached print is George C. Hemmens, ed., *Urban Development Models* (Washington, D.C.: Highway Research Board, 1968).

[8] J. P. Herbert and B. H. Stevens, "A Model for the Distribution of Residential Activities in Urban Areas," *Journal of Regional Science,* 2, no. 2 (Winter, 1960), 21-36.

[9] Britton Harris, *Linear Programming and the Projection of Land Uses,* P. J. Paper 20 (Philadelphia: Penn-Jersey Transportation Study, 1962).

[10] Britton Harris, Josef Nathanson, and Louis Rosenberg, *Research on an Equilibrium Model of Metropolitan Housing and Locational Change* (Philadelphia: Institute for Environmental Studies, University of Pennsylvania, 1966).

the cost of development.[11] The constraints upon this objective were the demand for various types of development (such as residential, industrial, and commercial); limitations on land uses within zones, usually based upon density of development; and ratios of land uses relative to other land uses in a zone, established by zoning and other land use controls. The linear programming model was used for the general problem, expressed by

$$\text{Min } c_t = c_1x_1 + c_2x_2 + \ldots + c_nx_n \qquad \text{(objective cost function)},$$

subject to

$$d_1x_1 + d_2x_2 + \ldots + d_nx_n = E_k \qquad \text{(demand constraint)},$$
$$x_1 + x_2 + \ldots + x_n \leq F_m \qquad \text{(use limitation)},$$
$$x_n \leq Gx_m \qquad \text{(ratio constraint)},$$
$$x_n \geq 0 \qquad \text{(nonnegativity constraint)},$$

where

c_t = total costs of development for period t,
c_i = cost coefficient,
x_i = type of land use,
E_k = demand for each land use,
d_i = service coefficients for supporting development, such as streets, utilities, and improvements,
F_m = limit on land use n in zone m,
G = ratio of land use n allowed relative to land use m in the same or different zones for the area.

The above linear programming problem is the generalized set of expressions for the comprehensive urban system's land use and development. Experience with the general model revealed that an urban system with 30 zones often yielded 400 decision variables and 60 constraints.

A trouble spot with the above model, often called the *SEWRPC land use design model*, is that the values for the x_i, or land use variables, are integers. For practical purposes the urban analysts used the simplex algorithm rather than integer programming and concluded that the approximation was 80 percent accurate. Nonetheless, the optimal solution is an approximation when solved by the simplex method.

An example of the industrial land use submodel is illustrative of the specific characteristics of the model. Considering only industrial land use, the linear programming problem within the SEWRPC land use design model is expressed by

[11] Southeastern Wisconsin Regional Planning Commission, *A Mathematical Approach to Urban Design: A Progress Report on a Land Use Plan Design Model and a Land Use Simulation Model* (Waukesha, Wis., 1966).

$$\text{Min } C_t = \sum_{i=1}^{J} \sum_{n=1}^{N} C_{in} I_{in} \quad \text{(objective cost function)},$$

subject to

$$\sum_{i=1}^{J} \sum_{n=1}^{N} I_{in} + SI_{in} = I_{id} \quad \text{(demand constraint)},$$

$$\sum_{i=1}^{J} I_{in} \leq I_{nz} \quad \text{(ratio constraint)},$$

$$\begin{array}{l} I_{in} \geq 0 \text{ if } I_{in} \, \varepsilon \, \{ \mathcal{J}_i \} \\ I_{in} = 0 \text{ if } I_{in} \, \varepsilon \, \{ \bar{\mathcal{J}}_i \} \end{array} \quad \text{(use limitation)},$$

where

C_t = total industrial land development costs (dollars) in period t,

I_{in} = industrial land for industry i developed in zone n (acres), $i = 1, 2, \ldots, J$ and $n = 1, 2, \ldots, N$,

C_{in} = cost of developing industrial land for industry i in zone n (dollars/acre),

I_{id} = total regional demand for industrial land in industry i (acres), $d = 1, 2, \ldots, D$,

S = service ratio or ratio of service land area to industrial land area,

$\{ \mathcal{J}_i \}$ = set of lands meeting requirements for industry i,

$\{ \bar{\mathcal{J}}_i \}$ = set of lands not meeting requirements for industry i,

I_{nz} = capacity limit for industrial land in zone n, $z = 1, 2, \ldots, Z$.

This linear programming program can be verbalized by saying that total costs of development for industrial land are minimized in planning period t, subject to the constraints that the land required for each industry must be satisfied and that industry does not locate on lands that do not meet requirements for that industry. The unusual data needed to calibrate the industrial land use submodel were collected through the execution of an original survey. Having solved the submodel for the 30 zones of the urban system, the optimal solution for industrial land use, which was a suboptimal solution for the comprehensive land use model, was linked to similar submodels for residential, service, agricultural, and special land uses.

COMBINED LAND USE AND TRANSPORTATION

Land use and transportation are integrated closely in real-world urban systems, and it stands to reason that a combined land use and transportation model would be valuable for urban analysis. Only a few attempts have been made in this direction. One of the most interesting attempts at an integrated model using the linear programming approach is still experimental.[12] We will simply present its format and suggest that it merits further experimentation and testing.

$$\text{Min } Z = \sum_{r=1}^{R} \sum_{j=1}^{J} \sum_{k=1}^{K} \sum_{i=1}^{I} C_{k(r,j)i} X_{k(r,j)i} \quad \text{(objective cost function),}$$

subject to

$$\sum_{j=1}^{J} \sum_{r=1}^{R} \sum_{i=1}^{I} \sum_{k=1}^{K} - a_{dk(r,j)i} X_{k(r,j)i} \geq -A_d^{\bar{s}d} \quad \text{(traffic flow capacity constraint),}$$

$$\sum_{r=1}^{R} \sum_{i=1}^{I} \sum_{k=1}^{K} - l_{jk(r,j)i} X_{k(r,j)i} \geq -L_j \quad \text{(residential land availability constraint),}$$

$$\sum_{j=1}^{J} \sum_{i=1}^{I} \sum_{k=1}^{K} b_{rk(r,j)i} X_{k(r,j)i} = B_r \quad \text{(labor requirements constraint),}$$

$$X_{k(r,j)i} \geq 0 \quad \text{(nonnegativity constraint),}$$

where

Z = total housing and travel-time-to-work costs,

R = number of plant locations, indexed by $r = 1, 2, \ldots, R$,

N = number of residential tracts, indexed by $j = 1, 2, \ldots, J$,

K = number of different types of possible housing structures containing one or more units, indexed by $k = 1, 2, \ldots, K$,

$I_{(r, j)}$ = number of routes connecting destination r to origin j, indexed by $(r,j)i = 1, 2, \ldots, I(r,j)$,

$X_{k(r, j)i}$ = number of people living in housing structures of type k at location j who take route $(r, j)i$ to plant r,

C_k = unit housing cost of structure type k,

$C_{(r, j)i}$ = twice the unit cost of travel (round trip) on route $(r, j)i$,

$C_{k(r, j)i}$ = sum of costs C_k and $C_{(r, j)i}$,

D = number of traffic lanes between two specified locations in the transportation network, indexed by $d = 1, 2, \ldots, D$,

$a_{dk(r, j)i}$ = unit of traffic flow over traffic lane d by people living in housing structure type k at location j traveling route $(r, j)i$,

$\bar{S}d$ = velocity per unit of flow over traffic lane d,

$A^{\bar{s}d}$ = flow capacity of traffic lane d at velocity $\bar{s}$,

L_j = total land available for residential land use in tract j,

[12] Jack Ochs, "An Application of Linear Programming to Urban Spatial Organization," *Journal of Regional Science*, 9, no. 3 (Dec., 1969), 451-459.

$l_{jk(r, j)i}$ = land required for housing by a person living in housing structure type k in tract j who travels route $(r, j)i$ to plant site r,

B_r = total work force required at plant site r,

$b_{rk(r, j)i}$ = a person who works at plant site r, lives in housing structure type k in tract j, and travels route $(r, j)i$ to work.

The above linear programming problem, which we can call the *Ochs transportation and land use model,* is a hybrid of the Penn-Jersey model and the transportation problem. It seeks to minimize the total costs that all people in an urban system pay for housing and travel to work as constrained by the traffic flow capacity constraint, which holds that the flow of traffic over a traffic lane cannot exceed the capacity of that traffic lane; the residential land availability constraint, which holds that the total land use for residential development in a tract cannot exceed the amount of land available for residential land use in that tract; the labor requirements constraint, which holds that the employment needs of each plant be satisfied; and the familiar nonnegativity constraint.

There are several assumptions built into the Ochs transportation and land use model — for example, *marginal cost prices* rather than other pricing mechanisms are assumed — and data problems which impede its full potential for urban systems planning, yet it is unique in what is attempted. With further modifications and improvements, and the benefit of fresh ideas on its use, it could be a prototype of linear programming applications for urban analysis in the future.

RECOMMENDED EXERCISES

1. Solve the following linear programming problem:

$$\text{Min } 1x_1 + 2x_2 + 1.5x_3 + 2x_4,$$

subject to

$$5x_1 + 12x_2 + 2x_3 + 8x_4 \geq 5,$$
$$6x_1 + 5x_2 + 12x_3 + 10x_4 \geq 10,$$
$$1x_1 + 1x_2 + 1x_3 + 1x_4 = 100,$$
$$x_i \geq 0.$$

Use the simplex algorithm for this problem and determine the optimal solutions for the primal and dual problems.

2. The Okefenokee Urban Development Commission wants to maximize the income of people within its urban system by allocating its scarce

resources of land, labor, capital, and water among new industries locating there. The urban analysts assigned to this problem devise a unit called the Okefenokee delivery dollar, *ODD*, which allows both resources and income to be expressed in common terms. This year only two industrial activities want to locate in the area, a paper mill and a glue factory. Working with the respective industrial representatives, the urban analysts found that the following resources were needed, measured in *ODD*'s for each new *ODD* generated within the urban system:

Resource	Paper Mill	Glue Factory
Land	0.60	0.70
Labor	0.30	0.40
Capital	1.30	0.35
Water	0.65	0.50

Resources within the Okefenokee urban system are not unlimited, and this year there are 4.30 *ODD*s of land, 2.40 *ODD*s of labor, 4.55 *ODD*s of capital, and 3.25 *ODD*s of water available for new industries. What is the maximum amount of new income that can be generated within the urban system under these conditions? How much income can be added to the above solution by adding one more *ODD* of land, labor, capital, and water? Use either geometric or simplex algorithms in your computations.

FURTHER READING

Levin, Richard I., and Rudolph P. Lamone. *Linear Programming for Management Decisions*. Homewood, Ill.: Richard D. Irwin, 1969.

   One of the few important works on linear programming that is written for nonmathematicians, it attempts to present the essential concepts of linear programming within the context of applications in business and industry. A particularly good section on the use of computers to solve linear programming problems, as well as the statements for a basic program written in FORTRAN IV, are invaluable to the reader who wants to know more about these matters.

Dantzig, George B. *Linear Programming and Extensions*. Princeton, N.J.: Princeton University Press, 1963.

   A more theoretical and mathematically oriented book than the above, it is written by the master of the subject. The book is difficult to get through, but the implications of the theoretical constructs of linear programming and the extensions made by Dantzig hold great promise for the sophisticated urban analyst.

We have mentioned that linear programming is the most popular, well-tested, and generally solvable form of mathematical programming. We would be somewhat remiss, however, if we did not examine the other important forms of mathematical programming, even though they are not generally popular among urban analysts, not well tested and tried in urban problems, and not always solvable for some problems. If little else, the very mathematical perplexity of mathematical programming, other than linear programming, is likened to the task of Sisyphus by many urban analysts. Experience offers little solace, since it is scant in this area of concern. With these conditions in mind, our discussion is primarily concerned with the potential applications which are considered to be worthwhile because of the interesting characteristics of mathematical programming.

When the objective function and/or the constraints are not adequately described by linear expressions but are nonetheless deterministic, *nonlinear programming* may be useful to the urban analyst. Urban problems that require multistage planning periods in which time is a major consideration in a step-by-step optimization may be solved by the use of *dynamic programming* in some cases. Variables which are inherently stochastic, regardless of the linearity or nonlinearity of the functional relationships, may necessitate some form of *stochastic programming*. Taken together, nonlinear, dynamic, and stochastic programming are the salient forms of mathematical programming other than linear programming. There are many variations of these methods and some special cases, which will limit our examination to basic precepts rather than detailed algorithms.

The utilization of nonlinear, dynamic, and stochastic programming in urban analysis is problematic because of the advanced level of mathematical methods that is required for solution of such formulations. Optimal solutions are difficult because the elegant simplicity of the linear programming solution spaces are almost entirely lost, and hence the computational advantages of the simplex method are effaced. Solution spaces for other than linear programming are often nonconvex, resulting in infinite extreme points of which only one is optimal. Dynamic formulations require a separate rationale and algorithmic theory called *backward induction,*

CHAPTER 8

Nonlinear, Dynamic, and Stochastic Programming

altogether different from our previous explorations. Stochastic variables must incorporate probabilistic methods that are devious to optimize.

The formidable problems of formulation, solution, and implementation of nonlinear, dynamic, and stochastic models are sufficient to daunt even the stout-hearted urban analyst. The potential of these approaches is exciting, however, because underlying theoretical structures reflect the complexity of the real world. Complex mathematical methods may be necessary for complex urban analyses. Advances in mathematical programming, being made daily, may ease the burden of computation in time. The possibilities for these methods are great, and future applications should be significant even though present success is meager.[1]

NONLINEAR PROGRAMMING

The mathematical foundation upon which we can build our construction of nonlinear programming is primarily an extension of the concepts discussed for the general form of the complex optimization problem and the optimal search routine. Nonlinear programming problems usually involve nonlinear objective functions, although it is possible to have nonlinear constraints as well. Nonlinear constraints, however, do irreparable damage to our efforts in that they create solution spaces which are nonconvex; hence we have an infinite number of possible extreme points and can never be absolutely sure that our answer is optimal. For example, consider two linear and one nonlinear constraints:

$$g_1 = 12 - x_1 x_2 \geq 0,$$
$$g_2 = 12 - x_1 \geq 0,$$
$$g_3 = 12 - x_2 \geq 0,$$
$$x_1, x_2 \geq 0.$$

The solution space S formed by these three constraints and the nonnegativity constraint can be mapped in the manner shown in Fig. 8:1. Within solution space S the extreme points are $(0,12)$, $(12,0)$, $(0,0)$, $a = (1,12)$, $b = (12,1)$, and an infinite quantity of extreme points lying on the curve ab. The best that could be done for such a solution space would be an approximation of the optimal solution if that solution were along or near

---

[1] Maurice D. Kilbridge, Robert P. O'Block, and Paul V. Teplitz, "A Conceptual Framework for Urban Planning Models," *Management Science*, 15, no. 6 (Feb., 1969), B-246–B-266.

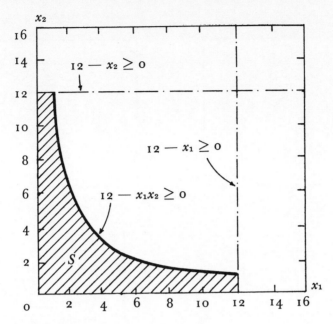

FIG. 8:1. Solution space for constraints g_1, g_2, g_3.

the curve $ab;$ if by some fortune the optimal solution for this particular example were coincidental with one of the finite extreme points, a heuristic solution could be computed.

Pragmatics dictate that we limit our sphere of concern to problems in which the solution spaces are convex. Even with this limitation, there are several problems which cannot be solved. There is no readily available algorithm, like the simplex method, by which we can compute optimal solutions for nonlinear programming. We can use any of three basic categories of algorithms for practical solution of urban problems: (1) *classical calculus,* (2) *method of Lagrange,* and (3) *gradient method.*

In addition to limiting the scope of solution spaces, one should limit the type of objective functions to be considered to *convex* or *concave nonlinear objective functions.* Convex and concave nonlinear objective functions take on bowl-like forms when mapped (see Fig. 8:2). Using linear constraints to guarantee convex solution spaces, one can solve many nonlinear programming problems. Extension of the optimal search routine implies that optimal solutions lying along a boundary can be found by some form of boundary search. Yet it can be seen that many types of non-

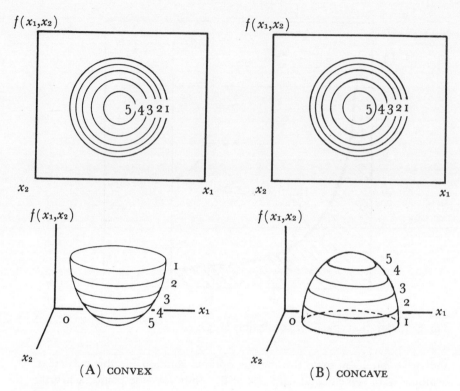

FIG. 8:2. Convex and concave nonlinear objective functions.

linear programming problems can have optimal solutions which are out-side the feasible area formed by the boundaries, which are called *exterior solutions,* or within the feasible area formed by the boundaries, which are called *interior solutions.* These can be seen in Fig. 8:3. Exterior and interior solutions require the use of algorithms that are similar to the mental process one uses in climbing a hill and attempting to determine precisely where he reaches the peak.

CLASSICAL CALCULUS

Classical calculus can be used to find optimal solutions to nonlinear programming problems where the objective function is convex or concave and the constraints form a convex set (these can be either linear or non-

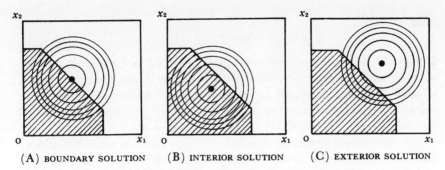

(A) BOUNDARY SOLUTION   (B) INTERIOR SOLUTION   (C) EXTERIOR SOLUTION

FIG. 8:3. Three hypothetical nonlinear programming solutions.

linear in form, although the former is obviously easier to deal with). Exterior, interior, and boundary solutions can be found using classical calculus methods. While we shall not cover them, there are some nonlinear functions in which no derivative exists that require a numeric search for possible optimal points.

The extension of the concepts of differentiation to include *partial differentiation* is most useful for our purposes. Partial derivatives, usually denoted by ∂, are the partial rates of change of one variable of a function with respect to another. A literal slice is made along an axis of the function with regard to that variable, ignoring all others. For example, consider

$$f(x_1, x_2) = 5x_1 + 8x_2 + x_1x_2 - x_1^2 - x_2^2;$$

taking partial derivatives,

$$\frac{\partial f}{\partial x_1} = 5 + x_2 - 2x_1,$$

$$\frac{\partial f}{\partial x_2} = 8 + x_1 - 2x_2,$$

setting these equal to zero (to determine a maximum value), and solving the simultaneous equations:

$$5 - 2x_1 + x_2 = 0$$
$$8 + x_1 - 2x_2 = 0$$

and

$$10 - 4x_1 + 2x_2 = 0$$
$$8 + x_1 - 2x_2 = 0$$
$$\overline{18 - 3x_1 \qquad = 0}$$

$$\hat{x}_1 = 6.$$

Substituting,

$$\hat{x}_2 = 7.$$

It might be added that second-order partial derivatives are used to test for strict concavity or convexity, although the manner is somewhat more complicated than was discussed for second-order derivatives. In the above example the objective function is strictly concave and unconstrained, so that we can consider optimality for $x_1^* = 6$ and $x_2^* = 7$.

The constrained nonlinear objective function presents some difficulties, but it is often possible to solve these problems with simple mathematical tools from calculus. Let us assume the following nonlinear programming problem:[2]

$$\text{Max } f(x_1,x_2) = 10x_1 + 20x_2 + x_1x_2 - 2x_1^2 - 2x_2^2,$$

subject to

$$g_1(x_1,x_2) = 7 - x_1 \geq 0,$$
$$g_2(x_1,x_2) = 8 - x_2 \geq 0,$$
$$g_3(x_1,x_2) = 10 - x_1 - x_2 \geq 0,$$
$$x_1, x_2 \geq 0.$$

Application of the optimal search routine shows that $f(x_1,x_2)$ is continuous for all real-number values of x_1 and x_2, and the solution space set is closed and bounded so that we can use classical calculus for optimization. This requires taking the partial derivatives:

$$\frac{\partial f}{\partial x_1} = 10 + x_2 - 4x_1,$$

$$\frac{\partial f}{\partial x_2} = 20 + x_1 - 4x_2.$$

Setting these equal to zero and solving the simultaneous equations yield $\hat{x}_1 = 4$ and $\hat{x}_2 = 6$. One could confirm that the objective function is strictly concave (in fact, the second partial derivatives are constants); hence, if $\hat{x}_1$ and $\hat{x}_2$ are feasible solutions, a maximum is guaranteed by the optimal search routine. Feasibility of solutions is checked by substitution of values in the original problem, and one can see that the maximum values are feasible — in fact, they lie on the boundary — which guarantees that $x_1^* = 4$, $x_2^* = 6$; therefore, $f(x_1^*,x_2^*) = 80$. This example is mapped in Fig. 8:4.

[2] For a more detailed treatment of this problem, see Charles R. Carr and Charles W. Howe, *Quantitative Decision Procedures in Management and Economics: Deterministic Theory and Applications* (New York: McGraw-Hill, 1964), pp. 236-248.

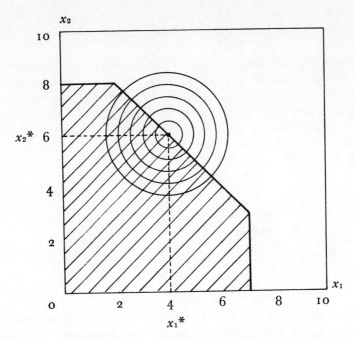

FIG. 8:4. Optimal solution of nonlinear programming example.

The example has a fortuitous optimal solution because the maximum points found by partial differentiation were feasible solutions, which means that an interior or boundary solution exists. Many examples are less fortuitous in that maximum or minimum points found by partial differentiation are not feasible solutions, but exterior solutions may exist. Assuming that the objective function is everywhere differentiable, this requires a boundary search according to the optimal search routine. Partial differentiation is useful in such a boundary search because it offers the ability to slice the function along axes formed by constraints — the procedure, nonetheless, is long and tedious for even simple problems.

METHOD OF LAGRANGE

Another category of solution algorithms for nonlinear programming borrows the name of Joseph Louis, Comte de Lagrange (1736-1813), the Franco-Italian mathematician who made such historic advances for mathematics in analysis, differential equations, maximum-minimum problems, and probability. The method of Lagrange is particularly useful for exterior solutions, even though it is applicable to boundary and interior solutions as well.

The nonlinear programming problem must be expressed in terms of an objective function, subject to equality constraints for the method of Lagrange. If one can achieve this, the method of Lagrange can be used to develop a new function, called the *Lagrangian function*, which incorporates the constraints into a single equation, thus allowing for the optimal solution of an unconstrained function. The general form which must be adapted is

$$\text{Opt} f(x_1, x_2, \ldots, x_n),$$

subject to

$$g_1(x_1, x_2, \ldots, x_n) = 0,$$
$$g_2(x_1, x_2, \ldots, x_n) = 0,$$
$$\cdot \qquad\qquad\qquad \cdot$$
$$\cdot \qquad\qquad\qquad \cdot$$
$$\cdot \qquad\qquad\qquad \cdot$$
$$g_i(x_1, x_2, \ldots, x_n) = 0,$$

where f and g are everywhere differentiable. Notice that the nonnegativity constraint is omitted since it is not necessary in this procedure.

The theory of the Lagrangian function is applicable to nonlinear programming if one considers some extensions of calculus. Assume that the nonlinear programming problem is expressed as

$$\text{Opt} f(x_1, x_2),$$

subject to

$$g(x_1, x_2) = 0.$$

The effect of the equality restriction is that the search for optimal x_1 and x_2 values should be limited to those values which equal zero as a function, $g(x_1, x_2)$. In essence, borrowing from the theory of linear models, we see that x_1 is interrelated to x_2 because of the equality constraint; hence x_2 is a function of x_1. Since this is so, we can define the calculus concept known as the *total derivative* in the following manner:

$$\frac{dg}{dx_1} = g_{x_1} + g_{x_2}\frac{d_{x_2}}{d_{x_1}} = 0.$$

It should be clearly understood that this expression is not the partial derivative of g with respect to x_1; rather, it represents the rate of change of g in the direction of x_1. The partial derivatives of g with respect to x_1 and x_2 are represented by g_{x_1} and g_{x_2}, such that

$$\frac{\partial g}{\partial x_1} = g_{x_1},$$

$$\frac{\partial g}{\partial x_2} = g_{x_2}.$$

Interpretation of the rate of change of x_1 simultaneously with x_2, within the constraint formed by $g(x_1,x_2) = 0$, is granted by the expression dx_1/dx_2. By manipulating the expression for the total derivative, one can easily verify that

$$\frac{dx_2}{dx_1} = -\frac{g_{x_1}}{g_{x_2}}.$$

This means that the simultaneous rate of change of x_2 with respect to x_1 is equal to the negative of the reciprocal of the partial derivative ratio. An example may be enlightening; let

$$g(x_1,x_2) = x_1 + 3x_2 - 6 = 0;$$

taking partial derivatives,

$$\frac{\partial g}{\partial x_1} = g_{x_1} = 1,$$

$$\frac{\partial g}{\partial x_2} = g_{x_2} = 3;$$

by rearrangement of terms

$$x_2 = \frac{6 - x_1}{3};$$

taking the first derivative results in

$$\frac{dx_2}{dx_1} = -\frac{1}{3}.$$

Then, by substitution for the terms ∂x_1, ∂x_2, and dx_1/dx_2 in the definition of the total derivative,

$$\frac{dg}{dx_1} = g_{x_1} + g_{x_2}\frac{dx_2}{dx_1} = 0,$$

$$\frac{dg}{dx_1} = 1 + 3\left(-\frac{1}{3}\right) = 0.$$

The same definitions hold for the objective function f, so that

$$\frac{df}{dx_1} = f_{x_1} + f_{x_2}\frac{dx_2}{dx_1} = 0.$$

By substitution of

$$\frac{dx_2}{dx_1} = -\frac{g_{x_1}}{g_{x_2}}$$

in the total derivative of f, one finds by manipulation of terms that

$$\frac{f_{x_1}}{g_{x_1}} = \frac{f_{x_2}}{g_{x_2}}.$$

This relationship shows that the ratios of the partial derivatives of f and g must be equal for optimization. Using the *Lagrangian multiplier* λ to stand for this proportion, we get the expression

$$\frac{f_{x_1}}{g_{x_2}} = \frac{f_{x_2}}{g_{x_2}} = -\lambda,$$

which also can be stated by

$$f_{x_1} + \lambda g_{x_2} = 0,$$

$$f_{x_2} + \lambda g_{x_2} = 0.$$

The theory of Lagrangian multipliers and functions is put to work in nonlinear programming by forming the Lagrangian function, which incorporates the constraints into the objective function. This can be seen from our preceding terms as

$$\text{Opt } L\,(x_1, x_2, \lambda) = f(x_1, x_2) + \lambda g(x_1, x_2).$$

The partial derivatives can be used to optimize this unconstrained Lagrangian function such that

$$\frac{\partial L}{\partial x_1} = \frac{\partial f}{\partial x_1} + \lambda \frac{\partial g}{\partial x_1} = 0,$$

$$\frac{\partial L}{\partial x_2} = \frac{\partial f}{\partial x_2} + \lambda \frac{\partial g}{\partial x_2} = 0,$$

$$\frac{\partial L}{\partial \lambda} = g(x_1, x_2) = 0.$$

Note that the partial derivative of the term with the Lagrangian multiplier is the original constraint expression. The partial derivatives form a set of simultaneous equations which can often be solved to find the optimal values of x_n^* and λ_i^*.

Referring to the example used in the discussion of classical calculus, we can change the constraints to illustrate a case where the classical calculus approach yields a set of maximum values which is not a feasible solution;

the existence of an exterior solution makes the method of Lagrange popular. Restating the original problem, we have

$$\text{Max } 10x_1 + 20x_2 + x_1x_2 - 2x_1^2 - 2x_2^2,$$

subject to

$$8 - x_1 - x_2 = 0.$$

Our previous solution to this problem, $\hat{x}_1 = 4$ and $\hat{x}_2 = 6$, is no longer feasible because of the equality constraint. We can form the Lagrangian function as follows:

$$\text{Max } L\,(x_1, x_2, \lambda) = 10x_1 + 20x_2 + x_1x_2 - 2x_1^2 - 2x_2^2 + \lambda(8 - x_1 - x_2).$$

The partial derivatives set equal to zero are

$$\frac{\partial L}{\partial x_1} = 10 + x_2 - 4x_1 - \lambda = 0,$$

$$\frac{\partial L}{\partial x_2} = 20 + x_1 - 4x_2 - \lambda = 0,$$

$$\frac{\partial L}{\partial \lambda} = 8 - x_1 - x_2 = 0.$$

Solution of these three simultaneous equations shows that $\lambda^* = 3$, $x_1^* = 3$, and $x_2^* = 5$. One can extend the use of the Lagrangian multiplier and function to more complex problems by using $\lambda_i[g_i(x_1, x_2, \ldots, x_n)]$ such that each constraint has a unique Lagrangian multiplier which can be incorporated into the Lagrangian function.

The Lagrangian multiplier not only serves as a useful algorithmic tool but it also represents a concept we have already discussed as part of the dual solution of linear programs. Specifically, we can state, although we will not take the space to prove, that the Lagrangian multiplier when optimized, λ^*, is the resource or shadow price found by the dual solution. The interpretation is that one can relax constraint g_i by one unit, and the improvement in the objective function will be the payoff rate of λ^*. To reiterate somewhat, this is most useful information for planning and programming of urban problem solutions.

GRADIENT METHOD

The third basic category of algorithms for solving nonlinear programming problems is a child of the computer age. While the mathematical theory of the gradient method is not new, the advent of large-scale computers with incredibly fast computational times has made this method more acceptable. Software and systems capabilities give further impetus for using the gradient method, since it is difficult to write programs for classical calculus and Lagrangian methods.

The gradient method develops a series of *successive approximations* by which one eventually gets closer and closer to finding an optimal solution to a problem. The term *gradient* comes from the formulation of a vector of partial derivatives of decision variables in the objective function which points the way toward values that increase or decrease the objective function efficaciously. The gradient allows an approximation of a quasi-complete enumeration, so to speak, by showing the analyst the most direct route or, as it is commonly called, the *path of steepest ascent*. An analogy, albeit a crude one, is that of a blindfolded person walking up a hill with a friend shouting directions from the foot of the hill — eventually, the shouts will be less meaningful and one can sense intrinsically and intuitively the steepness of the hill. When the steepness feels negligible, one can safely assume that he has reached the peak. Unfortunately, the mathematical equivalent of this process lacks the real-life test of removing one's blindfold to verify success.

Many methods and variations of the gradient method have been devised. For practical purposes we can say that there are two classes of algorithms within the gradient category: (1) *steepest ascent* and (2) *response surface*. The steepest-ascent class attempts to direct the analyst up (or down) the hill formed by the objective function in the most efficient way — this generally means a path that is perpendicular to contours of the objective function's bowl-like form.

An example of the steepest-ascent class is readily available for an unconstrained nonlinear function. Assume the nonlinear problem where one seeks to

$$\text{Opt} f(x_1, x_2, \ldots, x_n).$$

Letting f_{x_i} represent the various partial derivatives of the function and $X = (x_1, x_2, \ldots, x_n)$, the gradient is formed by

$$f_x = \begin{bmatrix} f_{x_1} \\ f_{x_2} \\ \cdot \\ \cdot \\ \cdot \\ f_{x_n} \end{bmatrix}.$$

A starting point must be selected for the computer to help one make the climb — this is usually an arbitrary selection based on intuition. Calling the starting point X_1, then by definition

$$X_1' = (x_{11}, x_{12}, \ldots, x_{1n}).$$

The next point up the hill should be in the direction indicated by the gradient, since that guarantees a perpendicular and steep climb over the contours. An element of the change vector can be denoted as

$$d_{1i} = f_{xi}(x_{11}, x_{12}, \ldots, x_{1n}), \text{ for } i = 1, 2, \ldots, n.$$

Many means exist for the computation of the next point, X_2, and all needed remaining X_m. The most widely used and pragmatic approach is to use an operator k to help guide the climber. The operator k is used as follows:

$$X_2' = x_{2i} = x_{1i} + k_1 d_{1i},$$

where

$$X_2' = (x_{21}, x_{22}, \ldots, x_{2n}).$$

Values for k_m are often constants, but some approaches use a variable arrangement for k_m. Selection of values for k_m is critical, since they must be sufficiently small not to bypass the optimal peaks. Ironically, however, values which are too small create extreme reiteration cycles and waste expensive computer time. Once again the judgment and intuition of the urban analyst become overriding factors. Having weathered this problem, the urban analyst awaits the computer's determination of when it is ready to quit climbing, although the machine must be carefully instructed on how to tell when the top (or bottom) has been reached. There are related problems of *saddle points*, which are conceptually similar to points of inflection, that must be dealt with, depending upon the given circumstances. A graphic analogy of the steepest-ascent approach is shown in Fig. 8:5.

Constrained nonlinear programming problems present somewhat more of a challenge to both urban analyst and computer. The Lagrangian function formulation is the most popular way to deal with the problem if such a function can be utilized. The response-surface class of algorithms has many variations for dealing with the constrained nonlinear programming problem — a practical approach uses a new function directing the climber.[3] The *Carroll algorithm* formulates a new objective function,

[3] C. W. Carroll, "An Operations Research Approach to the Economic Optimization of a Kraft Pulping Process," Ph.D. dissertation, Lawrence College, 1959.

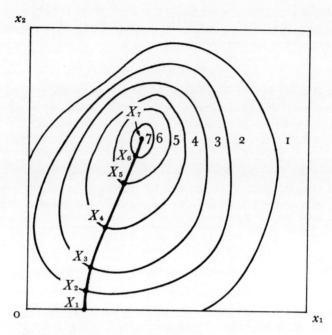

FIG. 8:5. Contour diagram and steepest-ascent path of hypothetical non-linear objective function.

$$A = E - r \sum_{i=1}^{m} W_i/R_i,$$

where

A = created response-surface function,
E = original objective function,
R_i = original constraints such that $R_i > 0$,
W_i = set of weighting penalties for each variable,
r = aggregate weighting criteria.

It should be noted that W_i and r tend to be somewhat arbitrary; hence experience and judgment can substantially reduce the number of iterations. A five-step algorithm is used:

1. Select a starting value for r (relatively small, say, one).

2. Maximize the A function.

3. Reduce the value of r and repeat maximization of A (r must not be negative).

4. Repeat steps 1, 2, and 3 until r gets very close to and $A \approx E$.

This algorithm uses the constraints as penalties, since they make the values for A small; eventually one reaches $r \approx 0$ and can assume an optimal solution.

SPECIAL APPROACHES

A number of special cases exist for nonlinear programming. An important approach used often in urban traffic scheduling is *quadratic programming*. This approach is used for special problems containing quadratic (second-order polynomial) and linear components in the objective function. Partial derivatives of the quadratic component are linear, and this characteristic allows the simplex method to be revived. *Separable programming* is used when the objective function is a sum of functions that can be dis-aggregated — a linear approximation of each allows the simplex method to be used. The *direct linearization* approach is simply the transformation of inherently linear functions to linear expressions and the use of the simplex method.

NONLINEAR PROGRAMMING APPLICATIONS

Significant applications of nonlinear programming techniques in urban analyses have been rare. Interesting applications have been executed by analysts working in quasi-private functions of urban government such as investment planning, bond financing and administration, and user charge-setting and administration. These uses often take advantage of the so-called *portfolio selection problem*. A fine example of the portfolio selection problem was developed by Charles R. Carr and Charles W. Howe.[4] The *Carr-Howe portfolio problem* has a linear objective function and a nonlinear constraint.

Portfolio Selection

The scenario for this problem is a portfolio selection limited to two securities — with no particular amount of total purchase limit established — and policy decisions to maximize dividend income and appreciation in the form of capital gains. The decision has been made to give twice the weight to appreciation as to capital gains. Since uncertainty is inherent, public

[4] Carr and Howe, *Quantitative Decision Procedures*, p. 253.

officials have suggested the use of a risk index for each stock, which we can take as given in the form

$$0.002x_1^2 + 0.003x_2^2 = 140,$$

where

$$x_1 = \text{first security},$$
$$x_2 = \text{second security},$$

while all other parameters stand for given risk factors which have been determined by past performance. Recent trends show that x_1 is expected to appreciate by 10 percent and have a dividend yield of 8 percent; x_2 is expected to appreciate by 15 percent and have a dividend yield of 4 percent over the next year.

The problem is formulated as

$$\text{Max } U(x_1, x_2) = 2(.10x_1 + .15x_2) + .08x_1 + .04x_2$$
$$= .28x_1 + .34x_2,$$

subject to

$$140 - .002x_1^2 - .003x_2^2 = 0.$$

The Lagrangian function is

$$\text{Max } L(x_1, x_2, \lambda) = .28x_1^2 + .34x_2^2 + \lambda(140 - .002x_1^2 - .003x_2^2);$$

partial differentiation yields

$$\frac{\partial L}{\partial x_1} = .28 - .004x_1\lambda,$$

$$\frac{\partial L}{\partial x_2} = .34 - .006x_2\lambda,$$

$$\frac{\partial L}{\partial \lambda} = 140 - .002x_1^2 - .003x_2^2.$$

Setting partial derivatives equal to zero and solving three simultaneous equations for the three unknowns gives

$$x_1^* = 187.87,$$
$$x_2^* = 152.74,$$
$$\lambda^* = 0.39,$$
$$U(x_1^*, x_2^*) = 94.66.$$

However, the real, unweighted return per year would be $62.91 on an investment of $340.61.

Nonlinear Traffic and Land Use

Some sparse work has been undertaken on the development of nonlinear traffic and land use models which have a sound capability for optimization through nonlinear programming. The *polimetric model,* an early if somewhat less successful version of the *Boston region empiric model,* is essentially a set of nonlinear equations for differences in activities in various zones. It was later used in the Philadelphia region under the acronym of *Resloc* in a modified format.[5] Both of these models represent the forefront of contemporary knowledge in using the capabilities and potentials of nonlinear models and inherent nonlinear programming for urban development problems.

DYNAMIC PROGRAMMING

Everything that we have examined in mathematical programming to this point has casually assumed that individual optimization decisions would result in overall optimization in the future or at the end of the planning period. Dynamic programming is based on the idea that some decisions must be made for the whole system in a sequence of time in a planning period in order to reach a true optimum. For example, in a 20-year planning period most mathematical programming techniques would hold that an annual optimization decision would result in an optimal urban system at the end of 20 years, even if simply by aggregation. Dynamic programming theory holds that the urban system must be optimized over the full period of 20 years in a sequence of optimal decisions which are related in time and space — hence time and space become critical, and one must optimize backward from the true optimum (backward induction).

Dynamic programming was originated by Richard E. Bellman in the late 1950s and early 1960s while he was a young scientist with the RAND Corporation. The theory and application of dynamic programming have been highly developed by Bellman, his colleagues, and several other scientists and mathematicians. Applications have been largely computer-based optimization of multistage decision problems, particularly in such areas as rocket trajectories and flight, inventory and production scheduling, feedback-controlled systems, and allocation of scarce resources. The last area is especially interesting to urban analysts.

The crux of dynamic programming theory is bounded by Bellman's *principle of optimality:* "An optimal policy has the property that, what-

[5] Ira S. Lowry, "Seven Models of Urban Development: A Structural Comparison," in George C. Hemmens, ed., *Urban Development Models* (Washington, D.C.: Highway Research Board, 1968), pp. 121-163.

ever the initial state and initial decision are, the remaining decisions must constitute an optimal policy with respect to the state resulting from the first decision."[6] The principle of optimality is one of those curious paradoxes of the English language in that its meaning is more complicated than its statement. Dynamic programming is based upon the mathematical notion that regardless of the starting point, all other points to be reached must be optimal. Such a notion is often called *recursion* because optimization must occur step by step over several stages. Thus the concepts of a state, or the instantaneous condition of a system — such as the discrete examples we used when discussing Markov processes for a toll booth — and a stage, or a particular point in time during the planning period, become crucial for dynamic programming. A major utility of dynamic programming is for urban analysis because it is a mathematical theory and method which inculcates the notion that one can change the state of a system by making decisions about it in optimal sequences of stages such that the overall outcome is an optimal system.

Dynamic programming is conceptually the most potent of the mathematical programming techniques, although, computationally, linear programming is more powerful. Algorithmic techniques for dynamic programming are many and varied, but the most well known are the *numeric search routine* and *classical calculus search routine*. The result of these conditions is that dynamic programming has considerable intellectual merit for urban analysis because questions become as important as answers. Complications arise in the real world in that sometimes there is a finite number of consecutive decisions to be made at each corresponding stage, called a *bounded horizon*, but sometimes there is an indefinite number of decisions to be made over an indefinite number of stages, called an *unbounded horizon*.

A general examination of recursive concepts and numeric search routines is valuable at this point for a problem with a bounded horizon. Let the given variable x be divided into n parts in such a way that the product is a maximum. Recursive programming is useful for this problem if we let $f_n(x)$ be equal to the maximum product. This simply means that we assume x to be fixed and let n vary over all positive integers; hence x becomes a function of n. We can define $f_1(x) = x$ as the initial state, and the initial decision can be represented by y. This results in the state just preceding the second decision being $x - y$. For $n = 2$, then

$$f_2(x) = \operatorname{Max} y f_1(x - y) = y(x - y),$$

[6] Richard E. Bellman, *Dynamic Programming* (Princeton, N.J.: Princeton University Press, 1957).

subject to

$$0 \leq y \leq x,$$

which is usually written in dynamic programming practice as

$$f_2(x) = \underset{0 \leq y \leq x}{\text{Max}}\{y(x-y)\}.$$

Taking the first derivative and setting it equal to zero allows one to solve this stage as $y^* = x/2$, which is a feasible solution. Since $n = 2$, the optimal decision sequence is $(x/2, x/2)$, or

$$f_2(x) = x^2/4.$$

Bellman's principle of optimality allows one to generalize the above to m parts or stages after the initial decision, which is written as

$$f_{m+1}(x) = \underset{0 \leq y \leq x}{\text{Max}}\{y f_m(x-y)\}.$$

Optimizing, this expression becomes

$$f_{m+1}(x) = y^* f_m(x - y^*).$$

We can explore this further by letting $n = 2, 3, \ldots, m$, and we can intuitively see that the optimal decision sequence will be y^* plus the mth decision for $x - y^*$. For example, for $n = 3$,

$$f_3(x) = \underset{0 \leq y \leq x}{\text{Max}}\left\{y\frac{(x-y)^2}{4}\right\}$$

and $y^* = x/3$, and the optimal decision becomes $(x/3, x/3, x/3) = x^3/27$. We can continue this recursion to generalize that the optimal decision will always be $(x/n, x/n, x/n, \ldots, x/n)$, so that

$$f_n(x) = (x/n)^n.$$

This generalizes to

$$f_{n+1}(x) = \underset{0 \leq y \leq x}{\text{Max}}\left\{y\left[\frac{(x-y)}{n}\right]^n\right\}.$$

Optimizing this expression yields $y^* = x/n + 1$, or the decision sequence $[n/(n+1)]x$, which is

$$[x/(n+1), x/(n+1), \ldots, x/(n+1)],$$

or

$$f_{n+1}(x) = [x/(n+1)]^{n+1},$$

and the same expression holds for m and $m + 1$.

This type of recursive programming is adaptable to computer program-ming but is limited in that only one constraint is easily handled. The classical calculus search routine is used when several constraints are in-cluded for a bounded-horizon problem. Consider a problem similar to the above: let $X = x_1, x_2, \ldots, x_n$ and solve

$$\text{Max} \, y = x_1, x_2, \ldots, x_n,$$

subject to

$$\sum_{i=1}^{n} x_i = X,$$

$$x_1 \geq 0,$$
$$x_2 \geq 0,$$
$$\cdot$$
$$\cdot$$
$$\cdot$$
$$x_n \geq 0.$$

Formulating a Lagrangian function, we find

$$\text{Max} \, L = x_1, x_2, \ldots, x_n + \lambda\Big[X - \sum_{i=1}^{n} x_i\Big].$$

The solution is either a subset $(x_1, x_2, \ldots, x_n)$ of $(x_1, x_2, \ldots, x_n, \lambda)$ or a boundary of one of the constraint planes where $x_i = 0$. Taking par-tial derivatives and setting to zero,

$$\frac{\partial L}{\partial x_i} = 0, \, i = 1, 2, \ldots, n,$$

$$\frac{\partial L}{\partial \lambda} = X - \sum_{i=1}^{n} x_i = 0,$$

one can find that

$$x_i^* = \frac{k}{n}, \, i = 1, 2, \ldots, n,$$

or

$$y = \left(\frac{k}{n}\right)^n.$$

The inherent distinction between the numerical and the classical cal-culus search routines is that the former changes a problem with n variables into n problems with one variable in each. The classical calculus search routine is more elegant, but partial derivatives may not always exist, and an optimal solution may lie along a boundary which will not be revealed by partial differentiation. Hence the computational aspects of the bounded-horizon problem are formidable. The future looks brighter in that modern computers and software are improving daily, and the numerical search abilities are becoming vastly improved.

Dynamic programming problems with an unbounded horizon have the effect of making a difficult problem of computation become almost unthinkable. Nevertheless, there is considerable interest in this sort of problem. The unbounded-horizon problem is characterized as one in which the number of optimal decision stages is not known or is indefinite. It is analogous to developing a plan for the future of an urban system with no particular end-point in mind — such fuzzy circumstances are not alien to urban systems planning. Few plans are made for urban systems that consider the end-point as absolute. As the planning period approaches the horizon stage, changes and modifications are made in plans. The dynamic programming technique is useful in such a process in that some problems have been solved which consider costs as the key variable. These problems use a discount rate for costs such that an average cost per decision can be determined over an indefinite, sometimes infinite, planning period. The mathematics is quite advanced and we shall not belabor it. Suffice it to say that integral series of equations can be formulated which operate under conditions such that the discounted costs are minimized, and discounted costs converge with the average cost per decision as the number of decisions approaches infinity.

DYNAMIC PROGRAMMING APPLICATIONS

The SEWRPC land use design model, which was discussed in its basic linear programming formulation, has a dynamic programming counterpart. This has been one of the few large-scale applications of dynamic programming to urban analysis.

Land Use Design Model

The allocation application is used for land as a resource which has alternative uses. The typical formulation is based upon

$$R(x_1, x_2, \ldots, x_n) = g_1(x_1) + g_2(x_2) + \ldots + g_n(x_n),$$

where $X = x_1 + x_2 + \ldots + x_n$ and $x_i \geq 0$. The function R is called the *return function* in that it represents the utility, such as minimum costs, etc., of allocating the scarce resource of land among X uses. This formulation is conceptually superior to linear programming because land uses can be integers and the return function can be nonlinear.

The basic resource-allocation algorithm of dynamic programming is used to reduce the necessity of a complete numeric search routine by using the procedure

$$f_n(X) = \underset{0 \leq x_n \leq X}{\text{Min}} [g_n(x_n) + f_{n-1}(X - x_n)],$$

where

$$f_1(X) = \text{Min} [g_1(X)],$$
$$n = 2, 3, \ldots, N,$$
$$x_n \geq 0.$$

This algorithm is used for the computation first of the minimum cost for each level of land assigned to the first land use. The first solution $f_1(X)$ is the minimum of the return function $g_1(x_1)$. The second-stage decision determines the minimum costs for the first and second land uses in combination by yielding

$$f_2(X) = \underset{0 \leq x_2 \leq X}{\text{Min}} [g_2(x_2) + f_1(X - x_2)].$$

Consecutive stages are minimized for costs of land development of land uses up to the nth stage — note that time is replaced by land uses in this formulation. The computation for the nth land use is interpreted to represent the minimum costs of all land uses for each level of land in the region. Using backward induction, the series of decisions $f_1, f_2, \ldots, f_n$ is programmed in a consecutive series starting with f_n, x_n; proceeding to the second stage (which is actually the next to the last stage, since this algorithm considers the last stage as the first stage), which is $f_{n-1}, X - x_n$; and continuing in the same fashion for $f_{n-2}, \ldots, f_1$. The final result is that all of the land in the urban system is assigned in order to minimize overall costs of development (note that the planning period is assumed to be a given year in the future).

Experience with the above approach has demonstrated that an alternative formulation is necessary for including several constraints. The classical calculus search routine can be employed and the problem restated as

$$\text{Min } R(x_1, x_2, \ldots, x_n) = g_1(x_1) + g_2(x_2) + \ldots + g_n(x_n),$$

subject to

$$\sum_{i=1}^{k} \left(\sum_{j=1}^{n} a_{ij} x_j \right) \leq x_i,$$
$$x_i \geq 0.$$

The return function is the cost of land development, and the constraints are all restrictions on the objective function, such as total land use demands and land use relationships that were formulated for the linear programming version. The Lagrangian function is

$$\text{Min } L(x_1, x_2, \ldots, x_n, \lambda) = \sum_{j=1}^{n} g_j(x_j) - \sum_{i=1}^{k} \lambda_i(x_i - \sum_{j=1}^{n} a_{ij}x_j).$$

Horizon Plan

The theory of dynamic programming was found useful for the planning of New Jersey's urban development.[7] Analysts working with various indicators and predictive models determined that the full urban development of New Jersey would occur around 2058 A.D. with a population of 20,000,000. This was considered to be the horizon point or the year beyond which no further predictions could be made. Over a period of years several alternative development plans were tested; using the backward-induction concept and numerical search routines, consecutive decision stages were devised which were called *subhorizon plans*. The analysts cautioned that the subhorizon plans for each alternative development strategy would have to be reviewed periodically as one got nearer and nearer to the horizon point. While the approach is not highly sophisticated in mathematical terms, it does imply that the theory of dynamic programming has great potential for urban systems planning.

STOCHASTIC PROGRAMMING

Each of the various types of mathematical programming that we have examined has been based upon the assumption that all of the parameters used are deterministic in nature — this is usually called *decision-under-certainty theory*. Real-world problems often appear to be based upon uncertainty about many matters which affect the parameters of mathematical programming — hence this general field of study is often called *decision-under-uncertainty theory*. Common practice among urban analysts is to develop deterministic mathematical programming models even where uncertainty is found in order to simplify the model, even if at the expense of

---

[7] There were numerous publications over a period of years emanating from this effort. The introductory monograph is New Jersey Division of State and Regional Planning, *The Various Alternatives of the Horizon Planning Concept* (Trenton, N.J., 1964).

rendering only an approximation of the real world. One should recall that this practice is logically sound in that by definition models are only representations of the real world. In some urban problems, however, uncertainty is too strong to allow for deterministic mathematical programming models to be used, and the urban analyst must employ stochastic mathematical programming models.

Stochastic mathematical programming has many variations and forms, and, in general, all problems are not readily solved. Stochastic mathematical programming models are considerably more complex than their deterministic counterparts in both mathematical and computational perspectives.

The simplest type of stochastic programming model is the *stochastic linear programming model*. One may recall that the linear programming model was expressed by

$$\text{Max} \, y = \sum_{i=1}^{n} c_i x_i,$$

subject to

$$\sum_{i=1}^{n} a_{ji} x_i \leq b_j,$$

$$x_i \geq 0,$$

where $i = (1, 2, \ldots, n)$ and $j = (1, 2, \ldots, m)$. In matrix terms

$$\text{Max} \, y = cx,$$

subject to

$$Ax \leq b,$$
$$x \geq 0.$$

Suppose that the a_{ji}, b_j, and c_i variables are all or partly random variables; one must restate the linear programming problem in corresponding stochastic terms.

Assume that the c_i parameters are random variables; then the objective function must be restated because it is not valid to optimize a decision variable with random-variable parameters in terms of determinism. The objective function can be cast in stochastic terms by the expression

$$\text{Max} \, E(y) = \sum_{i=1}^{n} E(c_i) x_i = E(cx).$$

The constraints would require similar restatements if they contained random variables. In practical applications urban analysts attempt to formulate stochastic linear programming problems with stochastic objective functions and deterministic linear constraints — this is the most elementary case.

Even with these simplifying assumptions, only certain cases can be solved. A sound approach has been developed in which stochastic linear programming problems of this type can be solved by assuming that the random variables can take any value within a finite set of values. This means that there will be only a finite number of combinations of parameter values to consider.[8] The algorithm uses a matrix M, where

$$M = \begin{bmatrix} c_1 & c_2 & . & . & . & c_n & 0 \\ a_{11} & a_{12} & . & . & . & a_{1n} & b_1 \\ a_{21} & a_{22} & . & . & . & a_{2n} & b_2 \\ . & . & & & & . & . \\ . & . & & & & . & . \\ . & . & & & & . & . \\ a_{m1} & a_{m2} & . & . & . & a_{mn} & b_m \end{bmatrix}.$$

Using matrices and vectors,

$$M = \begin{array}{c|c|c} & n & 1 \\ \hline 1 & c & 0 \\ \hline m & A & b \end{array}.$$

Since some of the elements of M are random, it can take on any of a finite set of possibilities, which can be represented by $_1M, _2M, _3M, \ldots, _nM$. If we let p_k stand for the probability of k, where $k = (1, 2, \ldots, n)$, then the probability that M will be $_kM$ would be

$$\sum_{k=1}^{n} p_k = 1.$$

Assuming that the probabilities can be estimated, we can let $c^{(k)}$, $A^{(k)}$, and $b^{(k)}$ represent the respective elements of $_kM$, so that

$$_kM = \begin{array}{c|c|c} & n & 1 \\ \hline 1 & c^{(k)} & 0 \\ \hline m & A^{(k)} & b^{(k)} \end{array}.$$

This means that $c^{(k)}$, $A^{(k)}$, and $b^{(k)}$ are what c, A, and b become when $M = _kM$. The most common decision situation would call for the solution of the optimization model for x_i before computing further information

[8] Frederick S. Hillier and Gerald J. Lieberman, *Introduction to Operations Research* (San Francisco: Holden-Day, 1967), pp. 530-536.

about M. In such a case the optimization problem, in matrix terms, is stated by

$$\text{Max } E(y) = \sum_{k=1}^{n} p_k c^{(k)} x,$$

subject to

$$A^{(k)}x \leq b^{(k)},$$
$$x \geq 0.$$

The simplex method can be used to solve this problem when the number of finite possibilities (n) is not unreasonably large. Special cases of the above problem may arise when values of x_i cannot be determined until values for random elements of M are known. In practical terms this results when decisions are made over different periods of time in a dynamic setting and when decisions are made by different decision-makers working at different parts of an urban system. Such special cases require that the decision variables x_i also take on a set of finite possibilities k and that various forms of $_kM$ be used where there are incomplete definitions of the elements. While somewhat cumbersome, this special case is solvable, although the computations are quite extensive.

Stochastic linear programming is based upon the assumption that the constraints must be satisfied in order for an optimal solution to be found. Since real-world problems often have a large number of various parameter combinations — because the parameters are random — it is sometimes practical to use a method which requires only that the constraints be satisfied by most of the parameter combinations. This approach to stochastic programming is called *chance-constrained programming*.[9] In essence, chance-constrained programming uses an algorithm which designates that nonnegative solution which probably will satisfy most of the original constraints as the random variables take on their different values.

The algorithm commonly used requires that the original constraints,

$$\sum_{i=1}^{n} a_{ji}x_i \leq b_j,$$

be replaced by

$$P\left\{\sum_{i=1}^{n} a_{ji}x_i \leq b_j\right\} \geq q_i,$$

where q_i is a constant such that $0 \leq q_i \leq 1$.

[9] A. Charnes and W. W. Cooper, "Chance-Constrained Programming," *Management Science*, 6, no. 1 (Jan., 1959), 73-80.

Still in its infancy, general algorithmic approaches to solving the chance-constrained programming model do not exist. Only special cases of the chance-constrained programming model can be solved using algorithms: (1) when a_{ji} are constants and some or all of the c_i and b_j are random variables, (2) when the probability density function of b_j is the normal model, and (3) when c_i is not functionally related to b_j. These special conditions allow for the use of a rather complicated algorithm which is basically an elaborate attempt to develop an equivalent linear programming model that can be solved by the simplex method. This procedure results in a considerable expansion of the original problem into an involved and extensive model with various combinations and permutations which must be considered for possible optimal solutions.

In order to overcome the problems of finding equivalent linear programming problems for stochastic linear programming models that become too large and cumbersome for practical solution, and to further incorporate the concepts of dynamic programming, much effort has been directed in recent years toward *stochastic dynamic programming models*. These models require forms of mathematics that we consider beyond the scope of our intended readers. The urban analyst will usually require the assistance of a mathematical programming specialist when dealing with such formulations. Interestingly enough, however, the stochastic dynamic programming model is only a little more difficult in strict mathematical terms than a deterministic dynamic programming problem.

Stochastic dynamic programming models are usually formulated as bounded-horizon problems and are used for such matters as distribution, transportation and routing, scheduling, inventories, forecasting, and complex decisions when expressed in networks, usually called *decision trees*. Random variables tend to appear in the objective function rather than in the states, stages, or other constraints. The concepts of sequential decisions and backward induction that are established in deterministic dynamic programming generally hold for stochastic dynamic programming models.

Several algorithms have been developed and tested for the solution of certain types of stochastic dynamic programming models which employ basic concepts connected with Markov chains. In fact, this type of problem is sometimes called *dynamic programming in Markov chains*. Most of the solvable models seek to minimize the costs, present value, or other economic factors associated with the probability of a system being in a given state. This conceptualization lends itself to Markov chains, which express such probabilities. For example, if one developed a decision tree which used a Markov chain to express the probability that the system would be in state

j, given that the decision d was made in state i, which is often expressed as

$$p(j|i,d),$$

then associated cost factors could be attached to a given sequential decision y_i. If we assume that the costs can be expressed by c_{ij} and the values must be discounted by some factor a in the expression ay_i, the generalized recursion for the stochastic dynamic programming is of the type

$$y_i = \underset{d \in D(i)}{\text{Min}} \left[\sum_{j=0}^{i-1} p(j \mid i, d) \, ay_i + c_{id} \right], \, i \neq 0 \text{ and } y_0 \approx 0,$$

where $D(i)$ is the set of possible decisions at state i.[10]

Recursive techniques and such others as *successive approximations* are used to solve many problems expressed in stochastic dynamic programming terms. Computer-based solutions are often mandatory, since the recursions are numerous, and the urban analyst would be wise to include an experienced computer programmer on any team that is organized for dealing with these problems.

APPLIED STOCHASTIC PROGRAMMING

We know of no major urban analyses that were based upon stochastic programming methods, although we have heard of several interesting theoretical and exploratory projects. Our comments on applications are limited to a few prospects and to a call for further research on the applications of these methods, since the concepts are so stimulating for urban problems.

The Center of Urban and Regional Studies at the University of North Carolina has pioneered in the development of residential growth models using Markov processes over a period of years.[11] Similar work concerning demography, migration, traffic, and economic growth is underway. Most of the models that we are familiar with can be cast in stochastic programming constructs with some additional effort and mathematical and computer programming expertise. This approach would allow for optimization of these models and would ease the mission of urban analysts and urban systems planners.

[10] Harvey M. Wagner, *Principles of Operations Research* (Englewood Cliffs, N.J.: Prentice-Hall, 1969), pp. 739-765.

[11] F. S. Chapin, T. G. Donnelly, and S. F. Weiss, *A Probabilistic Model for Residential Growth* (Chapel Hill: Institute for Research in Social Science, University of North Carolina, 1964).

PROSPECTS

We have purposely treaded lightly on the mathematical aspects of non-linear, dynamic, and stochastic programming, partly out of sympathy for the reader and partly because we believe that these are advanced methods which are more properly left to specialists and technicians. The basic concepts of the subject, however, should be within the grasp of urban analysts and should serve as a rallying point for the formation of inter-disciplinary teams to deal with these more advanced forms of urban analysis.

Concepts of nonlinear, dynamic, and stochastic programming that we believe are relevant would include nonlinearity, multistage programming, sequential decisions, planning periods and horizons, and Markov processes in mathematical programming. Most of these concepts are particularly new in terms of mathematical chronologies, and it should not surprise the reader that their very infancy has not yet allowed the development of rigorous methods for answering the questions that are raised. These concepts appear to us to lie at the frontiers of knowledge and will most certainly play a major role in future urban analysis.

RECOMMENDED EXERCISES

1. Write a brief essay showing the understanding you have acquired of the following concepts: nonlinearity in objective functions and constraints, sequential decision-making, and random variables in objective functions and constraints. How would you distinguish these concepts among the following forms of mathematical programming: linear programming, non-linear programming, dynamic programming, stochastic programming.

2. Develop several problems that you believe would be relevant for solution by using nonlinear, dynamic, and stochastic programming methods. What practical difficulties do you foresee in the solution of these problems and in the implementation of the results?

FURTHER READING

Wagner, Harvey M. *Principles of Operations Research.* Englewood Cliffs, N.J.: Prentice-Hall, 1969.

The most extensive treatment in one place that we know of concerned with operations research in general and nonlinear, dynamic, and stochastic programming in particular for management problems. The treatment of dynamic and stochastic programming is especially effective and sympathetic toward the non-mathematician.

Hadley, G. *Non-linear and Dynamic Programming.* Reading, Mass.: Addison-Wesley, 1964.

The classic mathematical treatment of nonlinear and dynamic programming theory. The material is written for the specialist and makes many demands on the reader. It will not be especially useful to the mathematically timid, but it will be indispensable to the reader seeking to develop greater knowledge in these areas.

Bellman, Richard E., and Stuart E. Dreyfus. *Applied Dynamic Programming.* Princeton, N.J.: Princeton University Press, 1962.

The classic work in which the originator of dynamic programming and his closest collaborator in theoretical development make the case for applications. The applications are managerial and scientific and not especially related to urban analysis, but there are some fascinating germs of ideas for urban problems.

Going around an obstacle is what we do in solving any kind of problem. People act like hens who solve their problems by muddling through, trying again and again, and succeeding eventually by some lucky accident without much insight into the reasons for their success.

George Polya, *How to Solve It* (1945)

PART IV

SIMULATION

Simulation is one of those terms which has come to mean many things to many people. Urban analysts often deal with the simulation of urban regions with regard to their economic, political, social, and physical components. Psychologists simulate the behavior of an individual person in an urban system — if such a person cannot behave well in an urban system, the therapist may prescribe forms of simulated learning to resolve the problem. Generals simulate the destruction of urban systems, and engineers simulate the mechanical properties of streets, buildings, and utilities of urban systems in order to build them. Thus simulation should be defined depending upon one's point of view of urban systems.

The term *simulation* is derived from the Latin, *simulatus,* which means to *imitate.* It may be recalled that earlier we said that the distinction between simulation and modeling was that the former *imitates* an urban system while the latter *represents* the urban system. Such fine distinctions are hardly needed for simulation and modeling because, in general, simulation is a way of *using* models. In another perspective one can say that representations of real urban systems are used in such a way that they imitate real urban systems. We can state an operational definition of simulation: an approach in which the characteristics, form, and appearance of urban systems are imitated in order to perform vicarious experimentation.

Major use of simulation is made for testing alternative solutions to urban problems by using models to imitate urban systems. This naturally means that experimentation can be perpetrated without disrupting the real world. It also means that colossal failures can sometimes be avoided by discovering errors in solutions. For example, a well-known simulation was conducted by a transportation planning agency in the New York urban system which tested various locations for a bridge between Long Island and Connecticut. The simulation showed that regardless of the location, the bridge would be saturated quickly after opening, and the traffic would become worse rather than better in the areas to be served.

FUNCTIONS OF SIMULATION

There are four major functions associated with the use of simulation in urban analysis.

CHAPTER 9

Simulation

1. *Optimization.* It often occurs that the optimization models we have examined cannot be used for a given problem, or it may arise that optimization models only deal with a part of the problem. Simulation can be used for linking models together in order to attain an overall optimization. This is possible because simulation allows for the approximation of several possible optimal configurations, one of which may be a good estimate of the overall optimization values for a given problem. Simulation also is useful when several possible outcomes could exist for an optimal solution; then its inherent ability to determine and test alternative solutions to problems can be utilized.

2. *Transitional Optimization.* Most of the deterministic optimization models yield optimal values for a steady state or final state of the urban system. Assuming that dynamic or stochastic optimization models cannot be formulated or are too difficult to formulate and compute for a given problem, it may be possible to employ advanced forms of simulation to determine optimal values for urban systems at various points of transition. This useful function of simulation allows for the determination of dynamic optimal solutions even when dynamic programming cannot be used.

3. *Parameter Estimation.* When all else fails in attempting to model an urban problem, it may be possible to use simulation to estimate the parameters of a suitable model. Problems that are most difficult to model are usually associated with poor and inadequate data. If past data are available or at least partial data on the problem in the past, and if the variables are known, simulation can be used to create artificially a data file from which parameters can be estimated. Even when no data are available, for a problem in the future, for example, it may be possible to generate hypotheses which can be used as a basis for simulating the problem and generating data in the artificial ways of simulation.

4. *Gaming.* It often occurs that the urban problem is too difficult, complex, and unwieldy to model. When these conditions occur, usually involving numerous outcomes of decisions and intervening human behavioral values, it is necessary to formulate alternative simulations of the problem. This function is called *gaming* and is dealt with separately in the next chapter because of its widespread popularity in urban analysis.

FORMS OF SIMULATION

Just as there are three basic forms of models, so there are three basic forms of simulation.[1]

1. *Analog.* This is the use of analog models to imitate the urban system. An interesting example of analog simulation is *MONIAC* at the London School of Economics. MONIAC is a series of hydraulic models — with pipes, fluids, outlets, and inlets — which simulate the flow of money in the British economy. Comparable simulations have been developed in the United States as well.

2. *Iconic.* This involves the use of iconic models in real or simulated environments to imitate urban systems. A familiar example from aeronautical engineering involves the use of scale-model airplanes in wind tunnels to simulate flight conditions — this is an iconic simulation under simulated conditions. Urban analysts have developed scale models of urban developments and tested them for drainage and sunlight conditions. Examples of iconic simulations under real-world conditions are found in such projects as the building of test highways which are opened for public use for a period of time.

3. *Symbolic.* This type of simulation involves *numerical* rather than *analytical* evaluation of variables and functions, using symbolic models. The general symbolic expression is

$$W = F(U_i, U_j),$$

where

W = characteristics of the urban system,
U_i = one or more control or noncontrol variables which generate values in a numerical function,
U_j = other independent variables and constants,
F = a numerical function.

Most symbolic simulations involve the random selection of a sample of random variables (U_i) and a set of deterministic variables or constants (U_j) to generate a probability density distribution (continuous) or probability distribution (discrete) for computing numerical values for the outcome (W). Since there can be different sets of values for U_i, there will be corresponding differences in W such that it is better to consider w_i, where $i = 1, 2, \ldots, n$. Thus optimal solutions, parameter estimates, and transitional optimization should be selected from the set $W \in \{w_1, w_2, \ldots, w_n\}$, and the expression is better stated by

$$w_i = f_i(u_i, U_j)$$

for $F = (f_1, f_2, \ldots, f_n)$.

[1] Russell L. Ackoff, *Scientific Method: Optimizing Applied Research Decisions* (New York: Wiley, 1962), pp. 346-351.

While we recognize the utility of analog and iconic models in many problems of urban analysis, we prefer to emphasize symbolic simulation. Symbolic simulation, which we shall simply refer to as simulation, is the most common type found in contemporary urban analysis, and the amount of research and development underway is astounding.

Methods of Simulation

Simulation is used generally in urban analysis when it is not possible to determine optimal solutions from optimizing models and mathematical programming. Such urban problems tend to involve complex interactions among variables and functions and several alternative solutions with varying associated costs and benefits.

There are no underlying, universal, and unified theories for the formulation and solution of simulation. Most simulations are *ad hoc* by nature and highly specific to particular problems. Simulations are even likely to be quite different for similar urban problems in different urban systems. The overall effect of this *ad hoc* nature of simulation is both a problem and a potential. The problem is that assumptions must be made frequently about the urban system even if there is scant knowledge about the characteristics for which assumptions are made. The potential is that simulation becomes a highly flexible and malleable scientific method that can be used for almost any urban problem no matter what the degree of complexity and data inadequacy. Ironically, a common complaint among urban analysts is that simulations are based upon much judgment and intuition in order to develop the *foundation of assumptions* upon which the simulation is built. This often makes it extremely difficult to measure the validity of the simulation without making further judgments and intuitive assumptions about whether or not the problem has been explained and resolved.

SIMULATION AND COMPUTERS

One often hears it said that simulation was made feasible by the development of the digital computer — some even prefer to call these scientific methods by the name *computer simulation*. Beyond a doubt, the speed and accuracy of the computer was the motivating force behind widened use of simulation, although it should be made clear that the theory and method of simulation were pioneered by seventeenth-century mathematicians with interests close to the gaming tables of the French Riviera. The methods were and remain cumbersome and computationally noisome, so that the computer brought an air of feasibility to simulation. Simulation is a numerical method, to reiterate, and requires special programming approaches for computer processing. The result has been a series of entirely new computer programming languages: *SIMSCRIPT, GPSS* (general-purpose system simulator), *DYNAMO,* and others. These languages allow for general algorithmic computation of many different kinds of system simulations.

One could solve simulation problems by "running them on paper," probably with a set of look-up tables for various measures and a trusty desk calculator. Simulation is not impossible without the use of computers. The more important question is whether running large simulation problems on paper is practical. Again we stress the point that computers cannot do anything that a man cannot do, but the computer, devoid of personality and fatigue, can do those things that man can do, like simulation, with incredibly better speed and accuracy. We would conclude this point by arguing that simulation usually requires the use of computers in order to relieve man of unreasonable burdens of computation, although this may be at the expense of voluminous reports from the output of the simulation which must be analyzed by man.

DETERMINISTIC SIMULATION

While most methods of simulation are stochastic, there are several types of simulation which are based on methods that are more deterministic than stochastic. Most of the deterministic simulations are uses of linked models which imply or assume randomness among the variables but which avoid stochastic expressions by using deterministic expressions based upon assumptions.

Many deterministic simulations have their historical roots in the evolution of *social physics,* which is the name given to a movement composed of theorists who attempt to utilize concepts of physical science for the solution of social science problems.[2] The most popular and well-known method of social physics has been the use of the *gravity model,* the simulation use of which is called *interaction simulation,* based upon the transfer of Newtonian mechanics to social and urban masses, be they people, jobs, traffic, sales, or cash flows.

[2] The reader interested in this school might refer to George K. Zipf, *Human Behavior and the Principle of Least Effort* (Reading, Mass.: Addison-Wesley, 1949).

Interaction simulation is historically derived from the *universal law of gravitation*, as expounded in the treatise *Philosophiae Naturalis Principia Mathematica*, written by Sir Isaac Newton (1642-1727). Newton was a mathematician who dedicated his life to the sound and coherent study of *mechanics*. His universal law of gravitation held that an attractive force or interaction between two masses was proportional to the ratio of the product of their masses to the square of the distance between them:

$$F = G \frac{M_1 M_2}{R^2},$$

where

$$F = \text{force of attraction or interaction,}$$
$$M_1, M_2 = \text{masses,}$$
$$G = \text{proportionality constant,}$$
$$R = \text{distance between } M_1 \text{ and } M_2.$$

Application of the universal law of gravitation by social physicists began in the nineteenth century and continued well into the twentieth century. The universal law of gravitation was modified by other laws: Boyle's law, Dalton's law, Charles's law, and Brownian movement. This modification allowed for the *kinetic* effects of forces to alter the interaction. For example, just as barometric pressure and temperature affect the interaction of gases, so do income and employment affect the travel of families. The earliest applications of interaction simulation, as based upon the universal law of gravitation, were concerned with the simulation of population and migration, traffic, communications, and human behavior.

The most common application of interaction simulation in urban analysis is for traffic movements. In this application the interaction simulation assumes a kind of probabilistic attraction which is based upon the universal law of gravitation, but the probabilistic basis is taken no further than an assumption — it is peripheral to computation.

We can develop the interaction simulation by looking at a hypothetical urban system with a population P and data gained from a survey of traffic (usually called an *origin-and-destination survey*) that allows us to measure the number of trips made within the urban system every day by the population.[3] For simplicity in development of these ideas, let us first assume that all of the various sub-areas of the urban system, which we will call *traffic zones*, are relatively homogeneous in size, population, race, income, occupa-

[3] Walter Isard, *Methods of Regional Analysis: An Introduction to Regional Science* (Cambridge, Mass.: M.I.T. Press, 1960), develops the basic concepts and this problem in much more detail for the interested reader. See especially Chapter 11.

tion, education, sex, and general character. We can remove this oversimplification later.

We can generalize our model and determine its mathematical expression if we use the precepts of the universal law of gravitation in its modified form. If we wish to first consider the movements between any traffic zone i to any other traffic zone j, we can assume for further simplicity that the relative costs and time of travel, usually called the *friction factor*, are equal, say zero. Then we can assume that the universal law of gravitation and its implied probability of attraction would hold: the probability of a person making a trip from traffic zone i to traffic zone j would be the ratio of the mass of the population of j to the total mass, P_j/P. For example, this probabilistic assumption would mean that in an urban system of $P = 1,000,000$, where $P_j = 100,000$, the probability of an individual making a trip from any traffic zone i to traffic zone j would be

$$P_j/P = 100,000/1,000,000 = 0.10;$$

more simply, there is a 10 percent probability that an individual will make a trip to traffic zone j from any other traffic zone i.

Since we know the total trips per day (T) from our survey, and the population (P), it can be readily seen that the per capita trips are $T/P = K$. Hence the probability that an average individual will make a trip to traffic zone j on a given day will simply be the per capita trips times the probability of making a trip to traffic zone j:

$$K\left(\frac{P_j}{P}\right).$$

For example, in our urban system of 1,000,000 and traffic zone j of 100,000, we can compute the per capita trips per week as 20. Thus the probability that an individual will make trips to traffic zone j is 0.10, and he is likely to make two trips per week to traffic zone j:

$$20\left(\frac{100,000}{1,000,000}\right) = 2 \text{ trips per week.}$$

If we want to know how many trips can be expected from any traffic zone i to traffic zone j, we simply multiply the per capita measure by the population of the traffic zone:

$$T_{ij} = K\frac{P_i P_j}{P},$$

where T_{ij} = total expected trips from all inhabitants of traffic zone i to traffic zone j for a stated time period (one day, one week, etc.). This same expression can be used to describe the total trips from all traffic zones, including within j itself, by using the summation expression:

$$\sum_{i=1}^{n} T_{ij} = K \sum_{i=1}^{n} \frac{P_i P_j}{P},$$

where $i = 1, 2, \ldots, n$.

This idealized interaction simulation is not practical because of our simplifying assumptions. We must remove these simplifying assumptions about homogeneity and friction factors in order to deal with real-world problems. Since we have an origin-and-destination survey available, however, we can eliminate the simplifying assumptions by incorporating all real-world deviations in a bit of mathematical sleight of hand. We can do this by developing a simple linear model of the real world and incorporating it into our interaction simulation. The simple linear model is computed by plotting the ratio of expected trips (T_{ij}) to observed trips (I_{ij}) against the distance from i to j (d_{ij}) on double logarithmic scales to insure linearity, as shown in Fig. 9:1. The simple linear model will take the familiar form $x = a + by$, or in our terms,

$$\log \frac{I_{ij}}{T_{ij}} = a - b \log d_{ij}.$$

The logarithmic values can be replaced by real-number values by taking the antilogs and letting c stand for the antilog of the constant a, which yields

$$\frac{I_{ij}}{T_{ij}} = \frac{c}{d_{ij}^b}$$

or

$$I_{ij} = \frac{c T_{ij}}{d_{ij}^b}.$$

We have previously said that the expected trips (T_{ij}) could be computed; thus, by substitution,

$$I_{ij} = \frac{c}{d_{ij}^b} \, K \, \frac{P_i P_j}{P} \, = \frac{c K P_i P_j}{d_{ij}^b P}.$$

We can factor out the constant cK/P and substitute another constant G to simplify the expression:

$$I_{ij} = G \, \frac{P_i P_j}{d_{ij}^b}.$$

This interaction simulation gives us the actual trips (I_{ij}) from traffic zone i to j, including all real-world empirical friction factors. By using the sum-

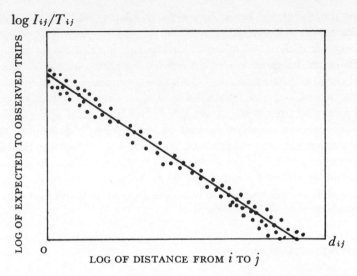

Fig. 9:1. Simple linear model of expected to observed trips by distance.

mation, we could compute total trips to traffic zone j from all other traffic zones:

$$\sum_{i=1}^{n} I_{ij} = G \sum_{i=1}^{n} \frac{P_i P_j}{d_{ij}^b}.$$

A double summation expression would yield all trips between all zones:

$$\sum_{i=1}^{n} \sum_{j=1}^{n} I_{ij} = G \sum_{i=1}^{n} \sum_{j=1}^{n} \frac{P_i P_j}{d_{ij}^b}.$$

This is the general form of interaction simulation, although many variations and special forms are used in practical urban analyses.

Interaction simulation, whether based on the gravity model or on other theoretical bases, is quite popular in many types of urban analysis. However, it has come under considerable criticism with increased application. The mathematical critique is that probability of interaction is an assumption which is not adequately proven or tested. Other mathematical assumptions have to do with the choice of the variable to signify mass; we have looked only at population, but income, jobs, retail sales, or any other reasonable measure of social mass could be used for urban analysis. The mathematical problem is that different choices of mass for the same problem can yield radically different results. Similarly, the selection of sub-areas, whether they be traffic zones, census tracts, blocks, etc., can significantly affect the results of interaction simulation.

A serious criticism has arisen regarding the justification of using the precepts of the universal law of gravitation for urban problems. The law is valid because it "averages out" deviations from unexplained forces. For example, interaction simulations have worked very well in practice for overall urban system problems, yet when they have been applied to sub-areas with special characteristics, such as low income, high income, black, low education, etc., the results have not been good. This situation arises because these special cases are averaged out of the overall system simulation and cannot be returned without special calibrations. This means that the urban analyst should carefully choose the type of problem and areas of application for interaction simulation.

STOCHASTIC SIMULATION

The most common and widely used form of simulation is the stochastic simulation of urban systems. Stochastic simulation entails the random sampling of probability density distributions and probability distributions. The heart of stochastic simulation is the *Monte Carlo method*. The romantic name for this method derives from its birthplace among the gambling tables and roulette wheels of the famous Mediterranean resort and casino. While the roots of the Monte Carlo method trace back to the seventeenth century, analysts did not begin to expand its applications until the early twentieth century. The major extensions were made by the Italian physicist Enrico Fermi (1901-1954), with major contributions by W. S. Gosset, John von Neumann, and J. W. Mauchly.

The method of stochastic simulation ordinarily entails a random sampling procedure by which a probabilistic numerical approximation of the problem is developed. The most frequently used device for obtaining *random numbers,* which one uses for random-sample selection, is the *table of random numbers,* the most famous of which was developed by an electronic roulette wheel built into a computer by the RAND Corporation.[4] There are several other tables of random numbers as well as numerous computer-based programs which automatically generate random numbers for random-sample selection according to some set of instructions about sample size and numerical specifications.

[4] RAND Corporation, *A Million Random Digits with 100,000 Normal Deviates* (Glencoe, Ill.: Free Press, 1955). The first page of random numbers from this effort is included here as Appendix G.

Random samples of data must be converted to random variables, in order to approximate the problem, from the probability density function that is given or artificially found. In general, the cumulative probability model is used, and a variety of different random-variable measures can be employed in order to approximate the problem. This sounds simple enough, and it is, although actual situations make the decision about efficient measures difficult. The mathematical basis, however, is not terribly sophisticated, and this accounts for much of the popularity of simulation.

Let us consider an example in which an urban analyst has been asked to simulate absenteeism in the sanitation department, which has been plagued by strikes, work stoppages, and inefficiency. There are 2,500 members of the sanitation department, and absenteeism is known to lie within the interval from zero to 1,000 per day. The urban analyst determines from past data that the cumulative probability for absenteeism is an s-shaped curve, as shown in Fig. 9:2. Using a table of random numbers (such as Appendix G), the analyst begins to select a random sample of values for the Y axis (absenteeism range and probability range) which is used to generate random-variable values along the X axis. For example, the random-number sample 715 is used to generate the random-variable value x. The values for X could simply be the actual values for the problem, such as absenteeism in our example, or some numerical derivative, such as logarithmic, exponential, or equidistributed random numbers — whatever proves most convenient and economic.

One can see easily that the trick is to find the *generating function Y = F(X)* that enables the use of random-number selection for values of the random variable. Often this is not a problem because past data are available which enable the determination of the generating function or an approximation of it. Yet even when $Y = F(X)$ is almost impossible to determine, simulation can be used if a working hypothesis can be found to approximate the generating function or, in extremely random problems, if random numbers can be used to approximate the generating function. Fig. 9:3 shows an example of a generating function that was approximated from incomplete past data and working hypotheses about the characteristics of the system. While this generating function has no neat mathematical expression, it can be used, even in its graphic form, with a computer to perform Monte Carlo method simulation.

Advanced forms of simulation are concerned primarily with improving the generating function by reducing the variance σ^2 of the estimates. There are a number of well-developed procedures for variance reduction of gen-

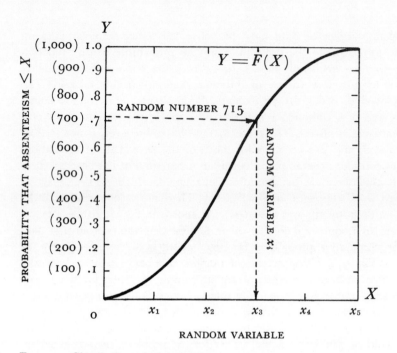

FIG. 9:2. Simulation of absenteeism.

erating functions.[5] As a general rule, we have found that the larger the sample of data from which the generating function is developed, the better the generating function's estimates and the less the variance. This same finding can be extended to say that the sounder the hypothesis used to approximate the generating function, the more likely it is that the estimates will have small variations from the real world.

The characteristics of the urban problem under consideration can be specified after a satisfactory number of iterations of the Monte Carlo method. Considering our previous example of the sanitation workers' absenteeism characteristics, the pattern of absenteeism can be simulated as shown in Fig. 9:4. Having described this pattern, useful information can be obtained by familiar statistical measures. For example, the expected value of absenteeism, or the mean of $F(\hat{X})$, can be computed in the familiar manner. Similarly, the standard deviation $\sigma_{F(\hat{X})}$ can be computed and the values mapped as the upper and lower limits. This particular

[5] See H. A. Meyer, ed., *Symposium on Monte Carlo Methods* (New York: Wiley, 1956), especially H. Kahn, "Use of Different Monte Carlo Sampling Techniques," pp. 146-190.

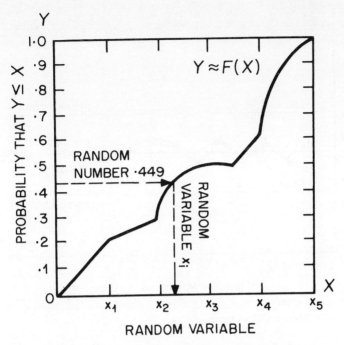

FIG. 9:3. Simulation with approximate generating function.

example has predictive and explanatory implications but relatively few optimization possibilities. Nevertheless, it could be used as input data to optimization models which consider control variables.

An illustrative simulation problem may be useful at this point. Let us consider a problem in which the urban analyst is requested to simulate traffic flow over a segment of a highway, as shown in Fig. 9:5.[6] The urban analyst uses a familiar traffic measure known as the *average daily traffic* (*ADT*), which is simply a statistical measure of the average number of vehicles in segment A per day for a period of a given month. The decision-makers have before them a proposal to close down the segment and add two more lanes because traffic jams are expected owing to the design capacity of 10,000 *ADT*s. The urban analyst is to simulate traffic over segment A for a period of 30 months in order to determine (1) what the *ADT* is likely to be and (2) what traffic tie-ups can be expected.

[6] This example is based upon a problem developed and solved in Giuseppe M. Ferrero di Roccaferrera, *Operations Research Models: For Business and Industry* (Cincinnati: South-Western Publishing Co., 1964), pp. 883-889.

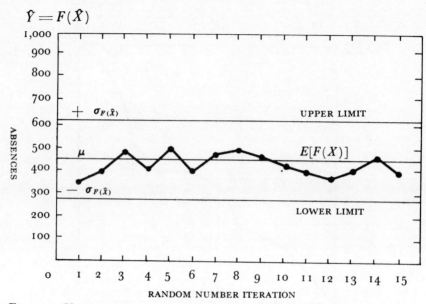

FIG. 9:4. Characteristic pattern of absenteeism by use of simulation using the Monte Carlo method.

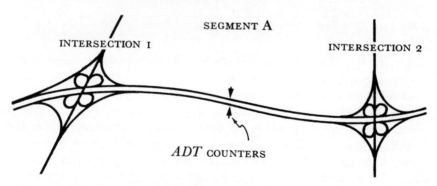

FIG. 9:5. Average daily traffic in segment A.

The *ADT* on segment A has been recorded for the last 40 months and is made available to the analyst, who then maps it as shown in Table 9:1 and Fig. 9:6; the latter uses the percent of observations of *ADT* by class, often called the *relative frequency*. The probability and cumulative probability are easily computed from Table 9:1 and are shown in Table 9:2.

The probability of a class of *ADT* is simply the conversion of the relative frequency into a probability scale ranging from zero to one. The cumulative probability is the accumulated total probability such that it represents the probability that a class is equal to or less than a given class, as shown in the last column of Table 9:2. The cumulative probability of *ADT* by class can be mapped as shown in Fig. 9:7. As can be seen, the *ADT* by class takes on the appearance of a Poisson model for a discrete class of random variables. This character in itself could be used for simulation, since *ADT* is independent of temporal or seasonal influences in our example.

Knowledge of the cumulative probability of the past 40 months for *ADT* by class is sufficient for the use of the Monte Carlo method for simulating the next 30 months. We can select a set of random numbers, which for convenience can range from 0 to 999 (or 1,000 random numbers); any set of random numbers is acceptable, although multiples of ten facilitate computations. The random numbers must then be assigned in proper proportion to the cumulative probability. This can be done simply enough

TABLE 9:1. *ADT* for segment A for last 40 months.

ADT by Class	Number of Months Observed
0– 1,999	2
2,000– 3,999	10
4,000– 5,999	15
6,000– 7,999	6
8,000– 9,999	3
10,000–11,999	2
12,000–13,999	1
14,000–15,999	1
16,000 or more	0
	Σ = 40

TABLE 9:2. Probability and cumulative probability.

ADT by Class	Number of Months Observed	Relative Frequency	Probability	Cumulative Probability
0– 1,999	2	5.00	0.050	0.050
2,000– 3,999	10	25.00	0.250	0.300
4,000– 5,999	15	37.50	0.375	0.675
6,000– 7,999	6	15.00	0.150	0.825
8,000– 9,999	3	7.50	0.075	0.900
10,000–11,999	2	5.00	0.050	0.950
12,000–13,999	1	2.50	0.025	0.975
14,000–15,999	1	2.50	0.025	1.000
16,000 or more	0	0.00	0.000	1.000
Total	40	100.00	1.000	—

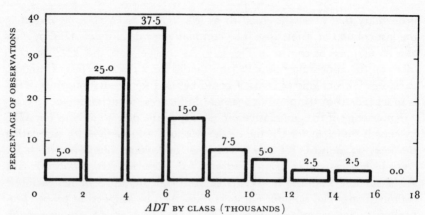

Fig. 9:6. *ADT* by class and percentage of observations for preceding 40 months.

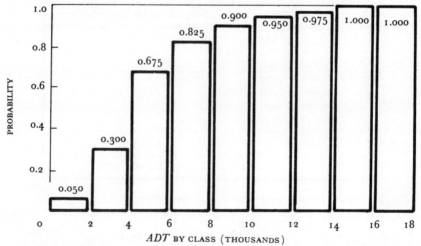

Fig. 9:7. Cumulative probability of *ADT* by class.

by converting the cumulative probability to an interval which is found by multiplying the cumulative probability by 1,000 and subtracting one (since our first random number is 0). For example, the first cumulative probability of 0.050 for the 0-1.999 *ADT* class can be converted to an interval of random numbers ranging from 0 to 049 — the next class would start at 050, etc. The quantity of random numbers can be computed by multiplying the difference between each cumulative probability and its imme-

TABLE 9:3. Assignment of random numbers to classes of *ADT*.

Cumulative Probability	Random-Number Interval	Quantity of Random Numbers
0.050	000–049	50
0.300	050–299	250
0.675	300–674	375
0.825	675–824	150
0.900	825–899	75
0.950	900–949	50
0.975	950–974	25
1.000	975–999	25
1.000	—	0
—	—	$\Sigma = 1,000$

diate predecessor by 1,000. For example, the first class would be (0.050 — 0)1,000 = 50, the second class would be (0.300 — 0.050)1,000 = 250, etc. These computations are shown in Table 9:3.

Since we have previously stated that 30 months are sought for the simulation, we should select 30 random numbers from Appendix G and determine the corresponding probability and *ADT* class. This can be done simply by comparing the selected random number with the assignments made in Table 9:3, or the random number can be plotted against the

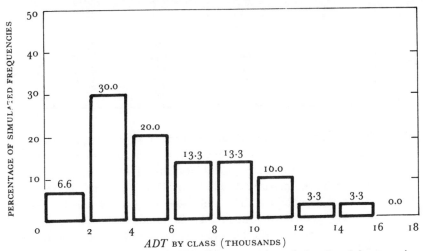

FIG. 9:8. Simulated *ADT* by class and percentage of simulated frequencies for next 30 months.

TABLE 9:4. Thirty random numbers and corresponding *ADT* classes.

Iteration	Random Number	Probability	*ADT* Class (thousands)
1	868	0.868	8–10
2	699	0.699	6– 8
3	937	0.937	10–12
4	681	0.681	6– 8
5	625	0.625	4– 6
6	935	0.935	10–12
7	113	0.113	2– 4
8	440	0.440	4– 6
9	173	0.173	2– 4
10	876	0.876	8–10
11	817	0.817	6– 8
12	013	0.013	0– 2
13	870	0.870	8–10
14	417	0.417	4– 6
15	957	0.957	12–14
16	030	0.030	0– 2
17	079	0.079	2– 4
18	069	0.069	2– 4
19	995	0.995	14–16
20	436	0.436	4– 6
21	755	0.755	6– 8
22	237	0.237	2– 4
23	946	0.946	10–12
24	182	0.182	2– 4
25	131	0.131	2– 4
26	190	0.190	2– 4
27	844	0.844	8–10
28	547	0.547	4– 6
29	426	0.426	4– 6
30	142	0.142	2– 4

cumulative probability, as shown in Fig. 9:7, and the resulting *ADT* class determined. In Table 9:4 we have selected 30 random numbers and determined the corresponding probability and *ADT* class. The data in Table 9:4 can be summarized as shown in Table 9:5, and the simulated frequencies can be obtained. The simulated frequencies can be mapped as shown in Fig. 9:8. This represents the 30-month simulation of the *ADT* by class for segment A of the highway under consideration. The question about traffic tie-ups because of exceeding the *ADT* capacity of 10,000

TABLE 9:5. Simulated frequencies of *ADT* class.

Expected *ADT* by Class over Next 30 Months	Simulated Frequencies
0– 1,999	2
2,000– 3,999	9
4,000– 5,999	6
6,000– 7,999	4
8,000– 9,999	4
10,000–11,999	3
12,000–13,999	1
14,000–15,999	1
16,000 or more	0

can be seen to be in the probability of 6:1. In other words, there is only one chance in six that a traffic tie-up will occur over the next 30 months. On the other hand, the urban analyst would point out that the simulation reveals that there will be five months in which the *ADT* will probably be over 10,000, which could result in horrendous traffic jams. The urban analyst might recommend that the highway improvements be made with dispatch. This example should point out the *ad hoc* nature of simulation, and the careful reader will no doubt be able to recognize many alternative simulations of this problem.

QUEUING THEORY

Queuing or waiting-line theory is a special class of the simulation approach in which analytical methods are employed. Queuing theory is the use of symbolic models with analytical and mathematical bases in order to simulate the characteristics of a system with random and nonrandom variables. The principal distinction from simulation is that queuing theory provides the ability to derive solutions from an analytical rather than a numerical approach, and hence optimization is possible.

Queuing theory deals generally with systems that are subject to congestion because of random *arrivals* or demands. We have briefly examined the rudiments of queuing theory in our examination of Markov processes. Making extensive use of the Poisson model and a special form of the gamma model known as the *Erlang model*, queuing theory allows the derivation of analytical solutions to such problems as waiting time, cost of waiting, length of queues, and number of servicing stations. The primary function of queuing theory is to provide solutions to systems which have problems of congestion owing to randomness of arrivals or demands.

We choose not to expend our energies on queuing theory, since the rudiments are simple but the methods are complex — complex not in mathematical terms but, rather, in the computational sense, which is admittedly cumbersome and depends upon iterative methods. Standardization of queuing theory expressions has caused some simplification in computation.[7]

CRITIQUE OF SIMULATION

Upon introduction, simulation has a tendency to blossom into love at first sight with many neophyte urban analysts. The mathematical foundations are not complicated with regard to computation, and digital computers ease most of the burden of computation anyhow. The versatility of simulation is exciting, and the inherent foundation of assumptions based upon judgment and experience, as well as intuition, appeal to many trained in the social sciences. Simulation appears almost too good to be true, but we offer the fatherly advice of putting off the wedding until one has learned more about the family and background of the intended.

We offer a critique of simulation not to dissuade the urban analyst from its employment but, rather, to alert the urban analyst to some of its drawbacks. One problem is that simulation is a somewhat imprecise approach, the results of which vary even with the same simulation and same problem because of the randomness of the method. This is both a drawback and a strong point. It is a drawback because imprecise solutions can result in bad decisions, yet we know precious little about urban systems and our data are imprecise. Thus it could be argued that simulation is a practical if imprecise approach for using the practical if imprecise data of urban systems. The counter-argument would be that such imprecise approaches do not leave the analyst with that arrogance of satisfaction and confidence that is often needed to approach the decision-maker and proffer the optimal solution to his problems. Once again the decision about whether or not to use the approach, in its present state of development, is largely a personal one to be made by the urban analyst.

The pragmatics of simulation have raised some basic issues related to

[7] The interested reader is directed to the following, which is written with some fine English insight: D. R. Cox and Walter L. Smith, *Queues* (London: Methuen, 1961).

the whole question of applying scientific methods to urban analysis. Simulation models, as we shall discover below, tend to become rather large, unwieldy, and fraught with built-in assumptions that are often forgotten. Few of the major simulations of urban systems are wholly understood by any one urban analyst — a team is almost always required, if only to keep track of the assumptions.

Since simulation is basically a numerical method, with the exception of certain queuing theory approaches, its value as a learning tool is dubious. The learning to be gained from simulation is directly proportional to the knowledge that was used in making assumptions. Obviously, shaky or questionable assumptions are not likely to reveal universal truths about problems in urban systems, even though perfectly adequate and approximately optimal solutions to the problems can be found. In other words, simulation is inwardly a pseudofunctional approach to urban problem-solving and does not deal with cause and effect in a direct way.

APPLICATION OF SIMULATION

Having made the above critique in good faith, we now turn to an examination of the major applications of simulation to problems of urban systems. Once again we notice the attractiveness of simulation as an approach to dealing with urban problems in cases where all else seems to fail. Witness the applications of simulation; they vary from highway traffic to hospital services to international relations.[8] The applications are many and varied. We have elected to examine two classes of simulation applications: *urban development simulation* and *urban dynamics simulation*.

URBAN DEVELOPMENT SIMULATION

Urban development simulation concerns the imitation of the physical growth of the urban system in terms of such components as housing, economy, population, traffic, and land use. One of the classic urban develop-

[8] Arno Cassel and Michael S. Janoff, "A Simulation Model of a Two Lane Rural Road," *Highway Research Record*, no. 257 (Washington, D.C.: Highway Research Board, 1968), pp. 1-17; R. B. Fetter and J. D. Thompson, "The Simulation of Hospital Systems," *Operations Research*, 13 (1965), 689-711; Harold Guetzkow et al., *Simulation in International Relations: Developments for Research and Teaching* (Englewood Cliffs, N.J.: Prentice-Hall, 1963).

ment simulation efforts was conducted in the Pittsburgh urban system.[9] There were several stages of the Pittsburgh simulation, which started out as a simulation in atemporal terms of one class of residential and three classes of retail employment land uses.[10] Later stages of the Pittsburgh simulation were concerned with extensions of the classes of land use to include commercial and manufacturing as well as retail and manufacturing employment and population.[11] The latter simulation was developed for the Pittsburgh Urban Renewal Program and is often called the *Pittsburgh urban renewal simulation.*

The Pittsburgh urban renewal simulation incorporated the methods of interaction simulation and a technique borrowed from economics known as *input/output analysis,* which essentially is a method for accounting for the flow of resources between industries. These methods gave the Pittsburgh urban renewal simulation a deterministic character, even though it would be more proper to consider it a hybrid of deterministic simulation with some basic probabilistic assumptions (that is, regarding interaction).

The Pittsburgh urban renewal simulation was an early attempt at application of simulation to urban analysis, and it proved to be somewhat cumbersome and expensive. The rationale for developing the simulation was to test alternative policies for urban renewal plans in order to determine the resulting effects on population, economy, and land use (linear programming was used to define optimal values). The major contribution of the Pittsburgh urban renewal simulation to applications of simulation to urban analysis was the successful design and implementation of a simulation that linked several submodels, such as housing, land use, economy, and population, in order to imitate overall urban development.

Stochastic simulation of urban development has been more popular than deterministic simulation. A long-term series of simulation experiments has been underway at the University of North Carolina since the early 1960s. Several of the experiments have resulted in operational simulations of residential development which are based upon the conversion of rural or vacant land to residential use.[12] The simulations are based upon the *theory*

---

[9] Ira S. Lowry, *A Model of Metropolis* (Santa Monica, Calif.: RAND Corp., 1964).

[10] A time dimension was added later; see John P. Crecine, *A Time-Oriented Metropolitan Model for Spatial Location* (Pittsburgh: Department of City Planning, 1964).

[11] Wilbur A. Steger, "The Pittsburgh Urban Renewal Simulation Model," *Journal of the American Institute of Planners,* 31, no. 2 (May, 1965), 144-150.

[12] There have been numerous reports. A good review is found in F. Stuart Chapin, "A Model for Simulating Residential Development," *Journal of the American Institute of Planners,* 31, no. 2 (May, 1965), 120-125.

of land use succession, which holds that land will be developed to its highest and best use according to a definable index of attractiveness. Attractiveness has been measured by such factors as accessibility, available utilities, street access, and nearness of schools to the given parcel of land.

The North Carolina residential simulation, as the above experiments are sometimes called, used various techniques of random sampling, including the Monte Carlo method, to simulate the development for residential purposes of parcels of land within grids of test urban systems. Numerous assumptions about the real world are built into this simulation in order to guide it. For example, inherent heuristic rules state that residential densities are predetermined through public policy, overdevelopment of land is not allowed, and spillover residential development goes to the nearest parcels not already developed.

Recent extensions of the North Carolina residential simulation have been directed toward the simulation of the behavioral patterns of developers and home buyers as constrained and shaped by public policies within an urban system.[13] This continuing research and development program for residential land development is most important because it has been directed to the major user of developed land (homes) and has dealt with pragmatic development and policy variables. The most recent extensions of the simulation have been based upon linked submodels within the simulation that deal with land prior to development, during development planning, as affected by residential preferences during marketing, and as an element of urban system structure after settlement. This linked-submodel approach allows for policy testing via simulation at the key points of leverage where decisions are needed by developers, public officials, and home buyers. Such a simulation is most practical for the real-world problems of residential land use planning and the provision of housing to satisfy demands in an urban system.

The most well-publicized stochastic simulation of urban development is the well-known *San Francisco housing simulation.*[14] This simulation was developed for the City and County of San Francisco for testing alternative policies to be used for the urban renewal program. Such public policies as zoning, rent subsidization, public housing, and mortgage guarantees were tested in alternative configurations and permutations for their effects on

[13] Edward J. Kaiser and Shirley F. Weiss, "Public Policy and the Residential Development Process," *Journal of the American Institute of Planners,* 36, no. 1 (Jan., 1970), 30-38.

[14] Arthur D. Little, Inc., *Model of San Francisco Housing Market* (San Francisco, 1966).

the future housing supply of the urban system. In this guise the San Francisco housing simulation is the best example of the use of urban system simulation in problems that cannot be expressed in the dynamic programming format because of complex interactions and relationships.

The San Francisco housing simulation was highly sophisticated in terms of its mathematical and functional structure, yet, like all other simulations, it was based upon a foundation of assumptions. The simulation essentially was concerned with housing stock by type over various time periods consisting of two-year intervals. Such aspects and characteristics as construction, demolition, physical condition, rent, price, and occupancy were simulated for various levels and degrees of public policies, which acted as both constraints and inducements to increasing housing supply.

The mathematical nature of the San Francisco housing simulation was somewhat novel. Rather than using the usual Monte Carlo method, the urban analysts employed Markov processes to develop transitional states and optimization. Such methodology is rarely found in urban problem analysis. The use of Markov processes allowed for probabilistic variables to be built into the equations that generated the simulated values for aging and deterioration of housing. This meant that the generating function was essentially part of the system description, and random sampling was minimized. While difficult in mathematical terms to formulate such expressions for urban problems, this method allows for more efficient use of digital computers for computations and output reporting.

The *raison d'être* for the San Francisco housing simulation was to test policies that could be used by the urban renewal officials in order to execute their basic charge of improving the housing supply and insuring that every family had a decent home.[15] Yet the critique that has arisen regarding the simulation is that the alternative policies that were tested tended to be expressible only in abstract terms. For example, on-off switches or flags were used to instruct the urban analyst about the probable ownership, occupancy, costs, and public policies for each of the sub-areas, which are called *fracts,* as affected by such policies as urban renewal programs of demolition, rehabilitation, and conservation within a perfect market environment. The result has been criticized as somewhat artificial and hypothetical. Further criticism has been addressed to the omission in the simulation of transportation and accessibility. The simulation more or less implies that each fract is independent of others and is equally accessible,

[15] Ira M. Robinson, Harry B. Wolfe, and Robert L. Barringer, "A Simulation Model for Renewal Programming," *Journal of the American Institute of Planners,* 31, no. 2 (May, 1965), 126-134.

and assumptions about preferences for types of housing replace such matters as commuting time and distances.

Nonetheless, the San Francisco housing simulation is a milestone in the application of simulation to urban problems. The complex and rigorous detail available from the simulation is new to urban analysis. The capabilities that the simulation has for testing many combinations of public policy provide a unique tool for planning and programming.

A recent spin-off from the San Francisco housing simulation has been a series of efforts concerned with the simulation of the future growth of the San Francisco Bay area. These efforts culminated in the *Bay Area Simulation Study* (BASS).[16] The BASS is a hybrid form of simulation that uses both deterministic and stochastic simulation methods. The BASS has three submodels:

1. *Aggregate Forecasting*. Simulates 21 kinds of industry and population distribution.

2. *Employment Location*. Allocates the 21 kinds of industry to 777 sub-areas within the urban system.

3. *Residential Location*. Distributes two types of housing for three income groups among the 777 sub-areas.

A rather large variety of methods is used to achieve the desired output, which ranges from complex linear models to transition matrices.

The BASS seems to be particularly oriented toward including transportation and accessibility characteristics that were missing in the San Francisco housing simulation. These characteristics are included through the use of a probabilistic time-distance matrix. The time-distance matrix describes probable average travel time and distance between centers of the 777 sub-areas according to mode of travel; the resulting matrix has 603,729 elements for each mode. This matrix allows the urban analyst to evaluate alternative transportation plans for their effect on employment and residential location for the urban system.

The BASS is still under development and refinement but promises to be a most useful simulation and perhaps another milestone in the application of simulation to urban analysis. Reviewers have called for a wider set of characteristics to be included in the simulation, even at the cost of making the simulation more complex and unwieldy than it is already. The future developments of BASS merit serious observation and analysis.

[16] Paul F. Wendt and Michael A. Goldberg, "The Use of Land Development Simulation Models in Transportation Planning," *Highway Research Record,* no. 285 (Washington, D.C.: Highway Research Board, 1969), pp. 82-91.

URBAN DYNAMICS SIMULATION

The most ambitious and perplexing application of simulation to urban problems has been the hybrid of *systems analysis* and simulation, developed to imitate the growth of urban systems.[17] Urban dynamics simulation was developed by Jay W. Forrester as an extension of his well-known concepts of *industrial dynamics*.[18] Industrial dynamics is a systemic approach to simulating the growth process of industries as reflected and effected through various managerial policies. Forrester has refined industrial dynamics so that urban systems can be simulated through the same methods used for industries.[19] Urban dynamics simulation is applied to a hypothetical urban system to simulate its growth and decay as represented generally by construction and migration.

The intellectual basis for urban dynamics simulation is more theoretical than the usual foundation of assumptions. Urban dynamics simulation is based upon the theory of systems as being inherently *counter-intuitive*. This theory holds that the intuitive answer to problems of systems will generally have adverse effects and may even compound the original state of problems. The reason for this is that intuitive selection of solutions to problems is made on the basis of our knowledge about *simple systems*, while industries and urban systems are actually *complex systems*. According to the theory, complex systems, unlike simple systems, have numerous states, many subsystems, internal relationships which are usually nonlinear, and interacting feedback loops. The result is that cause-and-effect relationships in complex systems are vague and almost impossible to identify; more important, they are shaped by historical events and forces from outside the system.

Urban dynamics simulation is an extremely large and complex simulation which is composed of 369 generating equations with 360 different variables, both deterministic and random. A special computer programming language had to be written in order to process the simulation; the language is called DYNAMO II and is an extension of the earlier DYNAMO, which was written for industrial dynamics problems. Nevertheless, despite the mathematical sophistication and Forrester's critique of assumptions made by other urban analysts who use simulation, the foundation is still primarily assumptions made about a hypothetical urban system as

---

[17] For further discussion of systems analysis for urban problems, see Anthony J. Catanese and Alan W. Steiss, *Systemic Planning: Theory and Application* (Boston: D. C. Heath, 1970).

[18] Jay W. Forrester, *Industrial Dynamics* (Cambridge, Mass.: M.I.T. Press, 1961).

[19] Jay W. Forrester, *Urban Dynamics* (Cambridge, Mass.: M.I.T. Press, 1969).

modified by theoretical constructs of the counter-intuitive nature of complex systems.

Urban dynamics simulation generates trend lines for 50- and 250-year periods to show the probable growth of the urban system according to various policies and programs. Its utility, then, is largely policy testing, although Forrester argues that it is a learning tool which should not be used for real-world problems until further testing is completed. The trend lines for growth are used to identify *sectors* of urban system growth, which usually means the following in urban dynamics simulation: (1) underemployed sector, (2) labor sector, (3) managerial-professional sector, (4) premium housing sector, (5) workers' housing sector, (6) underemployed housing sector, (7) new enterprise sector, (8) mature business sector, (9) declining industry sector, (10) tax sector, and (11) job sector. Like the North Carolina residential simulation, urban growth dynamics simulation uses an attractiveness scoring index which yields the probability of attraction of construction and people. The difference is that interacting feedback loops within the urban dynamics simulation are used to imitate growth. Policies such as urban renewal, political powers, and negative income taxes are used to test the impact that each, or combinations of each, would have upon the simulated growth of the hypothetical urban system.

The first run of the urban dynamics simulation showed the 250-year trend of growth, maturity, and stagnation for an urban system as generated by the numerous submodels used for the simulation (see Fig. 9:9). As can be observed, the simulation shows that urban systems begin on empty land and reach full development over the next 100 years. The simulation holds that when the land becomes filled, new construction decreases, and this results in spin-offs to raise the level of declining industries and underemployment. The higher level of underemployment creates adverse effects on the economy and affects skilled workers in a detrimental way. Similarly, too much housing goes to the underemployed housing sector, and more industries start to decline.

The interacting problems of the sectors of the urban system continue for less than 50 years. Somewhere around the 150th anniversary of the initiation of the urban system, the various sectors have been simulated to experience a mild renaissance, which becomes the foundation for an indefinite period of stagnation, although stability would be a kinder word.

The urban dynamics simulation is significant in that two assumptions are built into the generating models. The first assumption is that the environment in which the system is functioning is limitless. The second assumption is that the urban system is basically a closed system, although

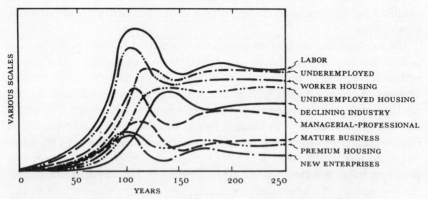

VARIOUS SCALES

LABOR
UNDEREMPLOYED
WORKER HOUSING
UNDEREMPLOYED HOUSING
DECLINING INDUSTRY
MANAGERIAL-PROFESSIONAL
MATURE BUSINESS
PREMIUM HOUSING
NEW ENTERPRISES

0   50   100   150   200   250

YEARS

FIG. 9:9. Urban dynamics simulation of hypothetical urban system.

Forrester muddies the water somewhat by arguing that the urban system is open but functions within a closed boundary.[20] The closed-boundary condition is essential if stagnation and decline in growth are to be simulated, since these states of the urban system are related to the amount of land that can be developed. Hence it is the basic resource of space for urban development that imposes a closed-system characteristic upon the urban dynamics simulation. Taken together, the limitless environment and closed boundary of the urban system result in a closed system which draws freely upon the resources of the environment without constraint and which interacts with other urban systems solely by attracting their migrants and investment dollars. No competition among urban systems exists in this simulation.

The basic critique of the urban dynamics simulation has been its closed-system milieu. While Forrester criticized other simulations which used simple simulation, the inherent closed-system characteristics make it really a simple system per se. John W. Dyckman commented several years ago about the wisdom of urban analysts' use of closed-system simulation:

Most of the [simulations] of theory, physical or social, are closed. The systems are in equilibrium usually shut off from upsetting shocks from outside the system. . . . Indeed, it might be argued that scientific analysis is impossible without closing the system which is being examined. We have not been able to devise intellectual constructs which can handle the open system, and the task of doing so may be inherently hopeless. Any system which is exchanging influence with its environment is open, and all of the phenomena of [urban systems] which we abstract for analy-

[20] Ibid., p. 12.

sis are in the process of interacting with some environment. Hence, all are open.[21]

Dyckman's comments are relevant to the urban dynamics simulation in that it was necessary to close the urban system, at least in terms of its use of land resources and competing neighbors, in order to make scientific analysis possible. Yet one must not lose sight of the truisms that urban systems do interact with their environments, do interact with other urban systems, and are rarely if ever in equilibrium. Hence urban systems are open systems, and the urban dynamics simulation does not portray open systems.

The urban dynamics simulation, ambitious as it may be, is based upon a constant supply of people, homes, and jobs which are attracted from unknown urban systems, as well as nonurban systems, outside the hypothetical urban system being simulated. In the real world urban systems compete with each other to attract people, homes, and jobs, and this results in some urban systems losing growth not because of stagnation but because of tough competition. The classic example is the last three decades of competition between Atlanta and Birmingham. Similarly, the notion of a limitless environment merits reconsideration. The people of the United States have become painfully aware of the foolishness of assuming that the environment, including its resources of land, water, air, quietude, and raw materials, can be constantly plundered by urban builders without all urban systems ever being affected. Obviously, there are limits upon the use of the environment, and it is no longer possible to exploit it without replenishment and economic use.

The severest criticism of the urban dynamics simulation has not been as much about its methods and assumptions as about its interpretations.[22] Forrester argues that interpretations should not be drawn too easily, but he nevertheless volunteers several interpretations for public policies in urban systems. The counter-intuitive bias inherent in the simulation naturally results in the criticism of most contemporary public policies for urban systems. For example, the urban dynamics simulation shows that any public policies that seek to improve the lot of the underemployed and poor are resisted by urban systems and result in decay and stagnation by attracting more underemployed and poor people to urban systems. The alternative is not discussed, however. Other interpretations offered are:

[21] John W. Dyckman, "Planning and Metropolitan Systems," in Melvin M. Webber et al., *Explorations into Urban Structure* (Philadelphia: University of Pennsylvania Press, 1964), p. 223.
[22] For example, see G. K. Ingram, "Urban Dynamics," *Journal of the American Institute of Planners*, 36, no. 3 (May, 1970), 206-208.

1. A somewhat Darwinistic purist ideology in that the urban dynamics simulation implies that rugged individualism and personal sacrifice result in overall urban system growth.

2. An argument that taxes penalize "those who contribute most to urban system growth" and encourage more people to move to urban systems, since they will receive better services without having to pay for them. The simulation, as one can easily see, is slanted toward high corporate profit taxation and progressive income and property taxes without any loopholes for the rich.

3. A vague charge that urban planners favor housing over industry and hence contribute to the decline of urban systems by attracting houses rather than factories. Forrester argues that industry should be the least restricted land use and should be allowed to do whatever it wants, since this is good for the growth of the urban system.

The counter-intuitive theory that is found throughout the structure of the urban dynamics simulation is simply a mathematical way of developing a biased imitation of the real world. The counter-intuitive theory can be used to develop a simulation that can prove just about anything that an urban analyst wishes to prove. The results of the urban dynamics simulation are thus reactionary in light of contemporary approaches to programming, planning, and action programs for solving the problems of urban systems. One must recall, however, that the counter-intuitive characteristics which Forrester insists be found in urban simulation are but untested assumptions themselves. This makes the interpretations unscientific in our viewpoint because the alternatives have not been analyzed and tested. Similarly, the use of these interpretations for decision-making would be inane because they are biased by the simulation methods per se.

The urban dynamics simulation has yielded landmark values and contributions which are not to be found in its learning, interpretive, and policy aspects:

1. The breadth and scope of the urban dynamics simulation are much greater and more synergistic than previous attempts at simulation.

2. The demonstration of the methods of simulation as a means of imitating real-world urban systems and testing policies for their improvement has been sound, qualified by our argument that other alternative simulations must be offered for fair and wise decision evaluations.

3. The effective use of abstract models which were linked to form the simulation, as well as the successful development of computational hardware and software, has been most impressive.

Any attempt at simulation of urban systems is prone to inherit much of the personal bias and beliefs of the urban analysts. This is especially true of large, unwieldy simulations which can only be understood by the originators. This should be minimized by the use of interdisciplinary teams and a large measure of give and take. Most of all, every simulation of urban systems should present a complete list of all the assumptions that were made so that any reasonable person can easily detect points to which one may or may not subscribe. This will probably mean that different persons and groups will favor different simulations, but this is the essence of modern programming and planning for urban systems and is the valid approach.

RECOMMENDED EXERCISES

1. Select a segment of a highway in your community that has been surveyed for traffic volumes in recent years. Develop a Monte Carlo method simulation of traffic for the highway segment over some period of time that is consistent with the available data.

2. Urban system simulations have tended to select characteristics for the system — that is, the W in our general expression — that often reflect the urban analysts' professional and intellectual backgrounds and interests. If you were asked to simulate an urban system, what characteristics do you believe would be most relevant? How quantitative are these characteristics? What assumptions would have to be made in order to employ scientific methods for the analysis of these characteristics?

FURTHER READING

Tocher, K. D. *The Art of Simulation*. Princeton, N.J.: Van Nostrand, 1963.
A classic book in the field of simulation which expounds upon the theory and methods of simulation in terms of general systems. The work is the major exposition of the theoretical basis of the methods of simulation and some of the implications that may be drawn from simulation. The author tends to view simulation as being as much an art as a science.

Forrester, Jay W. *Urban Dynamics*. Cambridge, Mass.: M.I.T. Press, 1969.
Any urban analyst seriously interested in the application of simulation to urban analysis should read Forrester's book and become well acquainted with it, not for its success or failures but, rather, as a case study of the methods involved. The simulation is indeed extensive, yet the book omits much technical detail in favor of attracting a wide audience.

Many urban problems resist attempts at modeling and simulation because variables and functional relationships are vague, interactive, and often unpredictable because of human behavioral inconsistencies and value judgments. Scientific methods of optimization for such problems are implausible, since so little is known about the structure of the problems; sometimes the problem cannot even be stated precisely. As we mentioned in the last chapter, such a seemingly hopeless situation can often be analyzed using the scientific methods found in that form of simulation called *gaming*.

Gaming is a special kind of simulation that allows the urban analyst to *learn* and *understand* more about urban problems by imitating the problems under simulated conditions. This generally entails *role playing* by persons in order to make decisions for hypothetical problems; sometimes actual data from real urban systems are used as well. Some theorists have argued that gaming can do even more in that playing the game over and over allows for the determination of certain patterns of behavior and decision-making by each role player. These patterns of behavior and decision-making can be described in models which can be used for predicting and estimating decisions. Our personal conviction is that such a use of gaming is dubious, if not dangerous, because this procedure amounts to little more than building models based upon variables and relationships found in artificial experiments. As a friend of ours once commented, "Let them play the game with real money, their own money, and there will be a world of difference in the way that the game is played."

The more commonly held rationale for gaming is that it is not a method to estimate and predict decisions but an approach to learning and understanding more about apparently nonquantifiable problems. Gaming can be used for teaching in cases where the problems can be well structured, and where the gamemaster believes that subtle points can be made by role playing which cannot be made in lectures. James S. Coleman, in responding to criticism of the use of gaming as a learning tool, made the following remarks:

Students have too long been taught things that are *known*, and have too seldom been allowed to discover for themselves the principles governing a situation. . . . The fascination with . . . games [is] the opportunity to learn about social organization by forming a *caricature* of such organization and then observing the caricature. . . . The student is learning how to incorporate this experience into his own life, learning to recognize the dominant aspects of social environment so that he can respond appropriately to them when he meets such an environment in his own life.[1]

Indeed, Coleman's notions have been widely accepted and adopted by many educators in various areas of urban analysis.

EVOLUTION OF GAMING

Gaming was first applied to real-world problems in military and defense contexts. Undoubtedly, the ideas of *conflicting goals* and *competing players* lend themselves well to battlefield and strategic planning and decision-making where there are two or more adversaries.[2] War games, which are simulated battles, were used by Greek and Roman generals both to teach their soldiers to fight efficiently and to learn about the behavior of soldiers under simulated battle conditions. Charlemagne was known to command his mathematicians to devise games which would reveal the most efficient ways to move large armies across rugged topography and rivers. The military use of gaming has continued up to the present with such games as *TEMPER* that use large-scale digital computers to assist role players in making decisions and then convert these decisions into simulated effects upon the technology, economy, politics, and militaries of various competing and conflicting countries throughout the world.[3] Gaming has been relatively successful and quite popular with the military, since it has proved to be a most useful method for learning and understanding strategic decision-making behavioral characteristics for adversary problems under conditions of *risk* and *uncertainty*.

The scientific and mathematical bases of gaming were raised to high levels of development through military and defense research, and with

[1] James S. Coleman, "In Defense of Games," *American Behavioral Scientist,* 10 (Oct., 1966), 4.
[2] For a discussion of basic problems of gaming in the military, see M. A. Geisler, W. W. Haythorn, and W. A. Steger, "Simulation and the Logistics Systems Laboratory," *Naval Research Quarterly,* 10, no. 1 (Mar., 1963), 23-54.
[3] For further discussion, see Walter C. Clements, "A Propositional Analysis of International Relations in TEMPER," in W. D. Coplin, ed., *Simulation in the Study of Politics* (Chicago: Markham, 1968).

this elevation there came an interest from industrial and business analysts. The landmark theoretical work was written by John von Neumann
and Oskar Morganstern, in which they extended the theoretical base of
gaming to include problems of economic behavior and decisions under
conditions of risk and uncertainty. Thus they set the stage for industrial
and business gaming.[4] Gaming has found extensive use in industry and
business, although not without much criticism, for such problems as management decision-making, personnel selection, advertising, marketing, and
sales by companies which are in competition with other companies. A
well-developed body of theory has arisen from these applications.[5] As with
military and defense applications, much criticism and controversy have
surrounded the employment of gaming as a learning and understanding
tool, but many applications have been relatively successful and popular.

The present evolution of gaming has been generic to such an extent that
the method can be applied to any type of problem, whether military, industrial and business, or urban.[6] The basic requirements are that the problems which are to be simulated involve decisions under conditions of risk
and uncertainty where two or more players are involved. The generic evolution of gaming has tended to result in a diminution of the conflicting-
goals and competing-players concepts. Gaming can be used in situations
where conflict and competition are vague and undefinable, although most
theorists believe that much of its effectiveness is lost in such applications.
The loss of conflict and competition in gaming as applied to urban analysis
has created several problems and much controversy over the usefulness of
the approach. There are, however, many urban problems which are subject to definable conflict and competition among two or more participants
in the decision-making.

The generic evolution of gaming usually has three purposes in urban
analysis:

1. Learning more about complex urban problems and understanding
the risks and uncertainties inherent in many of them.

2. Testing alternative solutions to complex urban problems and examining the risks and uncertainties attached to alternative solutions.

3. Approximating models of decision-making processes for complex
urban problems which are subject to conditions of risk and uncertainty.

---

[4] John von Neumann and Oskar Morganstern, *Games and Economic Behavior*
(Princeton, N.J.: Princeton University Press, 1944).

[5] For further background reading, see R. D. Luce and H. Raiffa, *Games and
Decisions* (New York: Wiley, 1957).

[6] Clark C. Abt, *Serious Games* (New York: Viking, 1970), explores the ramifications of this point in some detail.

Having already stated our belief that learning and understanding, the first purpose, is paramount for the use of gaming in urban analysis, we can briefly mention the other two. The second purpose, testing alternative solutions to complex problems, is a carryover from military applications. We have found that the testing of alternative solutions by the use of gaming does not result in clearcut findings for each solution but, rather, results in learning more about each alternative solution. Hence we believe that testing is actually a learning operation. Similarly, while several theorists have argued that gaming can be used for approximating models of urban problems when all else fails, we have found that gaming results in learning and understanding more about the behavioral patterns of decision-makers, from which analogies can be made with respect to the kinds of variables and functional relationships that may be relevant for modeling the decision process. Thus our basic position is that gaming is best considered a learning and understanding method which may have indirect benefits for testing alternative solutions and modeling decision processes.

GAME THEORY

Game theory, the underlying scientific and mathematical structure of gaming, has been largely oriented toward four types of games: (1) *two-person zero-sum games*, (2) *n-person zero-sum games*, (3) *nonzero-sum games*, and (4) *infinite games*. The mathematical complexities increase with this ranking of types of games.

The overwhelming bulk of research and development in game theory has been directed toward two-person zero-sum games, since they are the simplest. As the name implies, two-person games, the persons being armies, politicians, governments, individuals, or other suitable entities, consist of two persons with conflicting goals competing with each other. One person seeks to fulfill his goals at the expense of the other person. One person will lose a portion of his assets or resources, and the other person will acquire them; hence the sum of winnings and losses will be zero.

The real world of urban systems does not always involve only two competing persons. When such a situation arises, it may become necessary to use *n*-person zero-sum games in which any number (*n*) of persons may be competing. This will substantially increase the possible number of strategies to be selected. Games with a large number of persons become quite unwieldy, and digital computers are needed to keep track of the possible strategies and effects of moves by each player.

Nonzero-sum games are for two or n persons in which the sum of winnings and losses may not equal zero. This situation arises when *mutual advantages,* all players gaining by cooperative moves, are allowable. Cooperation is allowed at preplay and at-play periods and is based upon bargaining and negotiations between some or all of the players. *Trade-offs* occur, in which players may incur a loss in order to achieve a greater gain, such as one usually associates with such *parlor games* as Monopoly. The result is that competing persons with conflicting goals make moves in which all gain and none lose; therefore, the sum of winnings and losses will be less than or greater than zero but not equal to zero.

The infinite game is a situation in which the number of strategies is virtually unlimited. Such games usually encompass continuous, dynamic decision conditions that involve not only the strategy selection but the timing and phasing of strategies as well. It should appear obvious that one has the easiest mathematical task with two-person zero-sum games and the most difficult mathematical task with infinite games in which winnings and losses may or may not be equal to zero.

SIMPLE GAMES

We can learn much about the methods of game theory by examining a number of *simple games.* While these games are admittedly simplifications of real-world urban problems, this way of thinking about gaming applies to all games. As a general rule, simple games are usually taken to mean two-person zero-sum games.

TWO-FINGER MORRA

A sunny village square in southern Italy, with a warm wind blowing on groups of men drinking *vino* and playing a game, seems an unlikely setting to start our evaluation of simple games. These men will probably be engaged in the traditional game, often called *two-finger morra,* or any variation of it extending up to the full five fingers, in which they will passionately throw out fingers and attempt to predict the number of fingers thrown by an opponent, or throw a number of fingers such that the sum of fingers thrown will be odd or even. Ex-sandlot baseball players will probably recall playing a variation of this game, which we called Odds and Evens as young boys in New York, to determine which team got first "ups."

Two-finger morra, the elementary form of simple games, involves two persons who are allowed to throw either one or two fingers simultaneously. One player will choose evens, in which the total number of fingers must be an even number, i.e., two or four. The other player will have odds, which requires that an odd number of fingers be thrown, i.e., three. Let us assume that player A has chosen evens, and the winner will receive a dime from the other player. The game is a *fair game* in that each player has an equal chance to win, and we assume that payment will be made by the loser to the winner. This means that each player has only two strategies: each can throw either one or two fingers, let us say with the right hand. The strategies and possible rewards can be shown as a *payoff matrix*, as shown in Table 10:1. The payoff matrix is normally given for the first player only, player A in our example, in that it expresses the possible pay-

TABLE 10:1. Payoff matrix for two-finger morra.

		Player B	
	Strategies	Strategies	
		1	2
Player A	1	10	−10
	2	−10	10

offs for each strategy that the first player could select. The payoff matrix for the second player in zero-sum games is simply the negative of the first player's payoff matrix.

The entries in the payoff matrix, dimes expressed as pennies in our example, are sometimes called *utility values* and represent the effect of corresponding strategies. For example, if player A selects strategy 1 and player B selects strategy 2, player A will lose a dime to player B because the total number of fingers thrown will be odd. Utility values are expressed as money, commodities, votes, or any other quantifiable payoff possibilities. Sometimes in urban analysis utility values are expressed in qualitative measures when quantitative measures cannot be devised; the most common qualitative utility values are yes-no-maybe, go-no go, certain-uncertain, like–dislike–no response.

From a village square in southern Italy to the sandlots of New York to mathematical and scientific theory may seem like a long row to hoe, but this is the evolution of two-finger morra as a conceptual basis for game theory and its methods. The structure of the two-finger morra game is the same as most two-person zero-sum games: (1) strategies of player A, (2) strategies of player B, and (3) payoff matrix.

The heart of the method of game theory, as well as the applicability and relevance for urban analysis, lies in the development of criteria for selecting strategies, which are usually called *decision rules*. Decision rules can take any one of three forms for most games:

1. *Rational Strategy.* Assuming that each player is concerned solely with his own gains at the expense of the other players, he will select the strategy which corresponds to the decision rules which maximize utility values.

2. *Irrational Strategy.* Assuming that each player is concerned with his own gains but not necessarily at the expense of the other players only, he may select the strategy which is a variation of the decision rules for any of a variety of reasons.

3. *Nonrational Strategy.* Assuming that each player may or may not be concerned with his own gains and may or may not be concerned with the expense of the other players, he may select a strategy that is unrelated to decision rules.

Decision rules are of great interest to urban analysts. Urban analysts are involved with problems of decision-makers who require assistance; often the urban analyst can provide this assistance in the form of decision rules. Game theory is useful for determining decision rules based upon the rational strategy. Decision-makers can accept the advice of the urban analysts and apply the decision rules in order to act as "rational men." In many cases, however, the decision-maker will consider factors other than those related to the rational strategy and produce an irrational strategy — this is what one might call the "art of politics." Nonrational strategies are outside the realm of scientific methods, since they are random at best. Nonrational decisions are extremely rare in urban analysis, and few politicians and decision-makers can exist in today's urban systems by using nonrational strategies.

DOMINANT STRATEGY

A special case of rational strategy with considerable advantage and interest to urban analysts is called *dominant strategy*. The dominant strategy is that pleasant situation in which the strategy for rational selec-

TABLE. 10:2. Payoff matrix for dominant-strategy game.

Player B

Strategies		Strategies		
		1	2	3
Player A	1	3	2	5
	2	3	1	3

tion is obvious because there is no other strategy which will bring as high utility values regardless of the other player's moves. Considering Table 10:2 allows one to learn the nature of a dominant strategy. In this game the dominant strategy for player A is strategy 1, since it is at least as good as or better than strategy 2 no matter what player B may choose as a strategy. On the other hand, player B has a dominant strategy. Player B would eliminate strategy 3, since the other strategies are as good as or better than strategy 3 in terms of minimizing losses (since in this game player B cannot win anyway). Assuming that the two players are rational, player B would realize that player A will most likely select strategy 1 and therefore would select strategy 2 in order to minimize his losses. The result of this game would be that player A would receive a utility of 2 from player B — this is often called the *rational strategy value* of the game.

SADDLE POINTS

Unfortunately, the complex urban world does not always allow urban analysts to use games which have dominant strategies; if it did, digital computers could do the job nicely without human intervention. There are decision rules that can be used for two-person zero-sum games with rational strategy selection in the absence of dominant strategies. Considering Table 10:3, we can examine the special case of the *saddle point*.

There is no dominant strategy in this game, and hence no rational strategy is obvious. If player A were to select strategy 1, he could win 7 or lose 4, but since player B is assumed to be rational, he will realize that player A is most likely to select strategy 1; thus player B would select strategy 1 and player A would lose 4. If player A were to select strategy 3, he could win 6 or lose 5, but since player B is assumed to be rational, he would select strategy 3 and player A would lose 5. If player A were to select strategy 2, he could not lose anything and could win 3, but player

TABLE 10:3. Payoff matrix for saddle-point game.

		Player B			
		Strategies			
	Strategies	1	2	3	Minimum Payoff
Player A	1	−4	−1	7	−4
	2	3	0	3	0
	3	6	−1	−5	−5
	Maximum Payoff	6	0	7	—

B, still assumed to be rational, would select strategy 2, and hence player A would win nothing. The rational strategy value of this game would be zero.

Referring to Table 10:3, one can note that a column for *minimum payoff values* and row for *maximum payoff values* have been added. The minimum payoff to player A would be zero for strategy 2, and the maximum payoff to player B would be zero for his strategy 2. The corresponding utility value is also zero and lies in the second row and second column. This is called a *saddle point* in that it has the extraordinary function of setting both the upper and lower rational strategy values for the game.

Games with saddle points require that each player select strategies which minimize the maximum losses. Such a decision rule is called the *minimax criterion*. In our example, realizing that a saddle point exists, player B would select strategy 2, since it would be the smallest of his three possible maximum payoffs. Player A would apply the countervailing decision rule and attempt to maximize his minimum payoffs, which is called the *maximin criterion*, and hence player A would select his strategy 2. In other words, using the concept of minimizing losses, player A would select the strategy in which the minimum payoff is the largest, and player B would select the strategy in which the maximum payoff to player A is the smallest.

The saddle point establishes the upper and lower rational strategy values, as we mentioned, and these upper and lower values are usually the same in simple games. When the upper and lower rational strategy values are the same, a *steady state* is said to exist. The steady state is a game in which neither player can improve his own gains, since each player is assumed to be aware of the saddle point and is applying the maximin or minimax decision rules. The game will terminate at the steady-state value, which is zero in our example. Thus saddle-point games are fully predictable in that neither player is likely to depart from the decision rules if we assume rational strategy selections.

IRRATIONAL STRATEGY

Sometimes a simple game of the two-person zero-sum type can involve irrational strategies. Consider Table 10:4, which shows a game with no dominant strategy or saddle point. As can be seen, the least that player A could lose would be -3, and the least that he could win would be 3. Thus the lower rational strategy value of the game is -3, and the upper rational strategy value of the game is 3, using the minimax and maximin criteria. This means that there would be no rational strategy value for the game ($+3$ and -3 equals zero).

TABLE 10:4. Payoff matrix for irrational-strategy game.

		Player B			
		Strategies			
	Strategies	1	2	3	Minimum Payoff
Player A	1	0	-3	3	-3
	2	6	5	-4	-4
	3	1	2	-5	-5
	Maximum Payoff	6	5	3	—

However, it is doubtful that minimax and maximin criteria would be used. If player A were to select strategy 1, he would maximize his minimum payoff at -3; but if player B were to minimize his maximum payoff to player A, he would select strategy 3 and lose 3. This would not please player B, so he would ignore the decision rules and select strategy 2 and win 3. Anticipating this change, player A also would ignore the decision rules and select strategy 2 and win 5. Realizing this, player B would switch back to strategy 3 to try to win 4. Then player A would consider moving back to strategy 1, and the cycle would start all over again and conceivably never terminate. Such a game is called an *unsteady state* because the decision rules do not yield a termination point.

There is no simple way out of this dilemma. Game theory holds that the way to play such a game is to use an irrational strategy to try to outsmart the other assumedly rational player — in other words, to use irrationality to offset rationality. The scientific way to do this would be to select the random number, from an appropriate source, which corresponds to an available strategy. This would throw the opposing player off guard, since predictability would be lost. The result is that neither player knows in advance what the other player will do. Hence, if played to completion in this manner, a steady state will exist, and the winnings and losses of each player will be determined by chance. But at least the odds will be the same for both.

MIXED STRATEGIES

Rarely does the real world offer the opportunity to use a single strategy in order to win a game. Usually, *mixed strategies* are necessary. Game theory holds that a probability distribution can be assigned to the discrete number of strategies available to the players. This would take the form

x_i = probability that player A selects strategy i, where $i = 1, 2, \ldots, m$,
y_j = probability that player B selects strategy j, where $j = 1, 2, \ldots, n$.

Since these probabilities must sum to one, players A and B would assign values to each alternative strategy, the result being the probability distribution. The probability distribution determines the game plan, which is the mixed strategy of each player for strategies i and j. In order to not confuse actual and probable strategies, the original strategies are often called the *pure strategies*. The actual playing of the game requires each player to use mixed strategies as a method for determining which pure strategy to employ.

A useful measure for mixed strategies is called the *expected payoff*, which is essentially a measure of the demand for a strategy. The expected payoff is measured as follows:

$$E = \sum_{i=1}^{m} \sum_{j=1}^{n} p_{ij} x_i y_j,$$

where

E = expected payoff,
p_{ij} = probability that player A selects strategy i and player B selects strategy j.

The expected value is a useful measure in that it serves as an estimation and prediction of the average payoff if the game is played a number of times. The problem, however, is that this tells little about the risk and uncertainty of using probability distributions for strategy selection.

Many procedures exist for determining the decision rules when mixed strategies are used, although none are foolproof. Extensions of the minimax and maximin criteria can be made by using a number of game theory hypotheses even when the mixed strategies are based upon probabilities. Graphical methods have been developed by which the analyst can map the game and determine the decision rules. Even optimization models have been used to determine decision rules in mixed-strategy games. The equivalent linear programming model, for example, would be

$$\text{Max } E = \sum_{i=1}^{m} \sum_{j=1}^{n} p_{ij} x_i y_j,$$

subject to

$$\sum_{i=1}^{m} \sum_{j=1}^{n} p_{ij} x_i y_j \geq \text{lower value of the game.}$$

This is based upon the assumption that the optimal decision rules would be those that maximize the expected payoff such that it would be as good as or better than the lower rational decision value of the game. There are a very large variety and multitudinous versions of linear programming and other optimizing models for mixed strategies, none of which is necessarily better than the others.

CRITIQUE OF GAME THEORY

The basic critique of game theory is, "How realistic is it for real-world urban analysis?" We have said that models represent the urban system through simplification; this simplification is the inherent elegance of modeling. Game theory is used to formulate games which attempt to deal with the complexities of the real world through imitation of them, but not necessarily through simplification and sifting or winnowing. The result is that gaming may or may not imitate the real world, but critics argue that game theory does not provide an understanding of why urban systems function as they do or why residents behave in various ways.

Game theory sometimes serves as the basis for finding optimal solutions to urban system problems that seem to be *prima facie* impossible to model. The optimization takes form initially as decision rules that later become model parameters. The danger is that the decision rules are almost always based upon rational strategy selections, yet we have explained that even some simple games require irrational or mixed strategies.

Gaming uses real people to play roles and make decisions. The unfortunate result is that people often lose their uniqueness and individuality when they are told to assume a role, especially one in which they are uncomfortable and act as they think they "should act." On the other hand, it also has been found that different people playing the same roles in the same games will behave quite differently. Hence a variation is inevitable in gaming. The degree of variation found for several runs of any game may well affect its usefulness for urban analysis.

These are the most common and frequently heard criticisms of gaming. We believe it fitting to present them at this stage as an epilogue to theory and as a preface to applications. We consider many of these critiques to be serious, but we still hold to our earlier statement that the learning and understanding characteristics of game theory and gaming are the most valuable. Furthermore, we have found that despite these criticisms training is possible through gaming if and only if the roles are well understood by the persons conducting the game.

OPERATIONAL GAMING

A kind of trilogy exists in gaming in that games provide the conceptual and intellectual bases upon which game theory can be used for urban analysis. When games are concerned with urban problems, whether hypothetical or real, and when game theory is used to derive decision rules for urban analysis, the procedure is generally referred to as *operational gaming*. Operational gaming usually takes data from real urban systems and simulates problems, alternative solutions, and effects of moves. There are also cases in which real-world data have not been used, and data are manufactured from hypothetical urban systems.

While operational gaming did not catch on in urban analysis until the late 1950s, we already have three generations of games concerned with urban problems. "Generation" is perhaps too harsh a word in that it implies that some are old and impotent; this is not necessarily true. Nevertheless, the terminology is prevalent and we shall use it to examine applications.

FIRST-GENERATION GAMES

First-generation games for urban analysis first appeared in the late 1950s and were in wide use in colleges and universities by the early 1960s.

First-generation games are usually two-person zero-sum games, n-person zero-sum games, or infinite-strategy games.

A fine example of the two-person zero-sum game was developed in 1961 for teaching the economic aspects of urban redevelopment problems.[7] The game used for this purpose is often called the *prisoner's dilemma*. This intriguing name comes from the analogy of the police arresting two suspects for a crime and placing them in separate cells pending booking. The police will talk to each suspect individually in order to get a confession. Without collusion between each other, the suspects can choose not to confess. This would mean that they would be released or booked for a lesser offense. If both confess, the police might offer reduced charges or punishment. If one confesses and the other does not, it is likely that the confessor will receive light punishment for turning state's evidence. The prisoner's dilemma, then, is that separation prohibits collusion, so that the rational strategy selection for both prisoners would be not to confess even though both would benefit by confessing. If one prisoner knew the other would not confess, he could confess and minimize imprisonment.

The prisoner's dilemma game is applied to landlords with properties in declining areas by considering two adjacent properties with owner A and owner B. Each owner has made an initial investment in his property and is now deliberating on whether to make an additional investment for redevelopment. The strategy will be affected by the alteration in investment returns and by the strategy of the neighboring landlord.

The payoff matrix is defined on the basis of return rates on the original investments and return rates for idle cash reserves, which are assumed to be corporate bonds with 4 percent yields. The payoff matrix is shown in Table 10:5. The utility to each owner is shown in parentheses, with

TABLE 10:5. Payoff matrix for prisoner's dilemma game for urban redevelopment.

		Owner B	
		Strategy	
Owner A	Strategy	Invest	Not Invest
	Invest	$(.07, .07)$	$(.03, .10)$
	Not Invest	$(.10, .03)$	$(.04, .04)$

[7] Otto A. Davis and Andrew B. Whinston, "The Economics of Urban Renewal," *Law and Contemporary Problems*, 26, no. 1 (Winter, 1961), 103-117.

the right-side utility value representing the average return for owner A and the left side representing the average return for owner B. For example, this would mean that if both chose not to invest in redevelopment, each would continue to receive the 4 percent returns from corporate bonds. On the other hand, if both owners decided to sell their corporate bonds and invest in redevelopment of their properties, it is assumed that each would enjoy a yield of 7 percent.

The game has usually been played for apartment properties, in which such factors as quality of neighborhood, parking, and amenities are important in addition to rental costs. This would mean that if owner A invested in redevelopment, which would probably mean demolition and reconstruction of the apartments with adequate parking and amenities, he would be improving the quality of the neighborhood for owner B's tenants as well. Owner B's tenants would benefit from the improved neighborhood even though owner B had done nothing. It is highly probable that owner B, being a rational capitalist, would raise his rentals as soon as leases allow, since his property is now in a better neighborhood. The payoff matrix assumes that owner B's average return will rise to 10 percent, even though he has done nothing but raise rents. Owner A will only receive 3 percent return on his redeveloped property because it is in a neighborhood of unimproved properties and hence cannot attract higher-income tenants, as it might be able to do in an alternative location. The counterpart situation is shown in the matrix in the event that owner A did not invest and owner B did invest, assumed to be the reverse of the payoff described above.

This is a dominant-strategy game for the payoff matrix used in our example. Owner A would select not to invest, since he would receive a higher average return regardless of what owner B does. Similarly, the dominant strategy for owner B is not to invest, since he can receive a higher average rate of return regardless of what owner A does. The dominant strategies show that both owners of declining apartments in deteriorating neighborhoods will not invest in redevelopment, just as both prisoners would not confess. Even though both landlords would benefit by redeveloping both properties, they could benefit more as individuals by not investing. This is a simplified version of more elaborate prisoner's dilemma games that are used for teaching urban redevelopment and various other economic problems of urban systems. Critics have argued that it is an oversimplification of urban problems, but these simple games have been liked by both teachers and students.

Many of the first-generation games of urban analysts have been directed toward problems of land use and development, probably because of the simplifications possible. *New Town* is an *n*-person zero-sum game which uses 12 players; a two-person zero-sum version is also available.[8] The players assume various roles as private developers, planners, urban analysts, and elected and appointed officials in a hypothetical urban system that starts with no land developed. The game was designed to teach students and interested persons about the factors affecting decisions made by the various decision-makers and decision-influencers in the land development of urban systems. The New Town game will often confront such problems as development controls, suburban versus central city development, place of commercial and industrial land uses, competing and conflicting land uses, and urban redevelopment. While a simplified game, it has been somewhat popular with students and urban analysts because it combines elementary learning and understanding with some of the entertainment usually associated only with parlor games.

Two more serious and sophisticated games for urban development are infinite-strategy games. The first of these was developed by Richard D. Duke and others in order to learn and understand more about the complexities of nonquantifiable factors of urban development.[9] The game is called *Metropolis* and uses the tri-county Lansing, Michigan, urban system as a case study. Metropolis uses five categories of role playing:

1. *Politicians.* Settle conflicts arising over demands for urban space and other scarce resources.

2. *Businessmen.* Make basic decisions concerning the enterprises that determine the settlement patterns, as well as commercial and industrial projects, which affect the economic base of the urban system.

3. *Administrators.* Develop goals for the growth of urban systems as well as necessary controls on development.

4. *Educators.* Act as superintendents of human resources in the urban system.

5. *Judges.* Resolve conflicts that cannot be settled through compromises among the other players and establish the rules of the game for urban growth decisions.

Metropolis was developed for varying numbers of players with relatively unlimited strategies.[10] Playing becomes so complex that digital computers

[8] New Town was developed by Barry R. Lawson while he was a student at Cornell University. It is available from the New Town Company of Ithaca, N.Y.

[9] Richard D. Duke et al., *M.E.T.R.O.* (Lansing, Mich.: Tri-County Regional Planning Commission, 1960).

[10] A summary of the conceptual aspects is available; see Richard L. Meier and Richard D. Duke, "Gaming Simulation for Urban Planning," *Journal of the American Institute of Planners,* 32, no. 1 (Jan., 1966), 3-17.

are needed to assist the players with their decisions and determine the effects of decisions. Interaction and cooperation among players become quite involved, and computer models may be constructed to estimate and predict the by-products, spin-offs, and side effects of decisions. A simplified version is shown as Fig. 10:1.

A similar operational game experiment was taking place at Cornell University during the design and development of Metropolis, and it has became known as the *Cornell Land Use Game* or *CLUG*.[11] The interesting aspect of CLUG is that it does not define specific roles for the players. It establishes a set of definitions for the hypothetical urban system and allocates the resources of the urban system to the players, who then become the decision-makers.

CLUG has been very popular with students of urban analysis because it is somewhat entertaining, as is New Town. In terms of structure CLUG is a sophisticated hybrid of "chess and Monopoly."[12] This is because the strategies of the game are determined only by the rules of game; therefore, role playing is only a response to the rules of the game. The rules of the game for CLUG include a set of predetermined factors: (1) the location and efficiency of the highway network, (2) the location of major points of access to other urban systems, (3) a structure of real property taxation to pay for the building and maintenance of needed community services, and (4) a range of land use categories. Each player is given a fixed amount of capital with which he can buy land and construct buildings in order to get a return on his investment as well as to make profits from the operations of his investments (for example, he can spend part of his capital on advertising in order to bring customers to his shopping center).

The CLUG has undergone several modifications, one of which did away with the hypothetical urban system milieu by incorporating topographic and transportation features from the Syracuse, New York, urban system. The game has been used in both undergraduate and graduate courses at a number of colleges and universities as well as by civic groups and even as a parlor game. Some of the more advanced modifications require digital computers for record keeping and determination of the effects of decisions and strategies when a large number of players or infinite strategies are allowed.

The first-generation games of urban problems were modest and, we daresay, entertaining (a quality which does not exist in later games). The

[11] Allan G. Feldt, *The Cornell Land Use Game* (Ithaca, N.Y.: Center for Housing and Environmental Studies, Cornell University, 1966).
[12] Ibid.

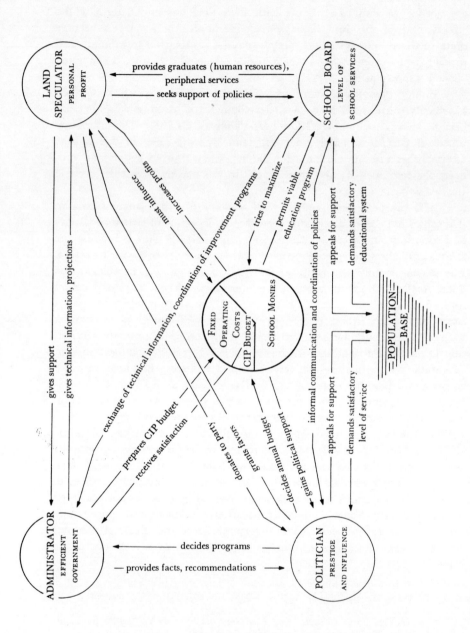

FIG. 10:1. Interactions between players in Metropolis.

games were developed solely for learning and understanding, with a dose of pleasantness for teaching. The originators of these games talked only in vague terms about the usefulness of operational gaming for modeling, simulation, and decision-making.

SECOND-GENERATION GAMES

Second-generation games were extensions of first-generation games to modeling, simulation, and decision-making for real urban systems. The two foremost examples of second-generation games, *Region I* and *City I,* were developed by the Washington Center for Metropolitan Studies in order to simulate problems of urban systems using data from case studies.[13] Region I is a somewhat elaborate extension of CLUG which incorporates several models of decision-making into the rules of the game.

City I is a game that attempts to simulate problems of various urban systems in order to test alternative solutions. Teams of players are needed to fulfill a number of roles for the political, economic, and social subsystems of the given urban system. A hypothetical version of City I deals with 625 squares representing land areas that could be developed. Unlike previous games, however, City I starts play with a fully developed central city and a partially developed suburban subcenter, as shown in Fig. 10:2.

There are nine teams needed for City I which represent entrepreneurial decision-making groups and government. A chairman is elected who acts as the mayor, and he in turn appoints four cabinet officers for highways, schools, public works, and zoning. The role of the governmental players is to find out the strategies of the entrepreneurial teams and estimate costs and benefits in terms of revenues and expenditures for alternative strategies. Government attempts to balance pressures from the teams that are seeking to maximize their investment returns with concerns for the public good.

The entrepreneurial teams build and manage property holdings, which they are given at the start of play. Each team has a portfolio of six types of properties: (1) heavy and light industry, (2) business goods (intermediate goods and machinery), (3) business services (accounting, computers, etc.), (4) personal goods (supermarkets), (5) personal services (medical, dental, and entertainment), and (6) residences. Each of the business types of properties may be developed at any of three levels of

[13] See *Region Manual* and *City I Manual* (Washington, D.C.: Washington Center for Metropolitan Studies, 1968).

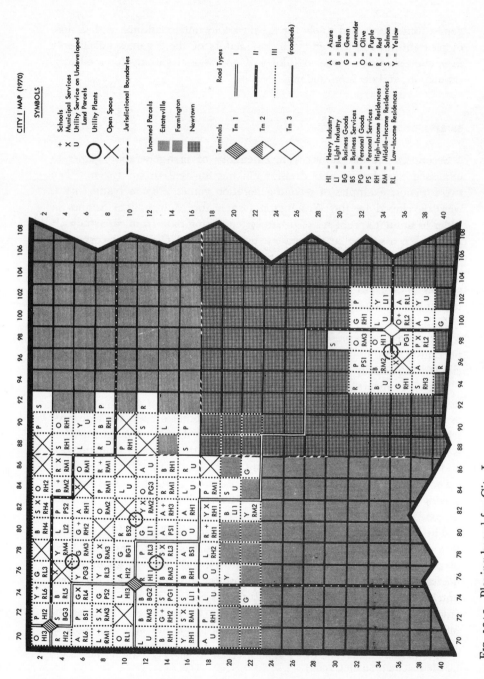

Fig. 10:2. Playing board for City I.

density, and there are low-, middle-, and high-priced residences. A digital computer informs each team of its holdings in such terms as income, sales, taxes, location, density, transportation costs, and price of goods.

City I allows for any degree of cooperation and wheeling and dealing among the teams that they wish. Much of the play actually consists of players attempting to persuade opposing players to sell, buy, or assist with the properties. Players also attempt to influence the government to grant privileges and immunities in such matters as zoning. The game is played for a prearranged time period, and the team with the highest returns from their portfolio development is the winner.

The problems simulated in the infinite-strategy game of City I are diverse. Political problems almost always arise in terms of which team can influence the government in legal ways. Basic qualities of management and finance are needed or must be developed by teams if they are to remain in the competition. In one game a team was particularly concerned about the high unemployment rate in a downtown ghetto area and decided to sponsor a Model Cities program by cooperating with the government. After much simulated trouble over boundary lines, federal regulations, and politics, the team was able to attract business and industry to the Model Cities area and effectively eliminate unemployment. The rest of the urban system suffered, however, in that unemployment rose in other parts of the urban system, an interesting point of speculation for real urban systems.

The City I game is complicated by a rather long playing time and the large number of players — 30 to 100 players are needed for the average session, which lasts two and one-half days. In order to overcome some of the drawbacks of City I, several variations have been developed in order to more effectively use it for teaching. *Telecity* is one version of City I which is played by remote terminals linked to a central computer which evaluates all player moves and strategies as well as keeps records. Telecity allows 25 to 60 players to play four or five rounds in a few hours.

The interaction between players in City I and Telecity is similar, as shown in Fig. 10:3. The inherent interaction pattern is that players seek to maximize personal gains by changing the status of the hypothetical or actual city. In order to achieve this, the entrepreneurial teams interact with players representing the economic, social, and governmental sectors, which serve to establish certain constraints upon change even in the perfect market mechanism which is assumed.

Region I, City I, and Telecity have been used as teaching devices in colleges and universities to the extent that several thousand students have played the game. But the teaching application has been almost entirely

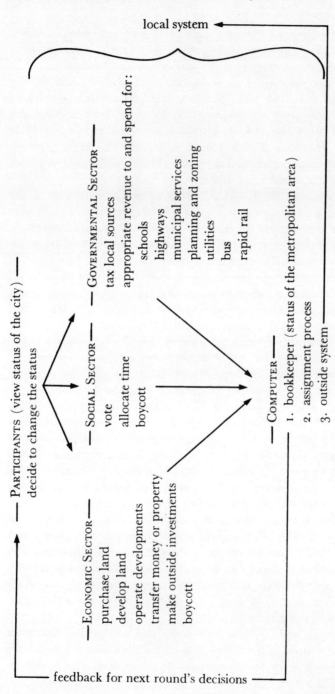

Fig. 10:3. Interaction between players in City I.

concerned with hypothetical urban systems, a point which critics often raise as indicative of a certain artificiality and irrelevance. Nevertheless, major contributions have been made to learning and understanding urban systems through second-generation games.

THIRD-GENERATION GAMES

Third-generation games are the latest stage of the evolution of operational gaming for urban analysis. These games are still experimental, and only a few are being played. The distinguishing feature of third-generation games is that they push the generality of the game to the full limit of scientific and technological capabilities in order to represent any urban system. The result is a highly generic game that can be customized to suit any given urban system by selecting the proper mix of characteristics.

Leaders in the design and development of third-generation games for urban systems argue that second-generation games, while quite successful for teaching, had little policy implications for decision-making in real urban systems.[14] In order to deal with this shortcoming, *Region II* was developed, which expanded upon the economic and governmental sectors of Region I. Similarly, *City II* expanded upon the economic and governmental sectors of City I in order to improve upon limited assumptions for strategies and to allow the players to utilize strategies based upon social consciousness.[15]

The current thrust of third-generation games is directed toward the development and implementation of *modular games*. Modular games are based upon the most common problem of simulation, the closed-system nature of the existing examples. Modular games are built upon five modules which represent five subsystems which interact to form the total system. The five modules are:

1. *National Module.* A computer simulates the measurements at the national level that affect all other urban systems at various lower levels.

2. *Regional Module.* Decisions are made concerning the allocation of industries to rural and urban systems and hence concerning the underlying employment base of urban systems.

3. *Metropolitan Module.* Different from the regional competition for

---

[14] Peter House and P. D. Patterson, "An Environmental Gaming-Simulation Laboratory," *Journal of the American Institute of Planners*, 35, no. 6 (Nov., 1969), 383-388.

[15] Environmetrics, Inc., *Environmental Modeling: The Method for Total Solutions* (Washington, D.C., 1970).

industries in that suburban and central areas now compete for industries and residences within the same metropolitan area.

4. *Central City Module.* The details of higher-level decisions are determined for such matters as zoning, politics, social problems, and voter preferences.

5. *Neighborhood Module.* The reaction and feedback of individuals are simulated. The social sector becomes very strong at this module, and citizen participation and advocacy of citizen causes are significant among the players. Thus the national module, almost entirely computer-based, sets the framework for urban systems in which to compete for economic, social, political, and physical gains. This is much more reflective of real urban systems in an open-system context, and the hierarchy of decision-making is realistic (see Fig. 10:4).

Having simulated the national module by digital computer, it is possible to use modular gaming for any given urban system with few structural changes. This is possible through the rather sophisticated rules of the game and use of the digital computer. One such experimental example of modular gaming, which is called the *environmental model,* allows for hundreds of players to make decisions for several different urban systems.[16] The developers of the environmental model argue that it not only has learning and understanding potentials but also allows real-world decision-makers and urban analysts to pretest programming and planning alternatives in order to simulate the effects both within and without the urban system.

While it is too early to judge the success or failure of such third-generation games as the environmental model, it has raised major issues for urban analysis. Somehow it seems reasonable for people to react to even the suggestion of large, complex simulations, with esoteric computer decision-making, as an approach for programming and planning urban systems. Yet to the urban analyst with a firm grasp of the proper role of scientific methods in urban analysis, the prospects are exciting.

A most ambitious third-generation game is called *Simsoc,* which derives from *simulated society.*[17] Simsoc is a teaching game for sociology, political science, and psychology courses concerned with urban problems. It differs from most other games in that it generates problems that the players must solve; the programmed rules of most urban problem games generate forces and factors that lead to problems. The salient feature of this approach is that players must come up with solutions from strategies that are quite numerous, sometimes infinite. The large number of strategies often results

[16] Ibid.
[17] William A. Gamson, *Simsoc: Simulated Society* (New York: Free Press, 1969).

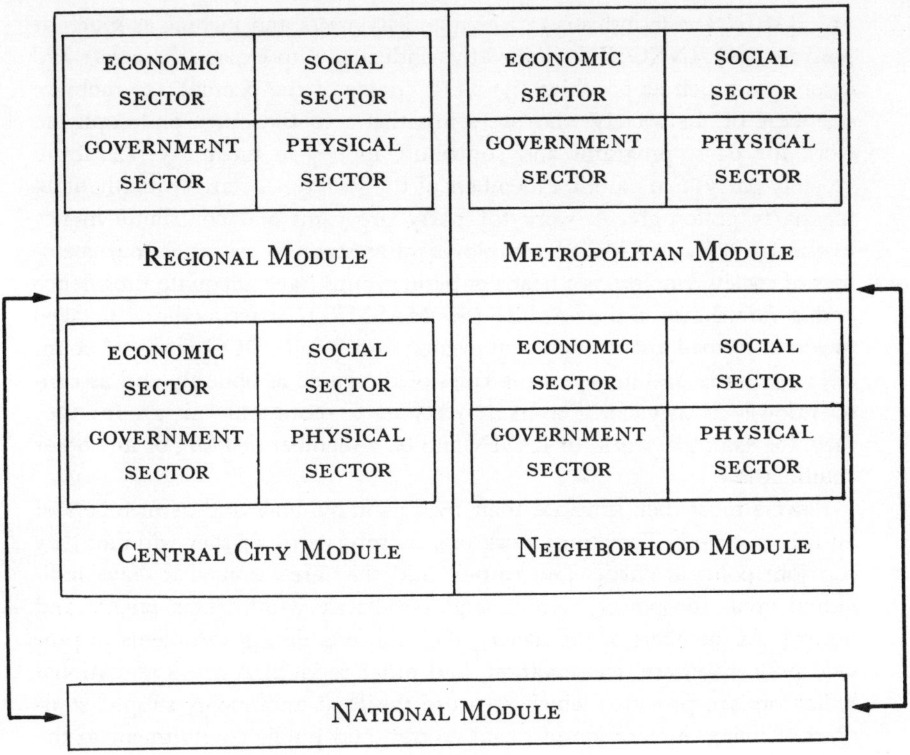

FIG. 10:4. Modular game structure.

in several strategies yielding solutions that work equally well — this is a basic point the game is designed to make.

Simsoc is similar to many of the stereotypes of war games in that specially designed rooms and equipment are suggested to improve play. Ideal facilities would involve laboratories which isolate teams of players representing various regions of an urban society but allow them communication capabilities. There also should be an observation station from which an instructor or game referee has some degree of control. Playing time varies from 60 hours and more, and the number of players can range from 20 to several hundred.

Players elect heads of seven groups which operate in four regions. Each of the seven groups offers employment possibilities for the remaining players if the players accept the overall objectives, which are as follows:

(1) BASIN (basic industry): to expand its assets and income as much as possible; (2) INNOVIN (innovative industry): to expand its assets and income as much as possible; (3) POP (party of the people): to mobilize members of the society who are sympathetic to the party philosophy to work for party programs and contribute money to the party; (4) SOP (society party): to mobilize members of the society who are sympathetic to the party philosophy to work for party programs and contribute money to the party; (5) EMPIN (employee interests): to see to it that members of society who are not heads of basic groups have adequate subsistence and a fair share of the wealth; (6) MASMED (mass media): to keep society informed about important events; and (7) JUDCO (judicial council): to clarify and interpret the rules of the game as honestly and as conscientiously as they can. Players may belong to more than one group: they may, for example, work for BASIN and be a member of POP, or any other combination.

Players must then simulate their lives as individuals and as members of an urban society. They must work to gain subsistence or they will die; they can join political parties and causes; and they are assumed to have individual goals for power, wealth, and popularity within their talents and powers. As members of the society, they can establish governments to provide police, welfare, conservation, and other services. A series of national indicators are provided which measure the food and energy supply, standard of living, integration of social groups, and public commitment to the society.

When the players have developed the society according to the rules of the game, the true learning objective can be introduced by the game referee. This consists of the introduction of problems for the players in the seven groups of the four regions to overcome. The usual problems are epidemics, earthquakes, and wars. Realism is possible in Simsoc by using various options in the game. Since there are four regions, it is possible to have some regions more wealthy in terms of resources and jobs than others. This will likely lead to rivalries between regions and concentration of political powers in the wealthy regions. Migration between regions is allowed through the use of the travel tickets which each player has received. He can move about the society in hope of finding his place and gaining wealth. To heighten the realism and introduce some Darwinistic concepts, unemployment, arrest, sickness, and death can occur.

Simsoc has been played in a number of colleges and universities and has been very worthwhile to students. Unlike most other third-generation games, Simsoc does not attempt to apply decision-making patterns to real-world societies. It is a modular game, however, and it is based upon the third-generation concepts of open systems and generic characteristics.

This discussion of first-, second-, and third-generation games has dealt only with what we consider to be the most significant and well-known games. In reality there is probably in existence or under development a very large number of games dealing with all or some urban problems. The very popularity of operational gaming gives rise to more and more experiments and new accomplishments, unlike many other aspects of scientific methods. With operational gaming, however, we enter into the twilight zone of science and art. We have explained science in a manner which relies upon judgment and intuition, but with gaming the scientific nature of the methods becomes somewhat vague.

RECOMMENDED EXERCISES

1. Select a problem which has received attention in the mass media of your community. Determine two principal decision-makers and formulate strategies for the two key roles. Determine through any means available what the possible political payoffs might be and enter these as the utility values in the payoff matrix. Develop a set of decision rules and find the rational strategy value.

2. Attempt to develop a simple game of hypothetical urban system. Borrowing from the Simsoc approach, make the game problem-oriented and introduce urban problems into the urban system. If possible, play several rounds of the game with interested colleagues.

FURTHER READING

Von Neumann, John, and Oskar Morganstern. *Games and Economic Behavior.* Princeton, N.J.: Princeton University Press, 1944.
While this famous work was not written necessarily for the layman, it is sufficiently lucid and well written that the interested reader can understand it. The book is a landmark work in that it formulates the framework for the application of the mathematical properties of game theory to real-world economic problems.

Gamson, William A. *Simsoc: Simulated Society.* New York: Free Press, 1969.
While just one of a number of important games, this work includes several

selected readings dealing with the theory and application of gaming to societal problems. It also provides detailed instructions and directions as well as all needed materials for the person who would like to play a third-generation game with the greatest of ease. All that is necessary is to convince several others to play the game.

Abt, Clark C. *Serious Games.* New York: Viking, 1970.

This highly readable book explores the work of the author and his firm, which is a leader in operational gaming for educational and instructional programs. Serious games are defined as operational gaming which simulates life and human conflicts. Examples of serious games are drawn from government, the military, and industry.

We may hope that machines will eventually compete with men in all purely intellectual fields. But which are the best ones to start with? Many people think that a very abstract activity, like the playing of chess, would be best.

A. M. Turing, *Can a Machine Think?* (1937)

PART V

URBAN INFORMATION SYSTEMS

Underlying the whole of urban analysis is a process for the collection, manipulation, interpretation, and dissemination of *data, information,* and *intelligence.* One can formally define data as the unitary relationship — one-to-one relationship — of an observation and a real-world phenomenon. For example, an item of data concerning population would be an observation of one person, one group, one race, or any other dis-aggregation. Data must be manipulated from their original state of *facts* into a more meaningful state of knowledge, which is the definition of information. Information is the use of data to determine the succinct and salient knowledge that is needed for urban analysis. An even higher form of information is intelligence, which is the inherent ability of a system to seize essential factors from complex information about complex urban problems. The definitional structure forms a hierarchy, as shown in Fig. 11:1, which can serve as our operational working hypothesis.

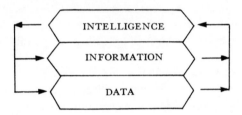

FIG. 11:1. Hierarchy of data, information, and intelligence.

Urban analysts rarely function as decision-makers, but they advise decision-makers on optimal choices. One can argue, then, that the main work of urban analysts is the provision of information and intelligence to decision-makers (assuming that most decision-makers have neither the intellectual equipment nor the desire to spend time on the personal evaluation of the data and analytical techniques used to generate information and intelligence). The urban analyst assembles data; manipulates data by use of predictive and estimating models, optimizing models, and simulation and gaming; interprets the results; and disseminates the intelligence to decision-makers with recommendations. The functional process of urban

CHAPTER 11

Urban Information Systems

analysis is greatly improved, then, if one has an effective and efficient system for data, information, and intelligence.

Systems of data, information, and intelligence are usually called *urban information systems*. An urban information system is a complex of people, equipment, and processes interacting to provide information and intelligence from input data for assistance in decision-making. The term *interaction* is critical in that it implies that men, machines, and knowledge — for example, science — must work together in a concerted action. This means that we can quickly dismiss myths about "machines taking over," "science gone wild," and "rampant technology." One can readily see that this approach is one in which machines are simply tools to ease the burden of manual mental work for urban analysts, and scientific knowledge acts as a constraint on the sophistication of this effort. The reason that we choose to stress urban information systems is that we view them as *overall, integrative, and coordinating mechanisms* for urban analysis. They provide convenient umbrellas over the whole of urban problems and enhance the information- and intelligence-providing responsibilities of urban analysts.

As a general rule, urban analysts are *users* rather than *collectors* of data. Urban analysts should resort to data collection at the source only when there is no feasible alternative for assembling data. Urban analysts are more concerned with the use of data in urban information systems than with detailed procedures for its collection.

Urban information systems facilitate the *accessibility, availability,* and *consistency* of data that urban analysts require for their activities. But urban information systems cannot be adequately developed if the models and simulations needed for the conversion of data into information and intelligence are not available or likely to become available. Hence, urban information systems are not likely to be used to their fullest capacities and capabilities without an underlying *analytical system* of models and simulations.

Constructs

Urban information systems are developed ideally to provide two types of information: (1) *management information* and (2) *programming and planning information*. Management information is the day-to-day operational information and intelligence needed for an urban system. It in-

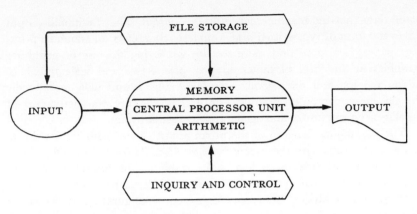

FIG. 11:2. Hardware configuration.

cludes such basic operations as billing, accounting, inventories, payrolls, and statistical summaries as well as more advanced management operations like budgeting, audits, personnel classification, and annual reports. Programming and planning information is related to longer-range information for comprehensive planning — physical, social, economic, and political — as well as for the programming of operations, both operating and capital. Urban analyses are involved with both types of information, depending upon the nature and temporal dimensions of the problems under examination.

The term *equipment* in our definition generally applies to the *hardware* of the urban information system. The generic hardware configuration for an urban information system is shown in Fig. 11:2. The *input* component allows the data and instructions for processing to enter into the *central processor unit*. The central processor unit performs computations as instructed within the capacity of its *memory* and the speed of its *arithmetic units*. When data are stored, the input must draw upon the *file storage*, which usually takes the form of *punchcards, magnetic tape*, or *magnetic drum* or any combination thereof. The *inquiry and control component* provides the *man-machine interface* or the interaction between operator and central processor unit. The urban analyst is rarely the operator of the hardware, although some advanced simulation and gaming approaches require that decisions be made before the machine can process further data, and hence the urban analyst must advise the operator on further processing. The result of the above components working together, with a set of instructions to the machine on what to compute, called *software*, and valid data that the machine can utilize, is *output*. The traditional output takes the form of typewritten *alpha-numeric* characters on standard print-out paper, but more and more we are witnessing the use of computer graphics in the form of tables, graphs, perspective and scale drawings, maps, movies, and televisionlike displays.[1] The future will undoubtedly herald more computer graphics, since they simplify the derivation of intelligence from information generated by the hardware.

The paramount concern of the urban analyst is not with the hardware configuration but with the *system configuration*. The system configuration of an urban information system is the result of the interfaces of man, machine, and knowledge; the latter takes expression in our definition through the analytical system. This system configuration is shown in Fig. 11:3.

A process must be developed by which urban analysts can use urban information systems as tools for assisting their analyses. The process involves the formulation of *questions* from *problems,* which can be translated into *queries,* that can be submitted to the hardware configuration.[2] This is not a semantic game but, rather, an operational definition. There are innumerable urban problems that can be posed in many terms, but there are relatively few that can be formulated into questions that are relevant for analysis and can be expressed in the analysts' terms by translation to queries. For example, one can argue that housing is a problem in a given urban system. This problem must be transformed into a series of questions if one is to explore it through analysis. Suitable questions might be, "What areas have poorer housing conditions than others?" "What is being done about poor housing in these areas?" "What should be done about poor housing in these areas?" Yet even these questions are not in the proper form for analysis using an urban information system. Queries are the analytical statements that can be made to the urban information system with its incorporated analytical system. Queries would take the following form: Given areas $A = (1, 2, \ldots, n)$, which have the housing supplies $X = (x_1, x_2, \ldots, x_n)$, what is the percentage of each element of X that has the following conditions $C = (c_a, c_b, c_c, \ldots, c_*)$ that we have defined as "poor"? What public and private programs are underway or completed in A that have reduced $f(X)$, where $f(X)$ is the percentage of poor housing? What optimal solutions are there to Min $f(X)$? Queries give the ques-

---

[1] For further details, see Anthony J. Catanese, James Grant, and Edward Kashuba, *Application of Computer Graphics to Urban and Regional Planning* (Atlanta: Georgia Institute of Technology, 1969).

[2] Kenneth J. Dueker, *A Recommendation for a State Planning Information System* (Madison: Wisconsin Bureau of State Planning, 1967), pp. 1-16.

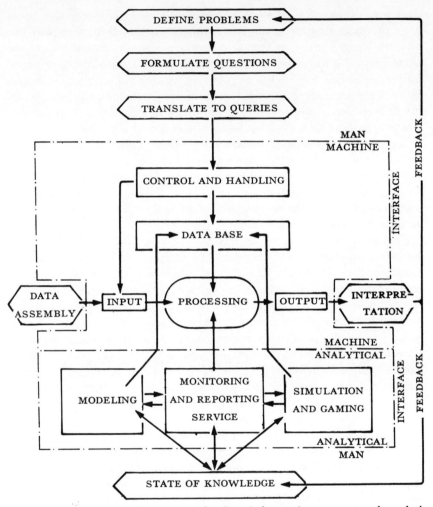

FIG. 11:3. System configuration of urban information system and analytical system.

tions raised by the problem statement a quantitative basis by which optimal solutions can be determined. In more and more cases this quantitative basis is integrated with a qualitative basis of judgment that both expands the reality of the information and still remains within our conceptualization of scientific methods.

Within the realm of activities performed by man in this system configuration are *data assembly* and *interpretation* of output. Data are collected at the source or assembled through familiarity or a search of available data. After the processing the urban analyst interprets the information and extracts relevant intelligence for presentation to decision-makers and as an aid in preparing recommendations. If the output is unsatisfactory or needs further processing, the analyst will refer to the original problem statement to check for accuracy, or he will consult the general body of knowledge on the problem for insights on how to make the modifications. This activity is called *feedback,* and the operation is often called the *feedback loop.*

The *state of knowledge* upon which the urban analyst has developed his models, simulations, gaming, and problem statements is largely an operation performed by man. We show an interface with the analytical system, however, because it has been our experience that the state of knowledge is often expanded by the development of an analytical system, which often uncovers new knowledge.

The analytical system, which has been the stuff of this book, is primarily an interrelated and complementary organization of models, simulations, and games which provides the urban analyst with the tools for data manipulation and problem-solving. We have included in Fig. 11:3 a box called *monitoring and reporting service* because this may be the major contribution of the urban information system in conjunction with the analytical system. The monitoring and reporting service is any coordinated set of techniques and methods that provides urban analysts and decision-makers with the following: (1) intelligence about conditions — social, economic, political, and physical — within the urban system at specified time periods; (2) "red flags" that show what conditions, areas, or groups are near a critical mass or trouble spot; (3) early warning signals that sound the alert for possible breakdowns in the urban system, such as traffic, fires, crime, etc.; (4) opportunity places or points of leverage and potential that can resolve future problems; and (5) progress reports on steps taken to solve problems and improve the urban system's performance and general quality of life. The monitoring and reporting system must draw heavily upon the analytical system, data, and processing capabilities in order to provide this worthwhile intelligence operation. It is, in this sense, the capstone of the intelligence function of an urban information system.

The machine realm of the urban information system is essentially the same as our previous description except that we incorporate a *data base* and somewhat expand the notions of *control and handling.* The data base is composed of all available and potentially available data, most often in machine-readable form. The control and handling component is expanded to include certain *real-time* operations, that is, the type of operation that uses a hardware configuration to perform ongoing functions such as regulating traffic control devices, locating fire alarms, directing emergency services, etc.

The set of interrelated operations from the man, machine, and analytical system realms provides an integrated and meaningful mechanism for the overall application of scientific methods to urban systems. It helps to place the role of the urban analyst in proper perspective as that of chief adviser to the elected and appointed decision-makers within the urban system.

Rationale of Urban Information Systems

We would be somewhat remiss in our presentation if we did not examine in some depth the arguments both pro and con regarding urban informations systems, since we have placed them in such a lofty setting. We must develop a rationale that is suited to contemporary urban systems if we wish to propose the development of urban information systems and complementary analytical systems.

Urban information systems are quite popular in many urban systems but for all the wrong reasons. Somewhat mystified and terrified at the same time by computers, mathematics, science, and technology, decision-makers and public and private officials concerned with the future of urban systems have rushed into the development of urban information systems. Their rationale has been that urban information systems (1) are efficient and economic and (2) free urban analysts and decision-makers, as well as general administrative personnel, from manual toil so that they can concentrate on more important matters.

Urban information systems are efficient and economic in the *long run*. For the initial period of system design and development and for that somewhat prolonged honeymoon period between the system and its new people-users, costs will be very high and efficiency will be the impossible dream. The first operating urban information system (in Alexandria, Virginia, with a population of 120,000) cost at least $100,000 to develop, and operating costs for the first year were $160,000. These are rather high (over $2.00 per capita), and there is little evidence that hardware and software costs will go down in the future (on the contrary, costs are rising). Over a period of years the operating costs of urban information systems may decrease in terms of unit costs, but it is a grievous error to argue that urban information systems reduce the costs of operating urban systems, except in the long run through optimum use of the intelligence such a system provides. Parenthetically, we might add that recent advances in *time sharing*, where many users share the same computer, and software development, where new programs are shared by users, have eased the cost problem somewhat, but inflationary price spirals quickly reduce the savings.

The traditional argument — urban analysts are freed from unexciting computational and data analysis tasks — is somewhat more acceptable. Our experience has shown, however, that the development of urban information systems requires more effort in these areas by urban analysts rather than less. We suspect the reason is that few urban analysts have integrated their models and simulations in a meaningful way into the analytical system that is required for an urban information system. Similarly, urban analysts must often fill the gaps in missing or poor-quality data for the data base. Hence we believe that urban analysts will be freed from their manual toils by an urban information system only after a period of time has expired and the system is operating smoothly.

A more pragmatic and sober rationale for having urban information systems can be developed if we are discreet in our arguments. We believe that a viable case for the development of urban information systems does exist when the following conditions are present in any given urban system.

1. When the scientific techniques and methods used for both management and programming and planning information are sufficiently complex and sophisticated, and the burden of computation can be eased by an urban information system. This condition is consistent with our basic position that urban information systems must be based upon analytical systems, since we see no particular advantage in having any kind of system which simply gives us more information to mull over without any analytical framework.

2. When the data base is sufficiently large and complex, and manual processing methods are inadequate. Analytical systems require voracious amounts of data, much of it complicated, and the problems of storage, retrieval, and processing become beyond human capabilities. We might add that in our view the major attractions of the digital computer are its processing speed and its memory capacity.

3. When there is a sincere desire among urban analysts and decision-makers to improve the quality of decisions by basing these decisions on better information and intelligence. We know of no case where an urban information system or an analytical system has been successful without the empathetic understanding and appreciation for potential improvements in

decision-making by those who make decisions and those who advise the decision-makers.

4. When the conviction exists that the urban system can be improved and the quality of life uplifted if changes are made at strategic points which are based upon programming and planning established on a sound data, information, and intelligence foundation. In essence, we are saying that the people in the urban system must be optimistic and have confidence that problems can be solved through programming and planning.

A Strategic Approach

Having defined our terms and established what we believe to be a workable rationale, we now turn to an examination of "how to do it." This aspect of urban information systems should not be underrated, since there have been several notable and costly failures by urban analysts who rushed head-long and zealously into these areas without a *strategic approach*. The strategic approach that we present has been tested to only a limited degree in three urban information system projects: (1) the state of Wisconsin, (2) the state of Hawaii, and (3) Fulton County, Georgia. All of these projects were done in a consultative capacity rather than as continuing staff. Nevertheless, we were impressed with the soundness of the logic and the subtlety of the conflict-resolution devices. We might add that the entire strategy was based on an operational heuristic: participation is the surest way to minimize dissent and encourage support of urban information systems. We now present our ten-step strategic approach for the design and development of urban information systems.

STEP 1. UNDERSTANDING OF THE URBAN SYSTEM

The first step in the design and development of an urban information system is to reconnoiter the entire urban system in order to understand as much as possible about it, without becoming entrenched in minutia. Particularly important is an understanding of the organization and functions of the governmental and private decision-making process. It is most important to identify decision-makers and the urban analysts, lobbyists, group leaders, and bureaucracies that advise them. Urban information systems should be based on the particular patterns of influence and rationality that prevail in a given urban system, lest it become an irrelevant plaything.

The interrelationship of the groups that make up the political, social, and economic structure of the urban system should be examined. The interactions of these groups provide a basis by which one can measure information flows. Since urban information systems seek to improve the flow of information, it is essential that these flows be well known by the designers of the system.

The practical usage of an urban information system will be in providing the management and programming and planning information needed by staff and line agencies of the government or cooperating governments of the urban system. This requires a sound understanding of the work programs and functions of all agencies. This will prove useful for later attempts to identify data, information, and intelligence needs.

STEP 2. FORMATION OF POLICY GROUP

The design and development of an urban information system have proven to be unsatisfactory without the full cooperation of all affected groups within the government of the urban system; possibly this could also be extended to private groups in some cases. Applying our operational heuristic of participation, we have found that the formation of a *policy group* and *task forces* is the soundest way to insure participation and establish a forum for debate and involvement.

The policy group can take on various structures, but we favor a hierarchy of groups arranged by functions, as shown in Fig. 11:4. The policy group is composed of all affected agency heads. This group should be formed by the chief executive and chaired by the agency head that will most likely be responsible for the long-term management of the urban information system. The policy group is responsible for all policy matters concerning the design and development of the urban information system and the rules and regulations governing its use and operations.

The *data task force* is composed of the chief technicians and urban analysts from the affected agencies who are knowledgeable about the raw inputs in the form of data that are needed for the urban information system. This task force should be concerned exclusively with the data needs and demands of the affected agencies and make recommendations to insure that an optimal data base be developed.

The *technical task force* is concerned with the software and hardware specifications of the urban information system. As such, it is not essential that every agency have a representative on this task force. The better

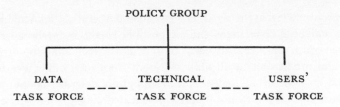

Fig. 11:4. Organization of policy group.

guideline is that the technical task force should be composed of the best resources available to the policy group. This will often require outside consultants that should report directly to the technical task force.

The *users' task force* is instrumental in the design and development as well as the continuing operations of the urban information system. The users' task force should be all-inclusive and open to all interested users and potential users of the urban information system. During the design and development period this task force would be concerned with the practical matters of analytical systems and demands for information and intelligence. During the continuing operations of the urban information system the users' task force would act as a feedback mechanism and provide suggestions and recommendations of ways to improve the operations, capacities, and capabilities of the urban information system.

STEP 3. DATA NEEDS AND SPECIFICATIONS

Data are the raw materials which are converted into the finished products of information and intelligence. This makes the determination of the data needed by the affected agencies and data that could be used if available (according to a consistent set of specifications regarding quality) a critical task. Such a task should be carried out by the data task force with the assistance and cooperation of all affected agencies and participating private groups. In our opinion this step will make or break the success of the urban system. Probably the most significant quotation from the early computer years was the immortal "GIGΦ — garbage in, garbage out." In less colorful terms any information system, or any computer usage, will be only as good as the data used as input.

There have been several attempts to specify a washlist of data that urban analysts should use in urban information systems. We frankly find these efforts to be useless. There is great variation among urban analysts and decision-makers as to what are considered useful data. Attempts to postulate universal data items cannot possibly be successful because they fail to recognize the very diversity that makes urban analysts, decision-makers, and urban systems all quite different from each other. We would argue that only the urban system can meaningfully describe its data needs. This *ad hoc* approach may not sound sophisticated, but it is the only operational approach we have encountered that will insure a certain level of success.

It may not be necessary to identify every item or category of data that is needed, but general specifications are necessary. These general data specifications should be developed through an objective analysis of the activities of all affected agencies and participating private groups. The general specifications should deal with four topics: (1) data identification, (2) data identifiers, (3) data files, and (4) privacy controls.

Data identification is more or less an inventory of what data are used, needed, and desirable. For each data identification, some assessment of its adequacy and availability will be needed. It is also important to study the flow of data between the affected agencies. In Figs. 11:5 and 11:6 we show the flow diagrams made in the data-needs study for Fulton County, Georgia. As can be seen, data flowed haphazardly between various agencies with no particular efficiencies or economies. The proposed flow, while idealistic, would make transactions between the various agencies speedier and more uniform, since data would be standardized.

Data identifiers are distinguished from data identification in that they are concerned with methods for retrieving data according to *codes* representing *spatial, person,* and *organizational* taxonomies. Spatial codes vary but are commonly based upon parcels, blocks, census tracts, voting districts, and other sub-areas in a geographical sense. Modern urban information systems use *grid coordinate* spatial identifiers, such as *X-Y* coordinates, since they are ordinal numbers that can be aggregated in any polygonal shape which coincides with any conceivable geographical area, and can be used for computations of distance, area, and related measures. A similar type of modern spatial identifier is the *address coding guide,* which is simply a look-up table used to generate coordinates or other areal aggregations of data. We would recommend that either grid coordinate identifiers or address coding guides be used, and we would argue against the traditional parcel-based spatial identifier, which is too rigid and inflexible for adequate urban analysis.

Person identifiers are somewhat more problematic because of *invasion of privacy* laws, rules, and regulations, as well as basic constitutional guarantees made to individuals concerning their right to live in privacy. We shall return to this subject below. Persons can be identified for this restricted type of data by Social Security numbers, in general, and by special codes when required. Similarly, data can be identified by organization in terms of which agency collects, uses, and analyzes the data; this is usually done simply by a devised code. The most important guideline for all three types of identifiers is to make sure that the maximum flexibility and usage of data are possible by having useful data identifiers.

Data files are the categories of structure given to the data base. As a general rule, urban information systems should contain (1) *property,* real and personal; (2) *person,* human and corporate; and (3) *transaction,* sales inventories, housing, etc., as a minimum file structure.[3] Another approach is to consider the data base as being highly interrelated; that is, transfers of data should be simplified. Hence we should think of *modes* of data: (1) *person mode,* for information on persons with respect to tax audits, vehicle registrations, health records, etc.; (2) *statistical mode,* for aggregation of data on persons, groups, and organizations in terms of percentages, means, and other statistical measures; (3) *administrative mode,* for the financial aspects of administration of urban systems; and (4) *plan test mode,* for testing plans, policies, programs, and proposals according to specified criteria and the available data base.[4]

Privacy controls cast a pall over all of the above matters and merit serious consideration. Invasion of privacy has been brought into the public eye through disclosures about the all-encompassing data base of government, especially the federal government, and certain abuses by such private groups as credit associations. Much controversy has been raised concerning the right of government to pry into the personal affairs of citizens and about what precisely government needs to know in order to manage urban systems. These questions have not been answered with any degree of adequacy and pose serious obstacles and considerations in the design of urban information systems.

No sound set of rules exists for determining what data are private and what are public knowledge. The urban analyst should review all pertinent laws, rules, regulations, and administrative guidelines when examining these questions. At a minimum, all private data must be controlled and protected

[3] Melvin M. Webber, "The Role of Intelligence Systems in Urban Systems Planning," *Journal of the American Institute of Planners,* 31, no. 4 (Nov., 1965), 289-297.
[4] Kenneth J. Dueker, "A Look at State and Local Information System Efforts," *Proceedings of the 1968 ACM National Conference* (Washington, D.C.: Association for Computing Machinery, 1969), pp. 133-142.

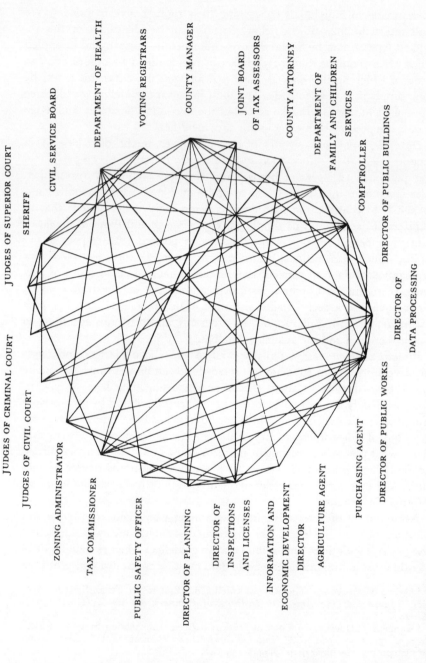

FIG. 11:5. Information flow found in Fulton County, Georgia.

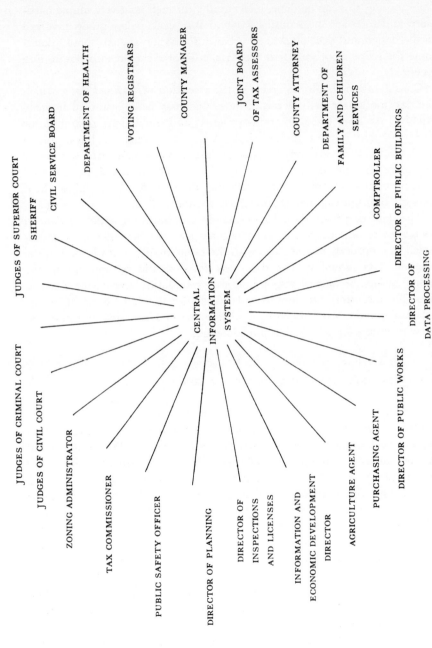

Fig. 11:6. Information flow proposed for Fulton County, Georgia.

from misuse; this can be done, incidentally, through relatively simple hardware and software mechanisms. Beyond that each policy group involved in the design and development of urban information systems should determine the scope of privacy that the data task force should incorporate into its efforts.

Consideration should be given to the retention of *archival data,* which are data no longer used or out of date, that may be of historical interest. Archival data are useful for testing models and simulations as well as for their inherent interest to historians. Adequate storage facilities can be made available at relatively low cost for retention of these data, but we by no means condone saving every scrap of data. The data task force should develop a set of guidelines that establishes the rules for determining which data are of historical interest and which are not.

The data task force should also include provisions for *updating data* in its design recommendations. Data become useless when they are not updated in an orderly manner and with the same quality controls used in the original data assembly. The data task force should recommend to the policy group the agency responsibilities for updating given data items or files. These recommendations should include details related to timing, characteristics, and costs of updating, and some set of safeguards to insure that these recommendations will be implemented.

STEP 4. ORGANIZATIONAL AND STRUCTURAL CONSIDERATIONS

A particularly difficult task that the policy group should settle at a relatively early date is the determination of the organizational and structural considerations of the urban information system. This is important because an error in this aspect could result in great inadequacies that could lead to failure as well as to possible agency abuses of information.

Problems arise in the organization and structure of the urban information system in four areas: (1) *administration,* (2) *operations,* (3) *costs,* and (4) *rules and priorities.* Administration of an urban information system must be fair and impartial, if only because the people who control the information of government tend to control the functions and operations of government. These people must be responsive to the needs of the government of urban systems, yet they must protect the privacy of the information that is not a matter of public record. The operations of the urban information system necessarily are affected by the administration of the system. An effective and flexible operational attitude should be developed so that the system runs well and can accommodate special or unusual queries. The costs of the urban information system must be fully understood, and economies should be sought wherever possible, especially at the expense of the inevitable gadgetry and empire building that tend to occur in many computer centers. Finally, there must be a viable set of rules and regulations, carefully spelled out, so that the urban information system can be utilized to its fullest advantage and priorities can be established for queries.

Since these tasks are somewhat more complex in the real world of urban systems and their governments than mere conjecture about their simplicity would suggest, we believe that these matters should be the primary responsibility of the policy group. This means that the policy group itself might tend to become somewhat institutionalized, but it must not become rigid and filled with special interests. The policy group must remain representative of the needs of urban analysts from many agencies and interest groups as well as of the day-to-day managerial needs of the government of the urban system.

Three basic organizational structures exist for urban information systems: (1) *centralized,* (2) *decentralized,* and (3) *federated.* The centralized structure would place all operational facilities and data bases within a high-level agency, usually independent of other agencies, directly responsible to the chief executive of the government. The decentralized structure would allow participating agencies to retain their own data bases and either share or individually develop their own operational facilities with only minimum regulation by a policy group. The federated structure is a compromise wherein participating agencies retain their own data bases and operational facilities, but all of these individual subsystems are interrelated by central switching facilities; in other words, machines would interact with other machines to form a pseudocentralization. The last structure is popular because agencies that have developed their own information subsystems still retain a degree of autonomy and control via rules and regulations that are built into the central switching facility. The centralized structure is the most economic, but it is sometimes difficult to develop such a structure when there are existing information subsystems which agencies do not wish to relinquish. The decentralized structure is the least desirable in a technical sense, since it is unnecessarily costly and inefficient, but there may be extreme situations in which it is the only acceptable alternative.

There is no optimal organizational structure for an urban information system, since urban systems and their governments are so different from each other. Special situations may require permutations of the three basic organizational structures. In all cases, however, an organizational structure for an urban information system is constrained by three forces: (1) *existing information subsystems,* (2) *agencies and their personnel,* and (3) *special interests.* Information subsystems, if and when they already exist, constitute an obvious limitation on the organizational structure of an urban information system in that they can rarely be completely erased or entirely incorporated into a new system. This is amplified by the attitudes of the participating agencies and the personalities of the individual decision-makers in these agencies. Similarly, special interest groups obviously will have special ideas on the nature and characteristics of the urban information system. To handle such problems, we again argue that the heuristic of participation in order to resolve conflicts should govern. If these matters can be debated and resolved through the forum provided by the policy group and task force design and development approach, then cooperation can be reasonably assumed.

STEP 5. TECHNICAL CAPABILITIES AND CAPACITIES

The major tasks of the technical task force are to develop the technical — hardware and software — capabilities and capacities of the urban information system. We find that this task is extremely difficult for non-technicians — which virtually all urban analysts would be — and recommend that the total technical resources of the urban system be put to work on these matters. There tends to be a furious competition among hardware and software companies which requires that all special interests be isolated from the technical task force; most certainly, politics should be completely removed from the technical decisions. This will require a general agreement among the participating agencies and a set of ground rules established from existing rules and regulations of the government as well as from new rules and regulations that the policy group devises. An especially important element of this task is the estimation of costs and personnel requirements. It almost goes without saying that this group should be fully aware of the decisions of the data task force.

STEP 6. OPERATIONS AND TESTING

Having completed the preceding steps, it is now possible to proceed with the initial operations and testing or *debugging* the urban information system. Initial operations would involve hardware, software, data base, and models. As a general guideline, problems should be expected no matter how carefully the design was developed. It can also be expected that adequate debugging will take patience, but not an unreasonable time period.

The testing should include the rules and regulations of the urban information system as well, in particular, (1) *priority assignments,* (2) *user identification,* and (3) *evaluation.* The manner in which queries are ranked for submission must be tested for fairness and efficiency. Such routine matters as accounting, payrolls, and billings will merit special priorities, since the government has responsibilities for these matters in which time is of the essence. On the other hand, *ad hoc* queries should not be placed so low on the priority assignment that they have unreasonable *turn-around times.* User identifications must be tested to insure that abuses are avoided and confidential and classified data are not violated. Evaluation of the urban information system should be regular and concerned.

The policy group has the responsibility for most of the above matters, but it should work closely with the users' task force. The users' task force should make regular evaluations which include grievances, enforcement of policies, adequacy of data and updating, and recommendations on the overall adequacy of the system. The users' task force also serves as the principal liaison between the urban analysts and the policy group with respect to the models and simulations that are to be made part of the urban information system.

STEP 7. MONITORING AND REPORTING SERVICE

The design and development of the urban information being highly advanced, the policy group can evolve an acceptable approach to the development of the monitoring and reporting service. This development would take the urban information system beyond the realm of management and programming and planning information processing to the higher realm of providing decision-makers with key indicators on the conditions and trends of the urban system. The use of indicators as a basis for intelligence for decision-making is not a highly sophisticated field, and innovation should be sought. The proper approach to the development of the monitoring and reporting service would seem to require the combined skills of policy group, data task force, technical task force, users' task force, decision-makers, and private groups. Each group has contributions to make to this endeavor which are vitally needed.

STEP 8. INTERGOVERNMENTAL INTERACTION

Although somewhat longer in range than preceding steps and subject to much variation among different urban systems, it is logical to assume that the urban information system may be enhanced by its extension to data sharing and interactions with other governmental information systems, for example, county, regional, state, and perhaps certain aspects of national information systems. Much functional interaction exists already between governments for information on such subjects as crime, traffic accidents, housing, health, and welfare. In time, and as constrained by privacy considerations, one can expect more extensive interactions between governmental information systems at all levels. The overriding concern, in our opinion, is not solely what data are available for sharing but what data are needed that are available from other governmental levels in order to carry out the management information, programming and planning information, and monitoring and reporting service functions of the urban system under consideration.

STEP 9. INVOLVEMENT OF DECISION-MAKERS AND THE PUBLIC

The involvement of the decision-makers and the public in the design and development, as well as evaluation, of the urban information system should permeate all other steps. We have found that ivory-tower planning of any sort, isolated from decision-makers and the public and shrouded with a veil of esoteric technicalities, is most unsatisfactory in modern urban systems. There are right-to-know considerations of the public, but, more important, people have a sincere desire to be kept informed of what government is doing and how it will affect them. Decision-makers should be informed so that they can foresee the benefits to their short- and long-range decisions and not be overwhelmed by outpourings of incomprehensible information or the arrogant claims of charlatans (there are such people involved in urban analysis, but we have found their numbers to be on the decrease).

The specter of invasion of privacy should always prevail over the development of urban information systems. Advocates of urban information systems have brusquely put aside these considerations, too often with the attitude that "anyone who has something to hide should be worried, but the ordinary citizen should be unconcerned." Such a flippant attitude is incorrect, if not unethical, and we seriously doubt that it could withstand the pressures of modern urban system residents. In fact, we all have something to hide no matter how trivial — how many of us would like it to be widely known that our fathers once owned Edsels? Is how much money we made last year really a matter of public record? Would urban analysts want widely known what grades they received in freshman statistics — or English? We may not be trying to hide anything, but urban life is filled with minor embarrassments that are best kept to ourselves. The public must be continually assured that government and its employees are not snoopers and tell-tale gossips. Privacy is a constitutional right in the United States and most free-world countries which must be preserved, especially in the face of technological change.

STEP 10. CONTINUITY

There is no end-point to the design and development process for urban information systems, since the tasks must be continually revised and updated. Feedback should occur on a continual basis and changes made when warranted. The urban information system should be expanded or contracted as valid needs develop.

DESIGN AND DEVELOPMENT NETWORK

Incorporating these ten steps into an orderly process is not simple, but it is essential. A network indicating the predecessor and successor steps is a beginning point in the formalization of the process. We have attempted such a network and display it in Fig. 11:7.

APPLIED URBAN INFORMATION SYSTEMS

There are so many applications of the concepts and technology of urban information systems that we would be foolhardy to oversimplify the numerous cases. Even if we were to present a general summary of urban information systems, it would be obsolete and dated upon publication. The more sensible approach, we believe, is to discuss three classic case studies

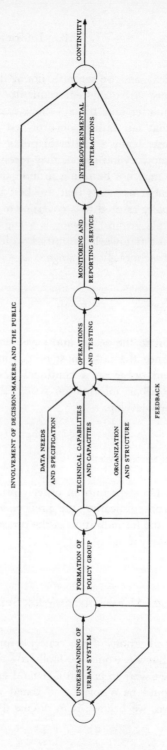

Fig. 11:7. Design and development network for urban information system.

which are timeless and represent the first major applications in this field. We are further justified in this tack because these three case studies have shown certain truths which are fundamental to further applications.

ALEXANDRIA, VIRGINIA, DATABANK

The first fully operational urban information system developed by a major city was the *Alexandria Databank,* which was implemented in 1964. The concept for Databank was an extension of the pioneering work by Edward F. R. Hearle and Raymond Mason as published in their early book, *A Data Processing System for State and Local Governments* (1963). The design and development of Databank were initiated by the city manager and the budget director, and all work was carried out by their respective staffs and consultants. The Databank is centralized in the Data Processing Department, which is responsible to the city manager. The organization and structure, as well as the design and development, are classic examples of centralization of urban information systems.

Databank was designed to provide information for management decisions and was specifically not to be used for such routinized functions as payrolls, accounting, and billings. The Data Processing Department was concerned with such daily clerical functions and had its separate system for meeting those needs. Databank accounts for approximately 10 percent of the operations of the Data Processing Department.

Two data files were designed for the original Databank: (1) *parcel file* and (2) *street section file.* The parcel file contained records for 20,000 parcels of land in the city and had 60 data identifications, such as location, size, zoning, land use, value, number of occupants, number of school children, and condition of improvements. The street section file was designed to aggregate data items by the street section, usually a block, for such items as traffic, pavement, services, and improvements. While most of the data were collected from existing data files among the city agencies, a special land use survey was conducted by firemen with rather good results owing to their familiarity with the city. As a general rule, data have been updated every quarter. This has proved to be troublesome, and efficiency has not been as high as anticipated during the design and development period. Problems of invasion of privacy have not occurred because the data were relatively noncontroversial in nature — crime data were collected but were aggregated to prevent person identifiers.

The success of the Alexandria Databank has been difficult to measure.

The highly centralized nature of Databank has resulted in some antagonism from affected agency personnel who feel that they were not adequately consulted during the design and development period. Other personnel, however, have become quite enthusiastic over Databank and use it regularly for their analyses. Some of the problems of centralization were overcome by the Data Processing Department's special courses and orientations for agency heads and key personnel to familiarize them with the potentials of the system. There have been strong signs, however, that many people are quite unfamiliar with Databank in particular and urban information systems in general. The near-legend story in Alexandria is that two city employees were watching workmen unload a new steel safe ordered by the city registrar when one asked the other, "Is that part of our new Databank?"[5]

The usage and costs of Databank have been difficult to evaluate. There has been some indication that usage was not as high as had been anticipated during the design and development period, and usage appears to be decreasing with time. Evaluators have linked this decline to unfamiliarity and lack of participation by agency heads and personnel, while others have blamed the problems involved in and lack of updating the data base. Many programs have been underway to resolve the low and declining usage of Databank.

The most frequent users of Databank have been the Planning Department, the city assessor, and the city manager. This was to be expected because of the parcel orientation and physical development character of the data base. Some observers believe that the data base was too oriented toward programming and planning information and not enough to the plethora of other data needed for urban analysis.

The significance of Databank lies not only in its historical claim but also in its place in centralized urban information systems. The influence of the Planning and Data Processing Departments has given the system a perspective that is not the major concern of many other agencies. The conscientious effort to isolate management information has served as an impediment to the dual functions of providing both management and programming and planning information that we have suggested. Nevertheless, the technical aspects of hardware and software have been well implemented, and few notable flaws have been found. There is apparent support for the assumption that while costs have been higher than anticipated

---

[5] System Development Corporation, *Urban and Regional Informational Systems* (Washington, D.C.: U.S. Department of Housing and Urban Development, 1968), pp. 15-25.

— running about $200.00 per query — the decision-makers have regarded the investment as a sound one.

METROPOLITAN DATA CENTER PROJECT

A federal demonstration grant was made to the Tulsa Metropolitan Planning Commission in 1961 to demonstrate how urban information system concepts could be applied to planning problems and analysis.[6] A group was formed with four other urban system planning agencies to explore possible applications, and the efforts have become widely known as the *Metropolitan Data Center Project*. The planning agencies each selected a distinct application area: (1) Denver — land use inventory, (2) Little Rock — school facilities, (3) Fort Worth — central business district, (4) Tulsa — community renewal program, and (5) Wichita — capital improvements program. Our interest in this unique experiment is in its historical perspective and in its implications for decentralized organization and structure of urban information systems.

The data needs and specifications were made by the participating agencies for the respective planning information of each. Since the data were entirely physical, the parcel was selected as the identifier. Data collection was largely through respective agencies in each area by a voluntary arrangement. Consultants and technicians were used to develop the system's capabilities and capacities. The system was fully operational by 1965, but within a few years it had virtually ceased to exist. Its demise was attributable to lack of funding and inherent problems of decentralization.

A disturbing amount of opposition to voluntary data sharing was found in the early stages of design and development. In each participating city urban analysts encountered difficulty in securing the data they needed from the regular data collection agencies. Observers related this to an unfamiliarity with the project and the feeling of being excluded from the club, so to speak, by data collection agencies. It was necessary in a few cases for the respective chief executive to intervene to secure the needed data.

Participants in the project concluded that this was the major drawback in the decentralized urban information system. They concluded that an urban information system designed solely for planning information would probably be unsuccessful in the future. The participating cities all noted the desirability of extending the data base to management data and of in-

[6] Metropolitan Data Center Project, *Final Report* (Washington, D.C.: U.S. Department of Housing and Urban Development, 1966).

cluding some mechanism for participation of agencies that were excluded. Some personnel of the respective planning agencies noted an actual feeling of having created problems for their ongoing planning functions by going it alone and having to coerce nonparticipating agencies to cooperate and share data; all agreed that this was most unfortunate.

Technical considerations of hardware and software were acceptable, although the computer used was probably too small, and the parcel identifier proved to be overly restrictive and inflexible. This was quite similar to the results of the Alexandria Databank. Most urban information systems are now designed with grid coordinate or street address coding guide identifiers to overcome the limitations of the parcel identifier. Costs were judged to be acceptable for hardware, software, and operations. The total project costs were $288,000, which included an estimated $0.72 per parcel for data assembly and $0.89 per parcel for data updates. The average query cost $73.87.

Important lessons were learned from the Metropolitan Data Center Project which should be etched indelibly on the minds of urban analysts. The go-it-alone philosophy proved extremely difficult to work with, as did the somewhat abstract concept of decentralization. Admittedly, this approach is probably an extreme example of decentralization. The failure to adopt the heuristic rule of participation to minimize conflict also proved to be an impediment to success. Another lesson is that while technical matters can be handled by technicians, there must be some familiarity with the basic concepts of hardware and software by the users; it was necessary to hold special training courses to overcome related problems. Perhaps the most important lesson, however, is that urban information systems must be as dynamic as urban systems themselves. It is an exercise in futility to design and develop urban information systems with models and simulations which are inadequate and data bases which are fixed and undynamic. Such systems, as evidenced by the Metropolitan Data Center Project, quickly outlive their usefulness and are left to wither away.

CALIFORNIA SYSTEMS

Urban systems in California have tended to experiment with information systems quite heavily, probably owing in part to the abundance of technical resources available in that state. The state of California undertook a series of explorations to determine the best design and development philosophies to follow by using aerospace and defense industry technicians as consultants. The most interesting results were found at the state level, largely stemming from a system design completed in 1965.[7] This system is officially known as the *California Statewide Integrated Information System,* but it is the intellectual and conceptual content used to describe the federated organization and structure that is best known.

Unlike many other urban systems in the United States, there were already much interest and partial implementation of urban information systems in California by the early 1960s. Similarly, there were rather extensive information system capability and development at the state level among the various functional departments. The designers were caught in the curious dilemma of how to integrate such an extensive, if uncoordinated, organization and structure of information systems. The solution proposed was the federated approach.

The operational heart of the federated information system is *information central,* which is described as "a computer-based communication system joining independent centers in an automated means for exchanging information."[8] The independent information systems are all participating urban, county, special district, and regional systems as well as the participating state departments. The conceptual network is shown as Fig. 11:8. A four-step routine is required for a typical query:

1. User requests information from information central using a remote terminal which is part of his agency's information system and is connected via telephone lines to the state information system.

2. Information central automatically determines the location of the information requested by the query.

3. Information central relays the query to participating agency with data or information.

4. Information central obtains requested information and relays it to the user that made request.

All of the above is done automatically with man-machine interactions at the originating and data-supplying terminals. An elaborate set of rules and regulations is built into information central to deal with problems of data specification and quality, user identification, protection of private information, and related problems.

The federated information system has been under development in California for several years. The original design anticipated a development time of at least ten years and total development costs of $98,000,000.

[7] Lockheed Missiles and Space Company, *California Statewide Information System Study* (Sunnyvale, Calif., 1965).
[8] Ibid., p. 6-1.

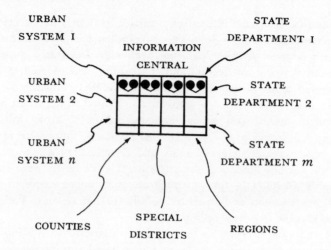

FIG. 11:8. Information central conceptual network.

Understandably, the work has been progressing slowly, since the proposal is somewhat monumental in scope, even for California. Several prototypes of the federated information system have been developed, the most notable of which is the Santa Clara land use information system, or *California Regional Land Use Information System* (CRLUIS), as it is officially known.[9] This prototype, as its name suggests, is solely concerned with land use data and was more concerned with experimentation than overall urban information system design and development.

The significance of the California systems at this relatively early stage lies in their breadth and scope as much as in their ambition. The concepts of federated organization and structure and information central are most interesting and will probably be relevant to future urban information systems.

RECOMMENDED EXERCISES

1. Select a nearby urban system, and design and develop a prototype urban information system. Deal with most of the problems raised in the above discussion, and utilize the full resources of the class or project group. This is a longer-term project, usually requiring at least one month, since

[9] TRW Systems Group, *California Regional Land Use Information System* (Redondo Beach, Calif., 1968).

many interviews must be conducted with affected agencies. Always approach such agencies in a sympathetic vein, and make it clear that this is a learning exercise.

2. Write a brief essay describing your personal interpretation of the question of invasion of privacy. You may use your understanding of the U.S. Constitution as formal background, but the major thrust of the essay should be directed toward subjective beliefs and leanings.

FURTHER READING

Hearle, Edward F. R., and Raymond Mason. *A Data Processing System for State and Local Governments*. Englewood Cliffs, N.J.: Prentice-Hall, 1963.

The classic book on the application of data processing and information system concepts to urban systems. While much of the technical material is dated, it constitutes a small part of the text. The significance of this work is the conceptual foundation which is established; as mentioned above, it was later applied to Alexandria, Virginia, and several other urban systems.

System Development Corporation. *Urban and Regional Information Systems*. Washington, D.C.: U.S. Department of Housing and Urban Development, 1968.

The final report in book-length form of the contract between the U.S. Department of Housing and Urban Development and System Development Corporation, in which the latter attempted to survey the theory, principles, case studies, and bibliography of urban information systems. The case studies are numerous but relatively embryonic. The bibliography is the most extensive we know of, but there are curious omissions of evaluative and critical publications. The most useful aspects of this work are the theory and principles.

APPENDICES

APPENDIX A. Values for chi square.

Probability

n	.99	.98	.95	.90	.80	.70	.50	.30	.20	.10	.05	.02	.01	.001
1	.000157	.000628	.00393	.0158	.0642	.148	.455	1.074	1.642	2.706	3.841	5.412	6.635	10.827
2	.0201	.0404	.103	.211	.446	.713	1.386	2.408	3.219	4.605	5.991	7.824	9.210	13.815
3	.115	.185	.352	.584	1.005	1.424	2.366	3.665	4.642	6.251	7.815	9.837	11.345	16.268
4	.297	.429	.711	1.064	1.649	2.195	3.357	4.878	5.989	7.779	9.488	11.668	13.277	18.465
5	.554	.752	1.145	1.610	2.343	3.000	4.351	6.064	7.289	9.236	11.070	13.388	15.086	20.517
6	.872	1.134	1.635	2.204	3.070	3.828	5.348	7.231	8.558	10.645	12.592	15.033	16.812	22.457
7	1.239	1.564	2.167	2.833	3.822	4.671	6.346	8.383	9.803	12.017	14.067	16.622	18.475	24.322
8	1.646	2.032	2.733	3.490	4.394	5.527	7.344	9.524	11.030	13.362	15.507	18.168	20.090	26.125
9	2.088	2.532	3.325	4.168	5.380	6.393	8.343	10.656	12.242	14.684	16.919	19.679	21.666	27.877
10	2.558	3.059	3.940	4.865	6.179	7.267	9.342	11.781	13.442	15.987	18.307	21.161	23.209	29.588
11	3.053	3.609	4.575	5.578	6.989	8.148	10.341	12.899	14.631	17.275	19.675	22.618	24.725	31.264
12	3.571	4.178	5.226	6.304	7.807	9.034	11.340	14.011	15.812	18.549	21.026	24.054	26.217	32.909
13	4.107	4.765	5.892	7.042	8.534	9.926	12.340	15.119	16.985	19.812	22.362	25.472	27.688	34.528
14	4.660	5.368	6.571	7.790	9.467	10.821	13.339	16.222	18.151	21.064	23.685	26.873	29.141	36.123
15	5.229	5.985	7.261	8.547	10.307	11.721	14.339	17.322	19.311	22.307	24.996	28.259	30.578	37.697
16	5.812	6.614	7.962	9.312	11.152	12.624	15.338	18.418	20.465	23.542	26.296	29.633	32.000	39.252
17	6.408	7.255	8.672	10.085	12.002	13.531	16.338	19.511	21.615	24.769	27.587	30.995	33.409	40.790
18	7.015	7.906	9.390	10.865	12.857	14.440	17.338	20.601	22.760	25.989	28.869	32.346	34.805	42.312
19	7.633	8.567	10.117	11.651	13.716	15.352	18.338	21.689	23.900	27.204	30.144	33.687	36.191	43.820
20	8.260	9.237	10.851	12.443	14.578	16.266	19.337	22.775	25.038	28.412	31.410	35.020	37.566	45.315
21	8.897	9.915	11.591	13.240	15.445	17.182	20.337	23.858	26.171	29.615	32.671	36.343	38.932	46.797
22	9.542	10.600	12.338	14.041	16.314	18.101	21.337	24.939	27.301	30.813	33.924	37.659	40.289	48.268
23	10.196	11.293	13.091	14.848	17.187	19.021	22.337	26.018	28.429	32.007	35.172	38.968	41.638	49.728
24	10.856	11.992	13.848	15.659	18.062	19.943	23.337	27.096	29.553	33.196	36.415	40.270	42.980	51.179
25	11.524	12.697	14.611	16.473	18.940	20.867	24.337	28.172	30.675	34.382	37.652	41.566	44.314	52.620
26	12.198	13.409	15.379	17.292	19.820	21.792	25.336	29.246	31.795	35.563	38.885	42.856	45.642	54.052
27	12.879	14.125	16.151	18.114	20.703	22.719	26.336	30.319	32.912	36.741	40.113	44.140	46.963	55.476
28	13.565	14.847	16.928	18.939	21.588	23.647	27.336	31.391	34.027	37.916	41.337	45.419	48.278	56.893
29	14.256	15.574	17.708	19.768	22.475	24.577	28.336	32.461	35.139	39.087	42.557	46.693	49.588	58.302
30	14.953	16.306	18.493	20.599	23.364	25.508	29.336	33.530	36.250	40.256	43.773	47.962	50.892	59.703

APPENDIX B. Standard r or R table.

Degree of Freedom	Number of Variables				Degree of Freedom	Number of Variables			
	2	3	4	5		2	3	4	5
1	.997	.999	.999	.999	24	.388	.470	.523	.562
	1.000	*1.000*	*1.000*	*1.000*		*.496*	*.565*	*.609*	*.642*
2	.950	.975	.983	.987	25	.381	.462	.514	.553
	.990	*.995*	*.997*	*.998*		*.487*	*.555*	*.600*	*.633*
3	.878	.930	.950	.961	26	.374	.454	.506	.545
	.959	*.976*	*.983*	*.987*		*.478*	*.546*	*.590*	*.624*
4	.811	.881	.912	.930	27	.367	.446	.498	.536
	.917	*.949*	*.962*	*.970*		*.470*	*.538*	*.582*	*.615*
5	.754	.836	.874	.898	28	.361	.439	.490	.529
	.874	*.917*	*.937*	*.949*		*.463*	*.530*	*.573*	*.606*
6	.707	.795	.839	.867	29	.355	.432	.482	.521
	.834	*.886*	*.911*	*.927*		*.456*	*.522*	*.565*	*.598*
7	.666	.758	.807	.838	30	.349	.426	.476	.514
	.798	*.855*	*.885*	*.904*		*.449*	*.514*	*.558*	*.591*
8	.632	.726	.777	.811	35	.325	.397	.445	.482
	.765	*.827*	*.860*	*.882*		*.418*	*.481*	*.523*	*.556*
9	.602	.697	.750	.786	40	.304	.373	.419	.455
	.735	*.800*	*.836*	*.861*		*.393*	*.454*	*.494*	*.526*
10	.576	.671	.726	.763	45	.288	.353	.397	.432
	.708	*.776*	*.814*	*.840*		*.372*	*.430*	*.470*	*.501*
11	.553	.648	.703	.741	50	.273	.336	.379	.412
	.684	*.753*	*.793*	*.821*		*.354*	*.410*	*.449*	*.479*
12	.532	.627	.683	.722	60	.250	.308	.348	.380
	.661	*.732*	*.773*	*.802*		*.325*	*.377*	*.414*	*.442*

APPENDIX B *(continued)*

Degree of Freedom	Number of Variables				Degree of Freedom	Number of Variables			
	2	3	4	5		2	3	4	5
13	.514	.608	.664	.703	70	.232	.286	.324	.354
	.641	*.712*	*.755*	*.785*		*.302*	*.351*	*.386*	*.413*
14	.497	.590	.646	.686	80	.217	.269	.304	.332
	.623	*.694*	*.737*	*.768*		*.283*	*.330*	*.362*	*.389*
15	.482	.574	.630	.670	90	.205	.254	.288	.315
	.606	*.677*	*.721*	*.752*		*.267*	*.312*	*.343*	*.368*
16	.468	.559	.615	.655	100	.195	.241	.274	.300
	.590	*.662*	*.706*	*.738*		*.254*	*.297*	*.327*	*.351*
17	.456	.545	.601	.641	125	.174	.216	.246	.269
	.575	*.647*	*.691*	*.724*		*.228*	*.266*	*.294*	*.316*
18	.444	.532	.587	.628	150	.159	.198	.225	.247
	.561	*.633*	*.678*	*.710*		*.208*	*.244*	*.270*	*.290*
19	.433	.520	.575	.615	200	.138	.172	.196	.215
	.549	*.620*	*.665*	*.698*		*.181*	*.212*	*.234*	*.253*
20	.423	.509	.563	.604	300	.113	.141	.160	.176
	.537	*.608*	*.652*	*.685*		*.148*	*.174*	*.192*	*.208*
21	.413	.498	.552	.592	400	.098	.122	.139	.153
	.526	*.596*	*.641*	*.674*		*.128*	*.151*	*.167*	*.180*
22	.404	.488	.542	.582	500	.088	.109	.124	.137
	.515	*.585*	*.630*	*.663*		*.115*	*.135*	*.150*	*.162*
23	.396	.479	.532	.572	1,000	.062	.077	.088	.097
	.505	*.574*	*.619*	*.652*		*.081*	*.096*	*.106*	*.115*

Italic: 1 percent confidence level.
Roman: 5 percent confidence level.

APPENDIX C. Values of t.

Degree of Freedom	Probability				
	0.50	0.10	0.05	0.02	0.01
1	1.000	6.34	12.71	31.82	63.66
2	0.816	2.92	4.30	6.96	9.92
3	.765	2.35	3.18	4.54	5.84
4	.741	2.13	2.78	3.75	4.60
5	.727	2.02	2.57	3.36	4.03
6	.718	1.94	2.45	3.14	3.71
7	.711	1.90	2.36	3.00	3.50
8	.706	1.86	2.31	2.90	3.36
9	.703	1.83	2.26	2.82	3.25
10	.700	1.81	2.23	2.76	3.17
11	.697	1.80	2.20	2.72	3.11
12	.695	1.78	2.18	2.68	3.06
13	.694	1.77	2.16	2.65	3.01
14	.692	1.76	2.14	2.62	2.98
15	.691	1.75	2.13	2.60	2.95
16	.690	1.75	2.12	2.58	2.92
17	.689	1.74	2.11	2.57	2.90
18	.688	1.73	2.10	2.55	2.88
19	.688	1.73	2.09	2.54	2.86
20	.687	1.72	2.09	2.53	2.84
21	.686	1.72	2.08	2.52	2.83
22	.686	1.72	2.07	2.51	2.82
23	.685	1.71	2.07	2.50	2.81
24	.685	1.71	2.06	2.49	2.80

Appendix C (*continued*)

Degree of Freedom	Probability				
	0.50	0.10	0.05	0.02	0.01
25	.684	1.71	2.06	2.48	2.79
26	.684	1.71	2.06	2.48	2.78
27	.684	1.70	2.05	2.47	2.77
28	.683	1.70	2.05	2.47	2.76
29	.683	1.70	2.04	2.46	2.76
30	.683	1.70	2.04	2.46	2.75
35	.682	1.69	2.03	2.44	2.72
40	.681	1.68	2.02	2.42	2.71
45	.680	1.68	2.02	2.41	2.69
50	.679	1.68	2.01	2.40	2.68
60	.678	1.67	2.00	2.39	2.66
70	.678	1.67	2.00	2.38	2.65
80	.677	1.66	1.99	2.38	2.64
90	.677	1.66	1.99	2.37	2.63
100	.677	1.66	1.98	2.36	2.63
125	.676	1.66	1.98	2.36	2.62
150	.676	1.66	1.98	2.35	2.61
200	.675	1.65	1.97	2.35	2.60
300	.675	1.65	1.97	2.34	2.59
400	.675	1.65	1.97	2.34	2.59
500	.674	1.65	1.96	2.33	2.59
1000	.674	1.65	1.96	2.33	2.58
∞	.674	1.64	1.96	2.33	2.58

APPENDIX D. Cumulative probabilities for Poisson model.

r	$\mu = .1$	$\mu = .2$	$\mu = .3$	$\mu = .4$	$\mu = .5$
0	.90484	.81873	.74082	.67302	.60653
1	.99532	.98248	.96306	.93845	.90980
2	.99985	.99885	.99640	.99207	.98561
3	1.00000	.99994	.99973	.99922	.99825
4		1.00000	.99998	.99994	.99983
5			1.00000	1.00000	.99999
6					1.00000

r	$\mu = .6$	$\mu = .7$	$\mu = .8$	$\mu = .9$	$\mu = 1.0$
0	.54881	.49658	.44933	.40657	.36788
1	.87810	.84419	.80879	.77248	.73576
2	.97688	.96586	.95258	.93714	.91970
3	.99664	.99425	.99092	.98654	.98101
4	.99961	.99921	.99859	.99766	.99634
5	.99996	.99991	.99982	.99966	.99941
6	1.00000	.99999	.99998	.99996	.99992
7		1.00000	1.00000	1.00000	.99999
8					1.00000

r	$\mu = 2$	$\mu = 3$	$\mu = 4$	$\mu = 5$	$\mu = 6$
0	.13534	.04979	.01832	.00674	.00248
1	.40601	.19915	.09158	.04043	.01735
2	.67668	.42319	.23810	.12465	.06197
3	.85712	.64723	.43347	.26503	.15120
4	.94735	.81526	.62884	.44049	.28506
5	.98344	.91608	.78513	.61596	.44568
6	.99547	.96649	.88933	.76218	.60630
7	.99890	.98810	.94887	.86663	.74398
8	.99976	.99620	.97864	.93191	.84724
9	.99995	.99890	.99187	.96817	.91608
10	.99999	.99971	.99716	.98630	.95738
11	1.00000	.99993	.99908	.99455	.97991
12		.99998	.99973	.99798	.99117
13		1.00000	.99992	.99930	.99637
14			.99998	.99977	.99860
15			1.00000	.99993	.99949
16				.99998	.99982
17				1.00000	.99994
18					.99998
19					1.00000

APPENDIX D (*continued*)

r	$\mu = 7$	$\mu = 8$	$\mu = 9$	$\mu = 10$
0	.00091	.00033	.00012	.00004
1	.00730	.00302	.00123	.00050
2	.02964	.01375	.00623	.00277
3	.08176	.04238	.02123	.01034
4	.17299	.09963	.05496	.02925
5	.30071	.19124	.11569	.06709
6	.44971	.31337	.20678	.13014
7	.59871	.45296	.32390	.22022
8	.72909	.59255	.45565	.33282
9	.83050	.71662	.58741	.45793
10	.90148	.81589	.70599	.58304
11	.94665	.88808	.80301	.69678
12	.97300	.93620	.87577	.79156
13	.98719	.96582	.92615	.86446
14	.99428	.98274	.95853	.91654
15	.99759	.99177	.97796	.95126
16	.99904	.99628	.98889	.97296
17	.99964	.99841	.99468	.98572
18	.99987	.99935	.99757	.99281
19	.99996	.99975	.99894	.99655
20	.99999	.99991	.99956	.99841
21	1.00000	.99997	.99982	.99930
22		.99999	.99993	.99970
23		1.00000	.99998	.99988
24			.99999	.99995
25			1.00000	.99998
26				.99999
27				1.00000

APPENDIX E. Values for y and y_a for gamma model.

y	y_a	y	y_a	y	y_a	y	y_a	y	y_a
.00	.5000000	.36	.55234633	.71	.59949158	1.06	.62018509	1.6	.6455077
.01	166108	.37	358965	.72	144048	1.07	094026	1.8	663340
.02	331088	.38	482273	.73	238267	1.08	169093	2.0	762335
.03	494925	.39	604568	.74	331825	1.09	243714	2.2	853382
.04	657603	.40	725862	.75	424729	1.10	317895	2.4	937540
.05	819111	.41	846165	.76	516987	1.11	391639	2.6	.7015677
.06	979438	.42	965491	.77	608607	1.12	464951	2.8	088511
.07	.51138573	.43	.56083849	.78	699595	1.13	537836	3.0	156639
.08	296508	.44	201253	.79	789961	1.14	610298	3.2	220568
.09	453237	.45	317712	.80	879710	1.15	682342	3.4	280727
.10	608755	.46	433238	.81	968850	1.16	753971	3.6	337487
.11	763057	.47	547842	.82	.60057389	1.17	825190	3.8	391165
.12	916141	.48	661536	.83	145333	1.18	896003	4.0	442040
.13	.52068005	.49	774331	.84	232689	1.19	966414	4.2	490353
.14	218649	.50	886236	.85	319464	1.20	.63036427	4.4	536319
.15	368074	.51	997264	.86	405665	1.21	106046	4.6	580126

.16	516282
.17	663277
.18	809061
.19	953640
.20	.53097019
.21	239205
.22	380204
.23	520025
.24	658674
.25	796161
.26	932495
.27	.54067685
.28	201741
.29	334674
.30	466493
.31	597209
.32	726833
.33	855377
.34	982850
.35	.55109265

.52	.57107426
.53	216730
.54	325189
.55	432812
.56	539610
.57	645593
.58	750771
.59	855154
.60	958751
.61	.58061573
.62	163629
.63	264927
.64	365479
.65	465291
.66	564375
.67	662738
.68	760389
.69	857337
.70	953591

.87	491298
.88	576369
.89	660886
.90	744854
.91	828279
.92	911168
.93	993527
.94	.61075362
.95	156678
.96	237481
.97	317777
.98	397571
.99	476869
1.00	555677
1.01	633999
1.02	711841
1.03	789208
1.04	866105
1.05	942537

1.22	175276
1.23	244119
1.24	312580
1.25	380662
1.26	448370
1.27	515706
1.28	582675
1.29	649279
1.30	715523
1.31	781410
1.32	846943
1.33	912126
1.34	976962
1.35	.64041454
1.36	105606
1.37	169420
1.38	232900
1.39	296049
1.40	358870

4.8	621942
5.0	661916
5.2	700182
5.4	736861
5.6	772060
5.8	805879
6.0	838406
6.2	869722
6.4	899901
6.6	929012
6.8	957116
7.0	984470

APPENDIX F. Probabilistic exponential model values.

x	e^{-x}	e^x
.01	.9900	1.0101
.02	.9802	1.0202
.03	.9704	1.0305
.04	.9608	1.0408
.05	.9512	1.0513
.06	.9418	1.0618
.07	.9324	1.0725
.08	.9231	1.0833
.09	.9139	1.0942
.10	.9048	1.1052
.20	.8187	1.2214
.30	.7408	1.3499
.40	.6703	1.4918
.50	.6065	1.6487
.60	.5488	1.8221
.70	.4966	2.0138
.80	.4493	2.2255
.90	.4066	2.4596
1.00	.3679	2.7183
2.00	.1353	7.3891
3.00	.04979	20.0886
4.00	.01832	54.598
5.00	.00674	148.41
6.00	.00248	403.43
7.00	.000912	1096.6
8.00	.000335	2981.0
9.00	.000123	8103.1
10.00	.000045	22026.0

APPENDIX G. Table of random numbers.

10097	32533	76520	13586	34673	54876	80959	09117	39292	74945
37542	04805	64894	74296	24805	24037	20636	10402	00822	91665
08422	68953	19645	09303	23209	02560	15953	34764	35080	33606
99019	02529	09376	70715	38311	31165	88676	74397	04436	27659
12807	99970	80157	36147	64032	36653	98951	16877	12171	76833
66065	74717	34072	76850	36697	36170	65813	39885	11199	29170
31060	10805	45571	82406	35303	42614	86799	07439	23403	09732
85269	77602	02051	65692	68665	74818	73053	85247	18623	88579
63573	32135	05325	47048	90553	57548	28468	28709	83491	25624
73796	45753	03529	64778	35808	34282	60935	20344	35273	88435
98520	17767	14905	68607	22109	40558	60970	93433	50500	73998
11805	05431	39808	27732	50725	68248	29405	24201	52775	67851
83452	99634	06288	98083	13746	70078	18475	40610	68711	77817
88685	40200	86507	58401	36766	67951	90364	76493	29609	11062
99594	67348	87517	64969	91826	08928	93785	61368	23478	34113
65481	17674	17468	50950	58047	76974	73039	57186	40218	16544
80124	35635	17727	08015	45318	22374	21115	78253	14385	53763
74350	99817	77402	77214	43236	00210	45521	64237	96286	02655
69916	26803	66252	29148	36936	87203	76621	13990	94400	56418
09893	20505	14225	68514	46427	56788	96297	78822	54382	14598
91499	14523	68479	27686	46162	83554	94750	89923	37089	20048
80336	94598	26940	36858	70297	34135	53140	33340	42050	82341
44104	81949	85157	47954	32979	26575	57600	40881	22222	06413
12550	73742	11100	02040	12860	74697	96644	89439	28707	25815
63606	49329	16505	34484	40219	52563	43651	77082	07207	31790
61196	90446	26457	47774	51924	33729	65394	59593	42582	60527
15474	45266	95270	79953	59367	83848	82396	10118	33211	59466
94557	28573	67897	54387	54622	44431	91190	42592	92927	45973
42481	16213	97344	08721	16868	48767	03071	12059	25701	46670
23523	78317	73208	89837	68935	91416	26252	29663	05522	82562
04493	52494	75246	33824	45862	51025	61962	79335	65337	12472
00549	97654	64051	88159	96119	63896	54692	82391	23287	29529
35963	15307	26898	09354	33351	35462	77974	50024	90103	39333
59808	08391	45427	26842	83609	49700	13021	24892	78565	20106
46058	85236	01390	92286	77281	44077	93910	83647	70617	42941
32179	00597	87379	25241	05567	07007	86743	17157	85394	11838
69234	61406	20117	45204	15956	60000	18743	92423	97118	96338
19565	41430	01758	75379	40419	21585	66674	36806	84962	85207
45155	14938	19476	07246	43667	94543	59047	90033	20826	69541
94864	31994	36168	10851	34888	81553	01540	35456	05014	51176

APPENDIX G *(continued)*

98086 24826	45240 28404	44999 08896	39094 73407	35441 31880
33185 16232	41941 50949	89435 48581	88695 41994	37548 73043
80951 00406	96382 70774	20151 23387	25016 25298	94624 61171
79752 49140	71961 28296	69861 02591	74852 20539	00387 59579
18633 32537	98145 06571	31010 24674	05455 61427	77938 91936
74029 43902	77557 32270	97790 17119	52527 58021	80814 51748
54178 45611	80993 37143	05335 12969	56127 19255	36040 90324
11664 49883	52079 84827	59381 71539	09973 33440	88461 23356
48324 77928	31249 64710	02295 36870	32307 57546	15020 09994
69074 94138	87637 91976	35584 04401	10518 21615	01848 76938

BOOKS

Abt, Clark C. *Serious Games.* New York: Viking, 1970.

Ackoff, Russell L. *Scientific Method: Optimizing Applied Research Decisions.* New York: Wiley, 1962.

Bellman, Richard E. *Dynamic Programming.* Princeton, N.J.: Princeton University Press, 1957.

Bellman, Richard E., and Stuart E. Dreyfus. *Applied Dynamic Programming.* Princeton, N.J.: Princeton University Press, 1962.

Carr, Charles R., and Charles W. Howe. *Quantitative Decision Procedures in Management and Economics: Deterministic Theory and Applications.* New York: McGraw-Hill, 1964.

Catanese, Anthony J., and Alan W. Steiss. *Systemic Planning: Theory and Application.* Boston: D. C. Heath, 1970.

Chapin, F. Stuart, and Shirley F. Weiss, eds. *Urban Growth Dynamics in a Regional Cluster of Cities.* New York: Wiley, 1966.

Chou, Ya-lun. *Statistical Analysis with Business and Economic Applications.* New York: Holt, Rinehart, and Winston, 1969.

Churchman, C. West. *Prediction and Optimal Decision: Philosophical Issues of a Science of Values.* Englewood Cliffs, N.J.: Prentice-Hall, 1964.

Coplin, W. A., ed. *Simulation in the Study of Politics.* Chicago: Markham, 1968.

Cox, D. R., and Walter L. Smith. *Queues.* London: Methuen, 1961.

Croxton, Frederick E., and Dudley J. Crowden. *Applied General Statistics.* Englewood Cliffs, N.J.: Prentice-Hall, 1955.

Dantzig, George B. *Linear Programming and Extensions.* Princeton, N.J.: Princeton University Press, 1963.

Dorfman, Robert, Paul A. Samuelson, and Robert M. Solow. *Linear Programming and Economic Analysis.* New York: McGraw-Hill, 1958.

Draper, Norman, and Harry Smith. *Applied Regression Analysis.* New York: Wiley, 1966.

Forrester, Jay W. *Industrial Dynamics.* Cambridge, Mass.: M.I.T. Press, 1961.

———. *Urban Dynamics.* Cambridge, Mass.: M.I.T. Press, 1969.

Gamson, William A. *Simsoc: Simulated Society.* New York: Free Press, 1969.

Guetzkow, Harold, et al. *Simulation in International Relations: Developments for Research and Teaching.* Englewood Cliffs, N.J.: Prentice-Hall, 1963.

Hadley, G. *Non-linear and Dynamic Programming.* Reading, Mass.: Addison-Wesley, 1964.

Hearle, Edward F. R., and Raymond Mason. *A Data Processing System for State and Local Governments.* Englewood Cliffs, N.J.: Prentice-Hall, 1963.

Bibliography

Hemmens, George C., ed. *Urban Development Models.* Washington, D.C.: Highway Research Board, 1968.

Hillier, Frederick S., and Gerald J. Lieberman. *Introduction to Operations Research.* San Francisco: Holden-Day, 1967.

Isard, Walter. *Methods of Regional Analysis: An Introduction to Regional Science.* Cambridge, Mass.: M.I.T. Press, 1960.

Lazarsfeld, Paul F., ed. *Mathematical Thinking in the Social Sciences.* Glencoe, Ill.: Free Press, 1954.

Levin, Richard I., and Rudolph P. Lamone. *Linear Programming for Management Decisions.* Homewood, Ill.: Richard D. Irwin, 1969.

Lipschutz, Seymour. *Theory and Problems of Finite Mathematics.* New York: Schaum, 1966.

Luce, R. D., and H. Raiffa. *Games and Decisions.* New York: Wiley, 1957.

Meyer, H. A., ed. *Symposium on Monte Carlo Methods.* New York: Wiley, 1956.

Newman, James R., ed. *The World of Mathematics.* New York: Simon and Schuster, 1956.

Pearl, Raymond. *Introduction to Medical Biometry and Statistics.* Philadelphia: W. B. Saunders, 1940.

Perlis, Sam. *Theory of Matrices.* Reading, Mass.: Addison-Wesley, 1952.

RAND Corporation. *A Million Random Digits with 100,000 Normal Deviates.* Glencoe, Ill.: Free Press, 1955.

Roccaferrera, Giuseppe M. Ferrero di. *Operations Research Models: For Business and Industry.* Cincinnati: South-Western Publishing Co., 1964.

Rogers, Andrei. *Projected Population Growth in California Regions: 1960-1980.* Berkeley: University of California, 1966.

Taylor, Angus E. *Calculus with Analytic Geometry.* Englewood Cliffs, N.J.: Prentice-Hall, 1959.

Tocher, K. D. *The Art of Simulation.* Princeton, N.J.: Van Nostrand, 1963.

Von Neumann, John, and Oskar Morganstern. *Games and Economic Behavior.* Princeton, N.J.: Princeton University Press, 1944.

Wagner, Harvey M. *Principles of Operations Research.* Englewood Cliffs, N.J.: Prentice-Hall, 1969.

Webber, Melvin M., et al. *Explorations into Urban Structure.* Philadelphia: University of Pennsylvania Press, 1964.

Wolfe, Henry Dean. *Business Forecasting Methods.* New York: Holt, Rinehart, and Winston, 1966.

Zipf, George K. *Human Behavior and the Principle of Least Effort.* Reading, Mass.: Addison-Wesley, 1949.

REPORTS

Arthur D. Little, Inc. *Model of San Francisco Housing Market.* San Francisco, 1966.

Catanese, Anthony J., James Grant, and Edward Kashuba. *Application of Computer Graphics to Urban and Regional Planning*. Atlanta: Georgia Institute of Technology, 1969.

Chapin, F. S., T. G. Donnelly, and S. F. Weiss. *A Probabilistic Model for Residential Growth*. Chapel Hill: Institute for Research in Social Science, University of North Carolina, 1964.

Chicago Area Transportation Study. *Final Report*, vol. 3. Chicago, 1962.

Crecine, John P. *A Time-Oriented Metropolitan Model for Spatial Location*. Pittsburgh: Department of City Planning, 1964.

Dueker, Kenneth J. *A Recommendation for a State Planning Information System*. Madison: Wisconsin Bureau of State Planning, 1967.

Duke, Richard D., et al. *M.E.T.R.O.* Lansing, Mich.: Tri-County Regional Planning Commission, 1960.

Environmetrics, Inc. *Environmental Modeling: The Method for Total Solutions*. Washington, D.C., 1970.

Feldt, Allan G. *The Cornell Land Use Game*. Ithaca, N.Y.: Center for Housing and Environmental Studies, Cornell University, 1966.

Hamburg, John R., et al. *A Linear Programming Test of Journey to Work Minimization*. Albany: New York State Department of Public Works, 1966.

Harris, Britton. *Linear Programming and the Projection of Land Uses*, P. J. Paper 20. Philadelphia: Penn-Jersey Transportation Study, 1962.

Harris, Britton, Josef Nathanson, and Louis Rosenberg. *Research on an Equilibrium Model of Metropolitan Housing and Locational Change*. Philadelphia: Institute for Environmental Studies, University of Pennsylvania, 1966.

IBM Technical Publications Department. *Concepts and Applications of Regression Analysis*. White Plains, N.Y.: International Business Machines Corp., 1966.

Lockheed Missiles and Space Company. *California Statewide Information System Study*. Sunnyvale, Calif., 1965.

Lowry, Ira S. *A Model of Metropolis*. Santa Monica, Calif.: RAND Corp., 1964.

Metropolitan Data Center Project. *Final Report*. Washington, D.C.: U.S. Department of Housing and Urban Development, 1966.

New Jersey Division of State and Regional Planning. *The Various Alternatives of the Horizon Planning Concept*. Trenton, N.J., 1964.

Southeastern Wisconsin Regional Planning Commission. *A Mathematical Approach to Urban Design: A Progress Report on a Land Use Plan Design Model and a Land Use Simulation Model*. Waukesha, Wis., 1966.

System Development Corporation. *Urban and Regional Information Systems*. Washington, D.C.: U.S. Department of Housing and Urban Development, 1968.

TRW Systems Group. *California Regional Land Use Information System*. Redondo Beach, Calif., 1968.

Voorhees, Alan M. *Factors and Trends in Trip Lengths*. Washington, D.C.: Highway Research Board, 1968.

Washington Center for Metropolitan Studies. *Region Manual: City I Manual.* Washington, D.C., 1968.

ARTICLES, PARTS OF BOOKS

Anderson, T. W. "Probability Models for Analyzing Time Changes in Attitude." In Paul F. Lazarsfeld, ed., *Mathematical Thinking in the Social Sciences.* Glencoe, Ill.: Free Press, 1954.

Cassel, Arno, and Michael S. Janoff. "A Simulation Model of a Two Lane Rural Road." *Highway Research Record,* no. 257. Washington, D.C.: Highway Research Board, 1968.

Chapin, F. Stuart. "A Model for Simulating Residential Development." *Journal of the American Institute of Planners,* 31, no. 2 (May, 1965), 120-125.

Charnes, A., and W. W. Cooper. "Chance-Constrained Programming." *Management Science,* 6, no. 1 (Jan., 1959), 73-80.

Clements, Walter C. "A Propositional Analysis of International Relations in TEMPER." In W. D. Coplin, ed., *Simulation in the Study of Politics.* Chicago: Markham, 1968.

Coleman, James S. "In Defense of Games." *American Behavioral Scientist,* 10 (Oct., 1966), 4.

Davis, Otto A., and Andrew B. Whinston. "The Economics of Urban Renewal." *Law and Contemporary Problems,* 26, no. 1 (Winter, 1961), 103-117.

Dueker, Kenneth J. "A Look at State and Local Information System Efforts." In *Proceedings of the 1968 ACM National Conference.* Washington, D.C.: Association for Computing Machinery, 1969.

Durand, David, and J. Arthur Greenwood. "Aids for Fitting the Gamma Distribution by Maximum Likelihood." *Technometrics,* 2, no. 1 (Feb., 1960), 55-65.

Dyckman, John W. "Planning and Metropolitan Systems." In Melvin M. Webber et al., *Explorations into Urban Structure.* Philadelphia: University of Pennsylvania Press, 1964.

Fetter, R. B., and J. D. Thompson. "The Simulation of Hospital Systems." *Operations Research,* 13 (1965), 689-711.

Geisler, M. A., W. W. Haythorn, and W. A. Steger. "Simulation and the Logistics Systems Laboratory." *Naval Research Quarterly,* 10, no. 1 (Mar., 1963), 23-54.

Herbert, J. P., and B. H. Stevens. "A Model for the Distribution of Residential Activities in Urban Areas." *Journal of Regional Science,* 2, no. 2 (Winter, 1960), 21-36.

Hill, Morris. "A Goals Achievement Matrix for Evaluating Alternative Plans." *Journal of the American Institute of Planners,* 34, no. 1 (Jan., 1968), 19-29.

House, Peter, and P. D. Patterson. "An Environmental Gaming-Simulation Laboratory." *Journal of the American Institute of Planners,* 35, no. 6 (Nov., 1969), 383-388.

Ingram, G. K. "Urban Dynamics." *Journal of the American Institute of Planners,* 36, no. 3 (May, 1970), 206-208.

Jourdain, Phillip E. B. "The Nature of Mathematics." In James R. Newman, ed., *The World of Mathematics,* vol. 1. New York: Simon and Schuster, 1956.

Kahn, H. "Use of Different Monte Carlo Sampling Techniques." In H. A. Meyer, ed., *Symposium on Monte Carlo Methods.* New York: Wiley, 1956.

Kaiser, Edward J., and Shirley F. Weiss. "Public Policy and the Residential Development Process." *Journal of the American Institute of Planners,* 36, no. 1 (Jan., 1970), 30-38.

Keyfitz, Nathan. "The Population Projection as a Matrix Operator." *Demography,* 1 (1964), 56-73.

Kilbridge, Maurice D., Robert P. O'Block, and Paul V. Teplitz. "A Conceptual Framework for Urban Planning Models." *Management Science,* 15, no. 6 (Feb., 1969), B-246-B-266.

Lowry, Ira S. "Seven Models of Urban Development: A Structural Comparison." In George C. Hemmens, ed., *Urban Development Models.* Washington, D.C.: Highway Research Board, 1968.

Meier, Richard L., and Richard D. Duke. "Gaming Simulation for Urban Planning." *Journal of the American Institute of Planners,* 32, no. 1 (Jan., 1966), 3-17.

Ochs, Jack. "An Application of Linear Programming to Urban Spatial Organization." *Journal of Regional Science,* 9, no. 3 (Dec., 1969), 451-459.

Pfouts, Ralph W. "Patterns of Economic Interaction in the Crescent." In F. Stuart Chapin and Shirley F. Weiss, eds., *Urban Growth Dynamics in a Regional Cluster of Cities.* New York: Wiley, 1966.

Robinson, Ira M., Harry B. Wolfe, and Robert L. Barringer. "A Simulation Model for Renewal Programming." *Journal of the American Institute of Planners,* 31, no. 2 (May, 1965), 126-134.

Rogers, Andrei. "A Markovian Policy Model of Migration." *Regional Science Association Papers,* 17 (1966), 205-224.

―――. "Matrix Methods of Population Analysis." *Journal of the American Institute of Planners,* 32, no. 1 (Jan., 1966), 40-44.

Steger, Wilbur A. "The Pittsburgh Urban Renewal Simulation Model." *Journal of the American Institute of Planners,* 31, no. 2 (May, 1965), 144-150.

Tinbergen, Jan. "The Hierarchy Model of the Size Distribution of Centres." *Regional Science Association Papers,* 20 (1968), 61-68.

Wallis, W. A. "The Poisson Distribution and Supreme Court." *Journal of the American Statistical Association,* 31 (1936), 326-380.

Webber, Melvin M. "The Role of Intelligence Systems in Urban Systems Planning." *Journal of the American Institute of Planners,* 31, no. 4 (Nov., 1965), 289-297.

Wendt, Paul F., and Michael A. Goldberg. "The Use of Land Development Simulation Models in Transportation Planning." *Highway Research Record,* no. 285. Washington, D. C.: Highway Research Board, 1969.

UNPUBLISHED MATERIALS

Carroll, C. W. "An Operations Research Approach to the Economic Optimization of a Kraft Pulping Process." Ph.D. dissertation, Lawrence College, 1959.
Catanese, Anthony J. "Separation of Home and Work Place in Urban Structure and Form." Ann Arbor, Mich.: University Microfilms, 1969.

AUTHOR INDEX

Index

SUBJECT INDEX